Christ and Culture in the New Testament

Christ and Culture in the New Testament

JAMES W. THOMPSON

CASCADE *Books* · Eugene, Oregon

CHRIST AND CULTURE IN THE NEW TESTAMENT

Cascade Books
An Imprint of Wipf and Stock Publishers
199 W. 8th Ave., Suite 3
Eugene, OR 97401

www.wipfandstock.com

PAPERBACK ISBN: 978-1-6667-3946-6
HARDCOVER ISBN: 978-1-6667-3947-3
EBOOK ISBN: 978-1-6667-3948-0

Cataloguing-in-Publication data:

Names: Thompson, James W.

Title: Christ and Culture in the New Testament / James W. Thompson.

Description: Eugene, OR: Cascade Books, 2023 | Includes bibliographical references and index.

Identifiers: ISBN 978-1-6667-3946-6 (paperback) | ISBN 978-1-6667-3947-3 (hardcover) | ISBN 978-1-6667-3948-0 (ebook)

Subjects: LCSH: Jesus Christ—Person and offices | Christianity and culture—Biblical teaching | Christianity and culture—History—Early church, ca. 30–600 | Bible. New Testament—Theology

Classification: BR115.C8 T46 2023 (paperback) | BR115.C8 (ebook)

03/31/23

For
Andrew Thompson
Elizabeth Bryant
Gabrielle Thompson
Benjamin Bryant

Contents

Abbreviations

BDAG Danker, Fredrick W., Walter Bauer, William F. Arndt, and F. Wilbur Gingrich. *A Greek-English Lexicon of the New Testament and Other Early Christian.* 3rd ed. Chicago: University of Chicago Press, 2000.

EDNT *Exegetical Dictionary of the New Testament.* Edited by Horst Balz and Gerhard Schneider. ET. 3 vols. Grand Rapids: Eerdmans, 1990–1993.

OTP *Old Testament Pseudepigrapha.* Edited by James H. Charlesworth. 2 vols. New York: Doubleday, 1983, 1985.

TLNT *Theological Lexicon of the New Testament.* C. Spicq. Translated and edited by J. D. Ernest. 3 vols. Peabody, MA: Hendrickson, 1994.

Introduction

The Enduring Problem

When the Thessalonians "turned to God from idols" (1 Thess 1:9), these gentile converts also turned away from a way of life and the dominant values of that society. These occurrences were not limited to Thessalonica, however, but took place in cities throughout the ancient world. Conversion involved the separation of families and withdrawal from much of civic life. It also disturbed the peace of the religious pluralism of the ancient society, creating hostility from the populace, which extended from the first century to the emergence of Christendom after Constantine. Hostility turned into inevitable periodic government-sponsored persecution because the Christian claim that Jesus is Lord was a challenge to the imperial claims that Caesar is lord. H. Richard Niebuhr declared that this separation of Christ and culture is "the enduring problem."[1] He observed that "ancient spiritualists and modern materialists, pious Romans who charge Christianity with atheism, nineteenth-century atheists who condemn its theistic faith, nationalists and humanists, all seem to be offended by the same elements in the gospel and employ similar arguments against it."[2]

After more than a millennium of a peaceful relationship between Christ and culture that began with Constantine, believers face a new challenge of defining their relationship to a changing world. Christians live in tension not only with totalitarian societies but with democracies as well. The claim that Jesus is Lord was an offense to the ancient pluralistic society, and it remains an offense in the modern world that honors the gods of nationalism, ideology, and personal fulfillment. As H. Richard Niebuhr declared:

---

1. Niebuhr, *Christ and Culture*, 1–44.
2. Niebuhr, *Christ and Culture*, 5.

1

> The Christ who will not worship Satan to gain the world's king-
> doms is followed by Christians who will worship only Christ in
> unity with the Lord whom he serves. And this is intolerable to
> all defenders of society who are content that many gods should
> be worshiped if only Democracy or America or Germany or the
> Empire receives its due, religious homage.[3]

The experience of believers in a pre-Christian culture has much in common with the experience of believers in a post-Christian culture. In this book I will examine what early Christian writers in the inhospitable environment of the first century offer believers who face the challenge of marginalization in contemporary society.

THE "AGE OF ENCHANTMENT" AND THE CONSTANTINIAN ERA

The church has defined its relation to culture in a variety of ways. From the edict of Milan, which declared the empire's toleration of Christianity in 313, to the emergence of secularism with the Enlightenment, church and society lived in relative harmony. Charles Taylor speaks of the "enchanted world" of the Middle Ages, when the environment was populated with supernatural forces and belief in God was self-evident. In the enchanted world, it was almost impossible not to believe, for belief was enshrined in family, civic life, education, and all institutions of society. Its place in the public square was evident in the majestic churches that stood at the center of every village.[4] In an earlier day, patriotism, religion, and a sense of family values shaped by religion seemed in lock step.

> Three sides of this triangle mutually supported each other. The
> family was the matrix in which the young were to be brought up
> to be good citizens and believing worshippers. Religion was the
> source of the values that animated both family and society; and
> the state was the realization and bulwark of the values central to
> both family and churches.[5]

This triad lived on until the middle of the twentieth century. Christian prayers were commonplace in the schools and other public events. In many parts of America, public schools were actually Protestant schools, and teachers were expected to uphold Christian values. At the school that

3. Niebuhr, *Christ and Culture*, 8.
4. Taylor, *Secular Age*, 25–26, 41.
5. Taylor, *Secular Age*, 506.

I attended, no events were scheduled for Wednesday night in deference to prayer meetings in Protestant churches, and no youth sports were conducted on Sundays. Politicians presented themselves to the public as virtuous Christians. While religion was rarely mentioned in television entertainment, the conduct of the characters in *Ozzie and Harriet, Father Knows Best*, and other family-oriented programs did not conflict with the values of most Christians.

Charles Taylor speaks of the time of "disenchantment," which began with the eighteenth-century Enlightenment and accelerated in the latter part of the twentieth century in a cultural transformation that included the sexual revolution and the challenge to traditional values. "Belief has lost many of the social metrices which made it seem obvious."[6] The number of those who regard themselves as atheists, agnostics, or to have no religion has increased dramatically. Intermediate positions also increase: many people drop out of active practice while still declaring themselves as belonging to some confession or believing in God.[7] The gamut of beliefs in something beyond widens, fewer declaring belief in a personal God, while more hold to something like an impersonal force.[8] Fewer people belong to any church. We have seen the remarkable growth of the "nones"—those who belong to no religious community. It has had a profound effect on the relationship between church and society, creating "a humanist alternative to faith" in which belief in God is no longer axiomatic.[9] The traditional Christian views about Christ, the Bible, heaven and hell, and morality were now regarded with disdain by a large segment of the populace, especially in the media and academia, creating tension between the church and society. Religious belief is no longer supported by communities, government, and education. The church has lost (or is losing) its place in the public square although the United States is the most religious nation among the advanced democracies.[10]

Since Niebuhr wrote, public prayer has been prohibited in the schools. The traditional Christian values of marriage and sexuality no longer have the support of the media or government. The rights of private institutions and businesses to determine their rules based on their religious convictions is the focus of numerous court cases. Even the practice of youth sports on Sunday morning reflects the diminishing influence of the Christian faith.

---

6. Taylor, *Secular Age*, 531.

7. See the quantitative analysis of the decline of religious affiliation in David E. Campbell, Geoffrey C. Layman, and John C. Green, *Secular Surge*, 1–12.

8. Taylor, *Secular Age*, 513.

9. Taylor, *Secular Age*, 77, 505.

10. David E. Campbell, Geoffrey C. Layman, and John C. Green, *Secular Surge*, 43, 209.

Secularization has changed the nature of moral discourse. Because moral discourse is no longer based on a transcendent reality, it is chaotic without a strong community consensus on the nature of the proper ends of human existence.[11] The transcendent foundation for morality is replaced by what Carl Trueman calls "the triumph of the therapeutic" and Charles Taylor calls "the culture of authenticity," which focuses on the individual's choice. Individuals have to discover their route to wholeness and spiritual depth; thus the focus is on individuals and on their experience. The language of morality as now used is really nothing more than the language of personal preference based on nothing more rational or objective than sentiments or feelings.[12]

I am not writing to lament this change in our culture or to call for the restoration of the Constantinian era, for Christianity has often flourished under difficult circumstances. My task is to gain insights from the past that will guide us in this changing situation. The demise of the Constantinian world is the occasion for Christians to reflect on their place in an increasingly secular culture. I am convinced that the New Testament, written for minorities in the Roman world, offers insights that are relevant in the present.

H. RICHARD NIEBUHR'S TYPOLOGY

Niebuhr maintains that the problem of Christ and culture has yielded no single Christian answer, but only a series of typical answers.[13] He adds that the purpose of *Christ and Culture* is to set forth typical Christian answers to the problem of Christ and culture. Employing the typological method, Niebuhr then categorizes the multiplicity of Christian responses to the "enduring problem" into five ideal types. Of the five responses to culture that he lists, the first two categories indicate the two extreme responses: Christ against culture (type 1) and the Christ of culture (type 2). Christ against culture uncompromisingly "affirms the sole authority of Christ over the Christian and resolutely rejects culture's claims to loyalty."[14] It calls for a withdrawal from the world and the rejection of cultural society. It is reflected in 1 John, Tertullian, Tatian, Benedictine monks, Tolstoy, and other Christian witnesses. The Christ of culture (type 2) is the accommodationist

11. Trueman, *Rise and Triumph of the Therapeutic Self*, 83. See Rieff, *My Life among the Deathworks*, 4, 12; MacIntyre, *After Virtue*, 8.

12. Trueman, *Rise and Triumph of the Therapeutic*, 85; MacIntyre, *After Virtue*, 11.

13. Niebuhr, *Christ and Culture*, 2.

14. Niebuhr, *Christ and Culture*, 45.

or assimilationist position. Christians emphasize the "ideal" in that culture, finding no major disagreement between this ideal and essential Christianity as reflected in Gnostic writings, Peter Abelard, and nineteenth-century liberals.[15] The former emphasized the conflict between Christ and culture while the latter emphasized the continuity between Christ and culture. Niebuhr then lists the three mediating positions. The "Christ above culture" (type 3) view seeks a synthesis between Christ and culture, acknowledges the wisdom of philosophers and scientists as represented by the apologists, Clement of Alexandria, Thomas Aquinas, and, to some extent, the Gospel of Matthew. Similar to type 3 ("Christ above culture") is type 4, "Christ and culture in paradox," which seeks to "do justice to the need for holding together as well as for distinguishing between loyalty to Christ and responsibility for culture."[16] They are acutely aware of permanent conflict between God and humans or between Christ and culture. Due to the pervasive effect of sin, the latter is corrupted and must therefore be kept within appropriate boundaries. Niebuhr attributes this view to Paul, Marcion, Luther, Kierkegaard, and Roger Williams. Finally, Niebuhr lists "Christ the transformer of culture" (type 5), which also holds a positive view of culture.[17] This view is rooted in three theological convictions: the creative activity of God in history, human nature as corrupted and in need of transformation, and the view that "to God all things are possible in a history that is fundamentally not a course of merely human events but always a dramatic interaction between God and men."[18] Consequently, type 5 Christians believe in the possibility of transformation of this reality, including culture, here and now.[19] This view is reflected in the prologue to the Gospel of John, according to which the divine incarnation in the world expresses faith in "God's wholly affirmative relation to the whole world, material and spiritual."[20] This view is also present in Augustine and John Calvin.

Niebuhr offers a critique of all but the latter view, which he supports. Writing in the early 1950s, he proposed a belief in Christ the transformer of culture. This was the view that liberal, mainline, American Protestantism favored. According to this view, the task of the church was to make America a better place to live, transforming society into something that corresponded

---

15. See Bargár, "Niebuhr's Typology Reconsidered," 298.

16. Niebuhr, *Christ and Culture*, 149

17. Niebuhr, *Christ and Culture*, 191.

18. Niebuhr, *Christ and Culture*, 194.

19. Bargár, "Niebuhr's Typology Reconsidered," 316 (here 299).

20. Niebuhr, *Christ and Culture*, 197.

to the Christian ideal.[21] This view was more plausible in 1951 than in the twenty-first century, for Niebuhr wrote within the context of the dominance of Christian influence in American culture. He wrote in the aftermath of the rise of totalitarianism in the preceding decades in Europe and the persistence of racial injustice in America. He was responding to accusations that Christianity has no positive contribution to civilization. The cultured despisers of Christianity said, in effect, that Christianity is a threat to a healthy situation. Progressive cultural ideals should thus be subordinated to cultural ideas, and traditional religion should be abandoned or brought into line with cultural ideals.[22] His principal agenda was the building of a unified culture, and he sought to find ways for progressive Christianity to contribute to civilization.[23]

In the seventy years since the publication of *Christ and Culture*, Niebuhr's typology has been greeted with both appreciation and critique.[24] While the typology is a useful starting point, it has numerous flaws, as Hauerwas and Willimon observe. Niebuhr's preference for "Christ Transforming Culture" had the effect of endorsing a Constantinian social strategy.[25]

"Culture" became a blanket term to underwrite Christian involvement with the world without providing any discriminating mode for discerning how Christians should see the good or the bad in "culture."[26] John Howard Yoder offered a comprehensive critique, maintaining that a) despite the word "Christ" in the title, Niebuhr's proposal actually runs counter to the message of Jesus,[27] who stood outside the existing culture; b) transformation is undefined by Niebuhr; and c) no ancient thinker actually fits the types inasmuch as most historical figures represent a mixture of the types outlined by Niebuhr.

---

21. Hauerwas and Willimon, *Resident Aliens*, 40.

22. Marsden, "Christianity and Cultures," 6.

23. Marsden, "Christianity and Cultures," 5.

24. For a positive response, see Gustafson, preface, in Niebuhr, *Christ and Culture*, xxi–xxxv. For the negative assessment, see Hauerwas and Willimon, *Resident Aliens*, 40: "We have come to believe that few books have been a greater hindrance to an accurate assessment of our situation than *Christ and Culture*."

25. Hauerwas and Willimon, *Resident Aliens*, 40.

26. Hauerwas and Willimon, *Resident Aliens*, 40.

27. Yoder, "How H. Richard Niebuhr Reasoned," 42–43: "Thus to summarize the core argument of the book, Niebuhr is saying, with careful refinement and pluralistic respect, 'Jesus would have us turn away from all culture, but we prefer not to do this because of our more balanced vision of the values of nature and history. Yet in our affirmative attitude to "culture" we do want to continue to show some respect for the criticism (or the "transformation") which flows from Christ's critical attitude toward it."

The prospects for Christ as the transformer of culture looked more promising in 1951 than today. Church membership and attendance were not only acceptable in this society but also widely encouraged. The triangle of patriotism, family values, and religion was still intact. Many in America found that they could demonstrate that they were good Americans by joining a church.[28] This situation has changed. The influence of the Christian faith has diminished, although it retains a powerful voice in American life, making the culture wars inevitable. The church now faces the new challenge of defining its relationship to culture.

Both evangelicals and liberals attempt to accommodate to the changing culture by being relevant and attractive to it or by having their moral convictions affirmed in the public square.[29] The evangelical seeker service is an attempt to create a worship experience that is attractive to the tastes of a secular audience. Worship services become an assortment of religious entertainments that serve to cheer and comfort us in largely therapeutic ways.[30] Churches are designed to resemble theaters and shopping centers. Preachers address themes that resonate with the secular audience.[31] George Marsden has observed that fundamentalism, although claiming to be based solely on the New Testament, has actually been shaped by American cultural traditions, confusing Christianity with certain dimensions of their culture.

The clearest example of their accommodation to culture is that many have lapsed into nationalism, virtually merging American patriotism with the cause of Christ. They sometimes speak as though America is the new Israel.[32] They make a concerted effort to restore an earlier time by engaging in political activities, attempting to restore a Constantinian order through political activism, frequently mixing patriotism with Christian faith, tying themselves to the Republican Party in hopes of passing legislation to enforce Christian values and American supremacy, "exchanging the gospel

---

28. See Taylor, *Secular Age*, 527.

29. See Hauerwas and Willimon, *Resident Aliens*, 32: "Both assume wrongly that the American church's primary social task is to underwrite American democracy."

30. Wood, *Contending for the Faith*, 20.

31. Norman Vincent Peale had great popularity before a liberal audience with his book, *The Power of Positive Thinking*, which was based on his sermons in New York. Peale was criticized by conservatives for leaving out Christian doctrine. A generation later, Robert Schuller, Peale's disciple, wrote books that were popular with conservatives. These include *Self-Esteem: The New Reformation*, *Self-Love*, *Believe in the God Who Believes in You*, and *The Be-Happy Attitudes*. "Not only have evangelicals caught up with their liberal rivals in accommodating religion to secular culture, they are now clearly in the lead" (Horton, *Christless Christianity*, 67).

32. Marsden, "Christianity and Cultures," 11–12.

of Christ's kingdom for the gospel of American power"[33] and advocating legislation on the beginning of life and the meaning of marriage.[34]

Similarly, the fundamentalist-evangelical church in North America, like its liberal antagonist, is in danger of exchanging the gospel of Christ's kingdom for the gospel of American power. William Willimon argued regarding Jerry Falwell, Pat Robertson, the Religious Right, and the Religious Left:

> Pat Robertson has become Jesse Jackson. Randall Terry of the Nineties is Bill Coffin of the Sixties. And the average American knows no answer to human longing or moral deviation other than legislation. Again, I ought to know. We played this game before any Religious Right types were invited to the White House. Some time ago I told Jerry Falwell to his face that I had nothing against him except that he talked like a Methodist. A Methodist circa 1960. Jerry was not amused.[35]

Dietrich Bonhoeffer's biographer Eberhard Bethge recalls with dismay his visit to an American church.

> As we entered the foyer, an usher stepped forward and gave me two badges to fasten to my lapel: the one on the left said, Jesus First and on the right, one with an American flag. . . . I could not help but think myself in Germany in 1933. . . . Of course, Christ, but a German Christ; of course, 'Jesus First,' but an American Jesus! And so to the long history of faith and its executors another chapter is being added of a mixed image of Christ, of another syncretism on the American model, undisturbed by any knowledge of that centuries-long and sad history.[36]

At the same time, evangelicals also adopt the cultural values of the period, embracing capitalism and patriotism while ignoring the desperate plight of immigrants and the needs of "the least of these." On the other

---

33. Metzger, "Christ, Culture, and the Sermon on the Mount Community," 25.

34. On the alliance between Evangelicals and the Republican Party and its leader, Donald Trump, a totally nonreligious politician, see Miller, *Religion of American Greatness*, 200–27. Trump identified himself with Christians, declaring, "We will respect and defend Christian Americans." In the 2016 campaign he said, "Your power has been totally taken away from you," but under a Trump administration, our Christian heritage will be cherished, protected, defended, like you've never seen before" (200). While the grassroots of white Evangelicals supported Trump, many influential Evangelical leaders spoke out against him.

35. Willimon, "Been There, Preached That," 6.

36. De Gruchy, *Daring, Trusting Spirit*, 200–201.

hand, their rejection of easy divorce, same-sex marriage, and abortion are indications of their resistance to culture.

Liberal Protestantism has also accommodated itself to culture, accepting the dominant cultural values, including same-sex marriage and abortion, accepting the Enlightenment culture's focus on the rights of individuals. Like evangelicals, mainline Protestants have also engaged in the political process, advocating their own moral values on matters of public policy. They take positions on both foreign and domestic policy issues of the state. On the other hand, they stand firmly against the culture on other issues: racism, sexism, and sexual exploitation. According to Marsden, "Let them be confronted by overt racism, sexism, or sexual exploitation and they will be up in arms thundering anathemas and warning their constituents to stay away from certain cultural practices."[37]

Both liberals and evangelicals take positions reflecting a residual Constantinian situation. After a millennium of peace between the church and society in the Constantinian-Christian society, the church in a post-Christian society now faces challenges similar to those faced by the church in a pre-Christian society. In this book I will examine Niebuhr's categories in light of the evidence of the New Testament. Niebuhr appealed to the New Testament books for support of his typology, but neither his typology nor his analysis of these writings is persuasive.[38] He does not acknowledge the complexity of the Johannine literature in its relation to the world. Nor does Paul, with his multiple writings addressed to different situations, fit in the category of "Christ and Culture in Paradox."

WHAT IS CULTURE?

The New Testament does not have a word for culture, although the issue is paramount everywhere. In most instances it uses such terms as "world," "human point of view" (*kata sarka*, cf. 2 Cor 5:16), "this age" (Gal 1:4), and the "wisdom of this age" (1 Cor 2:6). The world is divided between believers and the others, who are called "unbelievers" (*apistoi*, 1 Cor 6:6; 7:12–13; 14:23), "gentiles" (1 Cor 5:1; 12:2; Eph 2:11; 1 Thess 4:5), "unrighteous" (*adikoi*, 1 Cor 6:1, 9), "those outside" (1 Cor 5:12; Col 4:5; 1 Thess 4:11). While the New Testament never uses the term culture, the environment of the early believers fits the definitions. "Culture" does not mean the high culture of Shakespeare, Goethe, or Bach. Clifford Geertz has defined the term as "an historically transmitted pattern of meanings expressed in symbols, a

37. Marsden, "Christianity and Cultures," 11.
38 Volf, "Soft Difference," 16.

system of inherited conceptions expressed in symbolic form by means of which men communicate, perpetuate, and develop their knowledge."[39] The essential core of culture consists of traditions (i.e., historically derived and selected), ideas, and especially their attached values.[40] It includes the world of work, family, government, and commerce.

CHRIST AND CULTURE IN THE NEW TESTAMENT

According to Miroslav Volf, "To ask about how the gospel relates to culture is to ask how to live as a Christian community in a particular cultural context." He adds that "there is no other way to reflect adequately on gospel and culture except by reflecting on how the social embodiments of the gospel relate to a given culture."[41] Every writing in the New Testament reflects the struggle of the community to define itself in relationship to its culture. Therefore, the central question *Christ and Culture* poses is about how Christians should relate to their surrounding culture.[42]

In chapter 1 I will examine the struggle of Jews in the Second Temple period to maintain their identity. The Maccabean literature and apocalyptic writers of the Second Temple period resisted the influence of Hellenism, while other voices (e.g., 4 Maccabees, Philo) were influenced by philosophy but maintained resistance to the larger culture. Diaspora Jews undoubtedly provided a model for Paul's approach to the Hellenistic world.

Jesus never refers to philosophers or playwrights although Hellenistic influence was pervasive in Galilee. According to Joseph Klausner, Jesus endangered the existing culture by abstracting religion and ethics from the rest of social life. "Jesus ignored everything concerned with material civilization: in this sense he does not belong to civilization."[43] He refers to the state only when he is asked. The Sermon on the Mount was intended to create an alternative culture. In chapter 2, I will examine the response of Jesus to the culture of his time.

According to H. Richard Niebuhr, Paul held the church and the world in paradox. A more accurate description is that Paul holds a dialectical relationship to the world. He assumes that believers live within the institutions of the world but regards them as adiaphora. In chapter 3 I will examine the

---

39. Geertz, *Interpretation of Cultures*, 89.

40. Carson, *Christ and Culture Revisited*, 1.

41. Volf, "Soft Difference," 16.

42. Marsden, "Christianity and Cultures," 4.

43. Klausner, *Jesus of Nazareth*, 373–75.

relationship between Paul and his communities, demonstrating that Paul encourages both boundaries from the world and engagement with it.

According to Gal 3:28, "There is no longer Jew or Greek, slave or free, male and female" because the believers have been "rescued from the present evil age" (Gal 1:4). For Christians living in this new age, what was their relationship to ethnicity, slavery, and gender? Chapter 4 is an analysis of Paul's relationship with these realities, which continue to exist for believers but in a new form.

Although believers lived under Roman rule, they proclaimed that their "citizenship is in heaven," raising the suspicion of disloyalty to Rome within the populace. The claim that Jesus is Lord inevitably caused conflict with the authorities. Paul addresses this issue most clearly in Romans 13, acknowledging that believers still recognize the role of governmental authorities. Chapter 5 is a study in Paul's relationship to the state.

Paul mentions no philosophers in his writings, but he reflects an awareness of the philosophical and ethical language of his culture. To what extent did the philosophers shape Paul's theology and ethics? Chapter 6 is a study of the relationship between Paul and the philosophical currents of his day.

According to Niebuhr, 1 John is an example of "Christ against Culture," and John is an example of "Christ the Transformer of Culture." These categories are, at best, oversimplified. The Johannine writings are consistent in their view that "the world" is a hostile place, urging the community to unite in mutual love. In the Gospel of John, the community confronts a hostile world but envisions a mission to the world. Chapter 7 examines the insights from the Johannine writings.

Chapter 8 turns to other voices. Both Hebrews and 1 Peter appeal to members who are "exiles" in their own land, offering guidance on the Christian response to their culture. James warns against "friendship with the world." The book of Revelation reflects the most extreme tension between Christ and culture. At the same time, these voices reflect the influence of this culture on their own work, demonstrating their own inculturation through their facility with the language and images drawn from the wider culture.

Because the household codes have many similarities to the other household codes in antiquity, numerous scholars have maintained that they reflect a culture of accommodation to popular morality. Martin Dibelius described the expanded household code in the Pastoral Epistles as examples of "bürgerlich" (bourgeois, middle-class) morality, maintaining that the ethics of these letters are drawn from popular morality. Chapter 9 will explore the extent to which early Christians of the second generation practiced an ethic of accommodation.

The conclusion will demonstrate the unity and diversity of responses of New Testament writers to the "enduring problem" of Christ and culture. Their responses from a pre-Christian culture offer models for the church in a post-Christian culture.

I

Between Resistance and Accommodation

Hellenism and Second Temple Judaism

When the early Christians sought to define their relationship to the surrounding culture, their roots in Judaism provided them with models for their existence. As Martin Hengel demonstrated, Hellenism penetrated throughout Alexander's empire, including Israel.[1] The worldwide culture included Greek language, literature, religion, philosophy, the arts, and sports. In a tradition that had maintained an identity of separation from the nations (cf. Lev 18:3; 20:26), even in a time of exile,[2] this expansion of Greek culture presented a challenge to Jewish identity and practices in both Palestine and the diaspora, creating a crisis of plausibility for minority groups. The concept of holiness by separation from the gentiles inevitably created tension with the majority culture.[3]

---

1. Hengel, *Judaism and Hellenism*, 1974.

2. Cf. Ps 137:1–4, "By the rivers of Zion we sat down and there we wept when we remembered Zion. . . . For there our captors asked for our songs, and our tormentors asked for mirth, saying, 'Sing us one of the songs of Zion!' How could we sing the Lord's song in a foreign land?"

3. Wright, "Paul and Empire," 288: "The ancient traditions of Israel thus continued to put the Jewish people on a collision course with the all-embracing claims of human empire."

The separate identity of Jews led numerous ancient authors to express hostility to them during the Hellenistic age. Before Tacitus relates the fall of Jerusalem, he offers the most complete extant set of accusations against the Jews. They regard as profane everything that the Romans hold sacred (*Hist.* 5.5.1). Those who adopt their ways scorn the gods, abandon their own nation, and hold their parents, siblings, and children in contempt (*Hist.* 5.5.2). Jews throughout history were the most despised of subject peoples (*Hist.* 5.5.2).[4] Juvenal mentions Jews in five passages throughout the *Satires* (3.12–20, 3.292–96, 6.157–60, 6.542–5, and 14.96–106). Throughout these passages, Juvenal characterizes the Jews as a distinctly separate group, maligning their religious practices and cultural habits. In *Contra Apionem*, Josephus refutes slanders against the Jews—that they do not worship the Egyptian gods (*C. Ap.* 2.66) but instigate sedition (*C. Ap.* 2.68). He also responds to the ridicule that they refuse to eat pork (*C. Ap.* 2.137).

The pogrom against the Jews in Alexandria in AD 32/33 initiated by Flaccus is evidence of the tenuous relationship of Jews and the local populace. According to Philo, the local populace rose up against the large unassimilated group in its midst, questioning its loyalty to the best interests of the city. Over four hundred homes and shops were pillaged and Jewish families evicted. Outside the Jewish quarter individual Jews were set upon and some burned to death (*Flacc.* 96). Alexandrian crowds forced their way into Jewish synagogues and set up statues or busts of the emperor Gaius.[5]

When the conquerors brought a missionary zeal for Greek culture and a desire to institute a single world culture, abolishing all subcultures, Jewish identity was threatened in Palestine. In the diaspora, Jews under the cultural hegemony of Hellenism continued to find ways to reaffirm their ancestral heritage in the face of a dominant majority that devalued that heritage although some abandoned their Jewish traditions.

While none of the literature that has come down to us reflects total rejection of Hellenistic culture or total acceptance,[6] two major tendencies are present in the Jewish literature of the Second Temple: the tendency to embrace Hellenism within one's own identity as a Jew and the tendency to maintain strict Jewish distinctiveness. In some cases both of these tendencies are present in the same document.[7] Thus one may observe a continuum of responses that range from resistance to accommodation to Hellenistic culture. John M. G. Barclay describes the levels of assimilation among Jews

---

4. See Gruen, *Construct of Identity in Hellenistic Judaism*, 265.

5. Barclay, *Jews in the Mediterranean Diaspora*, 53.

6. Collins, *Between Athens and Jerusalem*, 24.

7. King, "Idolatry and Jewish Identity in Wisdom 13–15," 79.

in Alexandria. Those who exhibited a high degree of assimilation were fully integrated into the political and religious affairs of the state, married gentiles, and did not raise their children as Jews. As social climbers in Greek society, they gave up Jewish religious practices.[8] A large body of literature reflects various mediating positions that included both resistance and accommodation. Barclay distinguishes between the cultural convergence and cultural antagonism in the ancient literature.[9] This chapter offers representative examples of the responses to Hellenization.

THE LITERATURE OF RESISTANCE

The Maccabean literature describes the threats to Jewish identity by the Greeks' attempt to replace the Jewish way of life with Hellenistic culture. The Greeks collaborated with the Jewish elite in Jerusalem, whose path of accommodation is recorded in 2 Maccabees. When Jason obtained the high priesthood, "he at once shifted his compatriots over to the Greek way of life" (2 Macc 4:10).

> He took delight in establishing a gymnasium right under the citadel, and he induced the noblest of the young men to wear the Greek hat. There was such an extreme of Hellenization and increase in the adoption of foreign ways because of the wickedness of Jason, who was ungodly and no true high priest, that the priests were no longer intent upon their service at the altar. Despising the sanctuary and neglecting the sacrifices, they hurried to take part in the unlawful proceedings in the wrestling arena after the signal for the discus-throwing, disdaining the honors prized by their ancestors and putting the highest value upon Greek forms of prestige. (4:12–15)

The Maccabean literature indicates that the adoption of Hellenistic ways was an existential threat to Judaism and that the Jewish elite were complicit in the loss of Jewish identity. The heroes of 1 and 2 Maccabees engage in resistance to the encroachments of Hellenistic culture, leading the revolt that finally ends with independence under the Hasmoneans, whose

---

8. Barclay, *Jews in the Mediterranean Diaspora*, 107–9. The most famous case of high assimilation was Philo's nephew, Tiberius Julius Alexander, who rose to be a high-ranking officer in the army (Tacitus, *Ann.* 15.28). Josephus speaks of Joseph the Tobiad, who associated with high society in Alexandria (*Ant.* 12. 186–89). Philo speaks of those who engaged in allegorical interpretation but, unlike Philo, gave up distinctive Jewish practices.

9. Barclay, *Jews in the Mediterranean Diaspora*, chs. 6–7.

members had led the rebellion against Greek culture. In response to the conquerors' attempt to destroy the law (1 Macc 1:56–57), the motivating factor for the heroes and martyrs was "zeal for the law" (1 Macc 1:49; 2:22, 50, 58, 64, 67–68; 2 Macc 4:2). When the Greeks demanded the participation in the festival of Dionysus (2 Macc 6:7), prohibited circumcision (2 Macc 6:10), and forced the Jews to eat swine's flesh (2 Macc 6:17), those who had zeal for the law resisted to the point of death. The story of the torture and death of the seven brothers as their mother looked on appears in 2 and 4 Maccabees (2 Macc 7:1–42; 4 Macc 8:3–12:19). For the author, these heroes died for the preservation of their Jewish identity and were models for the readers as they faced the challenge of confronting Greek culture.[10]

Resistance literature continued as the Hasmonean ruling family became more Hellenized. The rulers of the Hasmoneans took on the trappings of Hellenistic monarchs as the names of the Hasmonean rulers (Hyrcanus, Aristobulus, Alexander, Antigonus)' suggest. Aristobulus called himself *philellēn*, lover of the Greeks.[11] The Qumran community, having determined that the priesthood and the ruling elite were corrupt, went to the desert, where membership is restricted to those who demonstrate their purity. According to the Community Rule:

> "And when these become members of the Community in Israel according to all these rules, they shall separate from the habitation of unjust men and shall go into the wilderness to prepare there the way of Him; as it is written, 'Prepare in the wilderness the way of . . . , make straight in the desert a path for our God' (Isa 4:3). This path is the study of the law." (1QS 8:12–15)

According to Philip Esler, "It is difficult to imagine a community which was more preoccupied with its own 'apartness,' its 'holiness,' or which could go to greater lengths than this one to distinguish itself from everyone else."[12] The theme of separation from the evils of the Jerusalem priesthood dominates the Dead Sea Scrolls.[13]

Separation is also a frequent theme in apocalyptic literature, which draws a sharp distinction between the righteous and the unrighteous. With

---

10. Although 2 Maccabees glorifies the resistance fighters, the book itself is cast within the tradition of Hellenistic historiography.

11. Collins, *Between Athens and Jerusalem*, 10. See also Gruen, *Heritage and Hellenism*, 31.

12. Esler, *First Christians in Their Social Worlds*, 81.

13. Flusser, *Judaism of the Second Temple Period*, 1:104: "It is an established fact that Qumran considered their separation from the community of sinners known as Israel to be the guiding principle, one rooted in the dualistic eschatology and institutionalized in their separatist organization that was closed to all on the outside."

its sharp distinction between the present evil age and the glorious future, apocalyptic literature encouraged a sectarian ethos and a separation from society as the community awaited divine intervention. According to 1 Enoch, the righteous suffer persecution at the hands of the wicked (1 En. 53:7; 62:11). The wicked are the enemies of the righteous—people of power, the kings of the earth, and mighty men (1 En. 46:4; cf. 38:4; 48:8; 53:5; 54:2; 62:1, 9; 63:1).[14] The Psalms of Solomon convey a Jewish community's response to persecution and a foreign invasion (cf. Pss. Sol. 2:3–6), a likely response to the Romans in the first century BC. The community identifies itself as "the pious" and "the righteous" in contrast to the outsiders and the apostate Jews. According to 2 Baruch, because Israel cannot be compared with other nations, it has not mingled with the other nations (42:4; 48:23).

ACCOMMODATION AND MAINTENANCE OF JEWISH IDENTITY

While some Jews abandoned the marks of Judaism and assimilated totally into the larger culture, our records reflect the variety of approaches during the period of the Second Temple. Some of the literature emerges in times of relative harmony between Jews and the dominant culture while others reflect the struggle to survive when the Jewish subculture struggled for its continuing existence.

The Epistle of Aristeas

The Epistle of Aristeas, which is famous for its legendary account of the translation of the Septuagint, was probably written under the Ptolemies in a time of peace by a Jewish author who had an excellent education and a high social position in Egypt.[15] The author's admiration for Greek culture is evident throughout this work. Indeed, the translators, according to the author, were "men of excellent education (*paideia*)" who had not only "mastered Jewish literature but also given considerable attention to the literature of the Greeks" (121–22). The author presents the Jews and Greeks as belonging to the same cultural world. According to a passage attributed to the Greek Demetrius, but actually written by the Jewish author:

> "God, the overseer and creator of all things, whom they worship,
> is He whom all men worship, and we too, Your Majesty, though

14. Gürtner, *Introducing the Pseudepigrapha of Second Temple Judaism*, 42.

15. Barclay, *Jews in the Mediterranean Diaspora*, 139. Trans. OTP.

we address Him differently, as Zeus and Dis; by these names men of old not unsuitably signified that He through whom all creatures receive life and come into being is the guide and lord of all." (16)

This statement reflects the theology of the book as a whole. While the author observes the law, the book suggests that both Jews and Greeks follow their separate paths; it gives no indication of the special place of the Jews or hints at proselytizing.[16]

According to the Epistle of Aristeas, both Jews and Greeks prize rational thought above bodily desires (5–8, 130, 140–41, 321); both extol moderation and self-control (122, 221–23, 237, 256); and both pursue virtue (*aretē*, 122, 200, 215) and justice (*dikaiosynē*, 18, 24, 125).[17] Both Jews and Greeks place great value on piety (2, 24, 37, 42, 131, 215, 229). Consequently, Jews are well integrated into the majority culture. Their leaders have even been appointed to high positions in various ministries (37).

Despite the high social position of Aristeas, he defends a social boundary over which the Jews may not pass.[18] "In his wisdom the legislator, in a comprehensive survey of each particular part, and being endowed by God for the knowledge of universal truths, surrounded us with unbroken palisades and iron walls to prevent our mixing with any of the other peoples in any matter, being thus kept pure in body and soul" (trans. OTP 139). He adds, "So to prevent our being perverted by contact with others or by mixing with bad influences, he hedges us all around with strict observances" (142). The author appeals to Greek values, indicating that the law is in accordance with reason. "In general, everything is similarly constituted in regard to natural reasoning, being governed by one supreme power, and in each particular everything has a profound reason for it, both the things from which we abstain in use and those of which we partake." The author offers examples.

> Everything pertaining to conduct permitted toward these creatures and toward beasts has been set out symbolically. Thus the cloven hoof, that is the separation of the claws of the hoof, is a sign of setting apart each of our actions for good, because the strength of the whole body with its actions rests upon the shoulders and the legs. The symbolism conveyed by these things compels us to make a distinction in the performance of all our acts, with righteousness as our aim. This moreover explains why we

16. Collins, *Between Athens and Jerusalem*, 180.

17. Barclay, *Jews in the Mediterranean Diaspora*, 141.

18. Barclay, *Jews in the Mediterranean Diaspora*, 147.

> are distinct from all other men. The majority of other men defile
> themselves in their relationships, thereby committing a serious
> offense, and lands and whole cities take pride in it: they not only
> procure the males, they also defile mothers and daughters. We
> are quite separated from these practices. (150–53).

The law is one symbolic expression of the truth that can also be discovered in other ways.[19]

While the author employs allegory to indicate the compatibility of Jewish laws with Greek rationalism, he also maintains the Jewish practice of separation from others. Thus the Epistle of Aristeas demonstrates Jewish accommodation to Greek culture and the boundaries that prevent complete assimilation to it.

Philo of Alexandria

Philo of Alexandria is the heir of a well-established Jewish community in Alexandria and of numerous predecessors who had responded to Greek culture. Some of Philo's contemporaries, including his nephew, Tiberius Julius Alexander, who rose to a high position in the provincial government,[20] abandoned all Jewish practices and assimilated to the dominant culture (Josephus, *Ant.* 20.100). Philo became a leading voice among the Jews, who maintained their Jewish identity while also being immersed in Greek culture. His brother, who held a high administrative position in Alexandria,[21] even donated the gold and silver plating for nine of the gates of the temple enclosure. His importance to Jewish life is suggested by the fact that he was once imprisoned by Gaius (cf. Josephus, *Ant.* 18.159–60, 165).

Philo's wealth enabled him to receive an elite Greek education in Alexandria (cf. *Legat.* 182). He evidently attended a gymnasium, which covered all the subjects that became the medieval trivium (grammar, rhetoric, dialectic) and quadrivium (arithmetic, geometry, music, astronomy [*Congr.* 11, 16–18, 75–76, 148]),[22] which comprise the *egkyklios paideia*. A typical gymnasium had statues of the Greek gods and a curriculum that included the

---

19. Collins, *Between Athens and Jerusalem*, 180–81.

20. Tiberius Julius Alexander became the governor of Egypt under Nero and then Titus's chief of staff in the Judean war (Josephus, *B.J.* 5.45–46, 6.237). Philo's debates with his nephew appear in *De animalibus* and *De providentia*.
See Schwartz, "Philo, His Family, and His Times," 14.

21. Schenck, *Brief Guide to Philo*, 10.

22. Schenck, *Brief Guide to Philo*, 10.

stories about the Greek gods. Philo undoubtedly became familiar with these stories, as he sometimes indicates in his writings (*Opif.* 133; *Cher.* 48–49).

As Philo argues in *De congressu*, the basic subjects are only the "handmaiden" to the study of philosophy (*Congr.* 9, 10, 14, 19, 23, 35, 72–74, 79, 121, 154–55; cf. *Leg.* 3.244), the knowledge of the higher things, which lead to wisdom and virtue (*Congr.* 79–80). Philo's heroes exemplify the path from the lower subjects to philosophy, and he himself exemplified this practice.[23] His knowledge of Greek literature, Homer and the poets (particularly Euripides), Demosthenes, Plato, and the Stoics, is evident on every page of his work.[24] He is especially indebted to Plato. His guiding principle was that Moses was a great philosopher whose writings cohere with Middle Platonism and Stoicism. In fact, according to Philo, the Greeks borrowed from Moses. He insists that the laws in the Pentateuch are in accordance with the law of nature, claiming the rationality of each commandment by using the Stoic method of allegory.[25] He finds philosophical truths throughout his commentaries on the Pentateuch. The creation narrative in Genesis is consistent with Plato's *Timaeus*; Philo finds two creations in Genesis: that of the intelligible world (*kosmos noētos*) and of the sensible world (*aisthētos kosmos*, *Opif.* 16). The Platonic view of the transcendence of the deity fits with Philo's understanding of God. Like the Middle Platonists, Philo employs negative theology, using the terms "unnameable" (*akatanomastos*), "unutterable" (*arrhētos*), and "incomprehensible by any idea" (*kata pasas ideas akatalēptou*) in reference to God (*Somn.* 1.67), claiming that these terms are consistent with the God of Genesis.

Although Philo was immersed in Greek literature and philosophy, he subordinated his love of Greek culture to his Jewish identity. The Jewish nation is

> One which makes the greatest profession, to be engaged in the supplication of the One who truly exists, who is the Creator and Father of all. For what disciples of the best philosophy learn from its teaching Jews gain from their laws and customs, that is,

23. Philo, *Congr.* 74: "For instance, when first I was incited by the goads of philosophy to desire her, I consorted in early youth with one of her handmaids, Grammar, and all that I begat by her, writing, reading, and study of the writings of the poets, I dedicated to her mistress. And again I kept company with another, namely Geometry, and I was charmed with her beauty, for she showed symmetry and proportion in every part. Yet I took none of her children for my own use, but brought them as a gift to my lawful wife."

24. John Dillon, *Middle Platonists*, 140.

25. On the Greek origins of allegory, see Kamesar, "Biblical Interpretation in Philo," 78.

knowledge of the highest and most original Cause of all, while they reject the deceit of created Gods. For no created thing is really God; it is only so in men's opinion, since it lacks the most essential quality, eternity. (*Virt.* 64–65)[26]

In his philosophical discourses he suggests that his Greek sources have borrowed their best ideas from Moses (*Prob.* 57; cf. *Aet.* 19; *Mos.* 1.1–3). This identity came into sharp focus in the crisis of AD 38, when long-standing tensions between Alexandrian Jews and other groups turned into violence. Jews were beaten, stabbed, dragged through the city, set on fire, and their bodies left to rot (*Flacc.* 65–71). What most affected Philo was when Flaccus declared the Jews of the city "foreigners and aliens" (*Flacc.* 53–54). After the crisis subsided, Philo led a delegation to Rome to see Caligula.[27]

Philo's loyalty to Judaism is evident throughout his writings. Although he provides extensive allegory on Jewish rituals, including circumcision, food laws, and the Sabbath, he is fully observant of the law. He gives an elaborate allegorical interpretation of circumcision as the elimination of pleasure and the passions (*Migr.* 92), but the literal practice was also important to him (cf. *Spec.* 1.8–11). Philo says, "Let us not abolish the law established concerning circumcision" (*Migr.* 92). In *Spec.* 1.1–12 Philo gives an extended defense of the practice of circumcision, noting that it was practiced by other peoples, including the Egyptians (*Spec.* 1.2). He counters those who mock this Jewish practice by arguing that 1) it prevents some incurable diseases (1.4); 2) it promotes the cleanliness of the whole body, preventing genital diseases (1.4); 3) it assimilates the circumcised member to the heart (1.6); and 4) it is beneficial for fertility, allowing the semen to "travel aright" (1.7). Thus as this defense of circumcision at the beginning of *De specialibus legibus* indicates, "circumcision is the entry to the law, because it signifies two fundamental principles of the law, the repudiation of pleasure, which is the chief cause of moral error, and faith in God."[28]

As one of the commandments of the decalogue, the Sabbath is of special significance to Philo, as his extended treatment in *De decalogo* indicates (*Decal.* 96–101; *Spec.* 2.260; *Somn.* 2.123; *Legat.* 158). He insists that the Sabbath is a holy, public, and universal holiday that celebrates the birthday of the world (*Opif.* 89; *Mos.* 1.207; 2.209–10; 2.59, 70). To keep the Sabbath is to follow the pattern of God (*Decal.* 100), who rested on the seventh day. This is the day to study wisdom (100).

---

26. Cited in Barclay, *Jews in the Mediterranean Diaspora*, 174.

27. Schenck, *Brief Guide to Philo*, 13.

28. Termini, "Philo's Thought within the Context of Middle Judaism," 117.

Philo gives several examples of things that Jews should not do on the Sabbath: "To light a fire or till the ground or carry a load or call a meeting or sit in judgment or seek deposits or recover debts or to do other things also allowed in those times that are not feast days" (*Migr.* 91). As in Exodus 20:10, the Sabbath rest is granted to servants and to animals (*Spec.* 2.66–70); Philo even includes plants (*Mos.* 2.22). The reduction of physical exertion is not to be understood as a provision for laziness or occasion for cheap entertainment (*Mos.* 2.211). It is instead a time to care for the soul. For this reason Jews assemble in synagogues on the Sabbath and listen to the reading and explanation of the Scriptures (cf. *Opif.* 128; *Abr.* 28–30; *Decal.* 98–101; *Mos.* 2.211–12, 215–16).

The Sabbath is of special significance because of the number seven. God is the transcendent One. "God, 'being One, is alone and unique'" (*Leg.* II.1). Philo concludes that the One is equivalent to seven, the ideal number, describing it in *Opif.* 100:

> It is in the nature of 7 alone, as I have said, neither to beget nor to be begotten. For this reason other philosophers liken this number to the motherless (ἀμήτορι) and virgin Nikē (i.e., Athena), who is said to have appeared out of the head of Zeus, while the Pythagoreans liken it to the ruler of all things: for that which neither begets nor is begotten remains motionless; for creation takes place in movement, since there is movement both in that which begets and that which is begotten. There is only one thing that neither causes motion nor experiences it, the original Ruler and Sovereign. Of him 7 may be fitly said to be a symbol (εἰκών). Evidence of what I say is supplied by Philolaus in these words: 'There is, he says, a supreme ruler of all things, God, ever One, abiding, without motion, like unto himself, different from all others.

Philo follows the allegorical interpretation of the *Letter of Aristeas* in his interpretation of Jewish food laws. The food laws under the general rubric of the tenth commandment, "Thou shalt not covet' (*epithumēseis*, desire)."[29] In Exod 20:17 the prohibition is directed against desiring wife or property of a neighbor, but in Philo it takes on a more general meaning. "None of the passions is so troublesome as covetousness and desire (*epithumia*) of what we have not" (*Spec.* 4.80), for it is the source of every sort of base passion (*Spec.* 4.84). After describing the desire for wealth, reputation,

---

29. See the extended treatment of desire (*epithumia*) in *Spec.* 4.79–118 as the heading for the explanation of the distinction between clean and unclean meat. The food laws are intended to mitigate excessive desire. See the other passages on the food laws in *Leg.* 2.105; *Post.* 148–49; *Agr.* 131–45; *Migr.* 64–67.

and office (*Spec.* 4.87–89), Philo concludes that the primal form of desire is connected with the stomach, because that is the seat of the "desiring" (*Spec.* 4.84, 92–94). Moses regulates the consumption of food by means of a series of laws that would encourage the virtue of *enkrateia* (self-control) and improve relations between men (*Spec.* 4.97). In describing the distinction between pure and impure animals, Philo mentions the pig and fishes without scales. They are forbidden because the tastiness of their meat excites the pleasure of the belly, provoking gluttony (121). The injunctions may be understood in an ethical sense to encourage a temperate lifestyle (*Spec.* 4.100–102). Moses prohibits the consumption of reptiles and insects that move on their belly or have four feet or more, for the belly is tied to pleasure, and the passions, the source of all vices (*Spec.* 4.113–115).[30]

Philo remained a loyal Jew, maintaining the boundary markers of circumcision, Sabbath, and food laws that frequently defined Jewish practice in the diaspora. He demonstrated how a loyal Jew could be deeply immersed in Greek education and remain faithful to the Jewish tradition. Scholars have observed parallels between Philo and both Paul and the author of Hebrews.

The Wisdom of Solomon

The significance of Hellenism for Jewish identity is apparent throughout the Wisdom of Solomon. Although the records do not give a date and place for the writing, this work probably also originated in Alexandria.[31] Indeed, the numerous echoes of Philo in this work suggest that the two come from a similar environment.[32] The author demonstrates a facility with Greek language and rhetoric. James M. Reese has pointed out that the vocabulary and style are not that of the LXX but of the Hellenistic environment in which the author lived.[33] Although it is addressed to "the rulers of the earth" (1:1; 6:1–5, 21), it is actually written to Jews who live as a minority group in a Hellenistic environment.

The Wisdom of Solomon is a protreptic address, a genre that called for the adoption of a meaningful philosophy as a way of life.[34] In contrasting the way of wisdom with the way of folly, it is intended to encourage continued adherence to the Jewish way of life "in a setting where the enticements of

---

30. Termini, "Philo's Thought within the Context of Middle Judaism," 121.

31. Collins, *Between Athens and Jerusalem*, 182. The book has been dated anywhere from the second century BC to AD 40.

32. See Winston, *Wisdom of Solomon*, 40–45, 59.

33. Reese, *Hellenistic Influence*, 3–31.

34. Reese, *Hellenistic Influence*, 118.

Hellenization and the ability of apostates to reject their heritage as of little value weigh heavily upon Jewish consciousness."[35] For a text that explicitly encourages one way of life over alternatives, the protreptic discourses of the philosophers provide the closest generic equivalents.[36]

Like other protreptic speeches, the Wisdom of Solomon it demonstrates encyclopedic learning throughout the work. The rhetorical skill is evident in the extended *synkrisis*, extolling wisdom (cf. 7:24, 28–30; 8:5).[37] Chapters 11–19 are structured by extended *synkrises* that contrast the misfortunes of the Egyptians with the deliverance of God's people[38] and the sorites in 6:17–20,[39] which traces the steps that lead from the wise man's search for training to his obtaining eternal royalty. The work is written in excellent Greek, and it has many connections with Philo.

A major component of Wisdom's attempt to promote loyalty to the Jewish worship of the one God is the way the author articulates and supports the appeal with concepts learned from Greek philosophy.[40] When borrowing from Greek philosophy, the author reflects the tendencies of Middle Platonism to create a viable synthesis drawn from Stoic and Platonic thought.[41] Part of the author's appeal to the readers, no doubt, was this incipient synthesis of the best of the Greek tradition with the Jewish tradition.[42]

Reese has demonstrated extensive philosophical vocabulary. The philosophical training is particularly evident in 13:1–9. The argument assumes that philosophical reasoning should lead to the conclusion that God created the world. The author's conviction that observation of these marvels of creation should lead to the perception of the Creator was shared by gentile philosophers such as Cleanthes.[43] Paul makes a similar argument in Rom 1:18–24.

Wisdom's anthropology connects with Platonic thought, as the author's reference to the preexistence of souls indicates (8:19–20). The soul enters the body, which is regarded as a burden for the soul, an "earthly tent"

---

35. DeSilva, *Introducing the Apocrypha*, 133.

36. DeSilva, *Introducing the Apocrypha*, 133.

37. *Synkrisis* is a common rhetorical device comparing two persons or objects in order to demonstrate the superiority of one over the other. Plutarch's *Parallel Lives*, a comparison between prominent Greeks and Romans, is an exercise in *synkrisis*.

38. Barclay, *Jews in the Mediterranean*, 189.

39. A *sorites* is a chain of syllogisms; the conclusion of each is used as the premise for the next.

40. Reese, *Hellenistic Influence*, 32–89.

41. Collins, *Between Athens and Jerusalem*, 200–201; Winston, *Wisdom of Solomon*, 33.

42. DeSilva, *Introducing the Apocrypha*, 146.

43. Cicero, *Nat. d.* 2.12–15; Collins, *Between Athens and Jerusalem*, 207.

that weighs down the soul (9:15). One may compare Plato, *Phaedo* 81C: "The body is a heavy load, my friend, weighty and earthly and visible." The author shares the Platonic idea of the immortality of the soul, stressing that one's moral character determines one's place in the afterlife.[44]

The author's ethical teaching provides a synthesis between the way of righteousness described in the Jewish tradition and Greek ethical instruction. The pursuit of God-given wisdom trains the devotee in the four cardinal virtues prized by Stoics and Platonists. Wisdom teaches the Greek cardinal virtues: "she teaches self-control [*sophrosynē*] and prudence [*phronēsis*], justice [*dikaiosynē*] and courage [*andreia*]" (8:7).

While not written necessarily during a time of persecution, Wisdom reflects a high degree of tension between gentile and Jewish groups.[45] Despite the affinity for Greek philosophy and rhetoric displayed by the author, the predominant theme is "the social conflict and cultural antagonism between Jews and non-Jews."[46] The author of Wisdom employs his considerable learning not to integrate his Judaism with his environment but to construct all the more sophisticated an attack upon it![47] He depicts a sharply polarized society where "righteous" and "ungodly" stand opposed in straightforward antagonism. God's people ("the righteous") stand in contrast to "the foolish" (3:2), "the ungodly" (1:16; 3:10; 5:14; 19:1), "the unrighteous" (4:18; 5:2), and "the wicked" (4:12). The author recalls transitional biblical characters who were saved by wisdom (10:1–2) before devoting a lengthy meditation on the salvation of God's people (11–19) and a critique of gentile religion (chs. 13–15). The author presents a lengthy argument against the legitimacy of gentile religion (13:1–15:19), using traditional Jewish criticisms (e.g., Isa 44:9–10; Ps 115:4–8; cf. Wis 14:15–16) as well as the common philosophical critique. All those who do not recognize the God of Israel as the creator are ignorant of God. These people are foolish by nature (*physei*). God's people are opposed by "enemies" and "foes" (11.3, 5, 8; 12:20, 22).[48] From the beginning of the polemic (13:1), the author draws a line between those who are ignorant and those who possess accurate knowledge of the divine.[49] While such a polemic would serve to reinforce the lines drawn between Jewish culture and the unenlightened Gentile masses, the points of contact with Greco-Roman philosophic texts suggest that the author sought to present

44. DeSilva, *Introducing the Apocrypha*, 136.
45. DeSilva, *Introducing the Apocrypha*, 137.
46. Barclay, *Jews in the Mediterranean World*, 184
47. Barclay, *Jews in the Mediterranean* World, 184.
48. Barclay, *Jews in the Mediterranean World*, 189.
49. King, "Idolatry and Jewish Identity," 83.

Jewish piety that was on a par with the tenets of the most enlightened Greco-Roman intellectuals.[50] Such rhetoric as we find in wisdom would have been a welcome reinforcement for Jewish commitment at any period and the one of hostility within the document may be intended to promote a "we versus they" mentality in order to guard against assimilation.[51]

Fourth Maccabees

Fourth Maccabees also reports the resistance to the conquerors who attempted to prohibit their religious practice with the collusion of Jason the high priest (4:19–20). The narrative focuses on the command for Jews to eat pork and food offered to idols (5:2–3, 14) and the tortures and death given to those who refused. The author records in vivid detail the tortures administered to the aged Eleazar (5:14–7:23) and the brothers, who ultimately died for their religion as their mother looked on (8:1–17:10). He is immersed in the Jewish traditions and the narratives of the Old Testament,[52] presenting Joseph (2:1–5), Moses (2:17), Jacob (2:19), and David (3:6) as examples of faithfulness to the law. When the mother speaks at the end, she recalls the stories of Cain and Abel, Isaac, Phinehas, the three young men in the fiery furnace, and Daniel (18:1–15) as examples of faithfulness to the law. She then cites Proverbs (18:16; cf. Prov 3:18), Ezekiel (18:17; cf. Ezek 37:2–3), and the song that Moses taught (18:32; cf. Deut 30:20; 32:19).

Although 4 Maccabees advocates resistance to those who prohibit the practices that define Judaism, it is also immersed in Greek philosophy and rhetoric. David deSilva describes this work as "acculturated resistance literature."[53] He has observed that the author writes in excellent Greek, following stylistic and rhetorical conventions that demonstrate a mastery of the language.[54] His command of the language suggests that he had undertaken the primary and secondary education and engaged in extensive reading in Greek literature.[55] As a book praising the virtue of reason and the martyrs who exhibited this virtue, 4 Maccabees is commonly described as epideictic

---

50. DeSilva, *Introduction to the Apocrypha*, 144; deSilva, *Introducing the Apocrypha*, 146.

51. DeSilva, *Introduction to the Apocrypha*, 133.

52. Niebuhr, *Gesetz und Paränese*, 216.

53. DeSilva, *Fourth Maccabees*, 66–91.

54. DeSilva, *Fourth Maccabees*, 10.

55. DeSilva, *Fourth Maccabees*, 10–31, demonstrates the author's skill with narrative, ekphrasis (the vivid description of a scene), the maxim, *synkrisis* and *prosopopoieia*.

oratory. With its exhortation to choose the course of action demonstrated by the martyrs, it also exhibits deliberative features.[56]

The opening words of 4 Maccabees demonstrate the author's engagement with philosophy, especially Stoicism. The subject for discussion, according to the author, is "most philosophical" (1:1). He begins with the proposition that "devout reason is sovereign over the emotions" (*tōn pathōn*), a claim that was commonplace in philosophical discussions. The work consists of two major sections framed by an exordium (1:1–12) and a *peroratio* (17:7–18:24).[57] The first section (1:13–3:18) contains the theoretical basis for the thesis, which the author announces in 1:1: "Devout reason (*ho eusebēs logismos*) rules the emotions (*pathē*)." This claim becomes the refrain for the entire book (1:1, 5–7, 9, 13–14, 19, 29; 2:4, 7, 9, 15, 24; 3:1, 5; 6:31; 7:1, 16; 13:1; 15:23; 16:1). Those who control the passions exhibit the cardinal virtues of justice (*dikaiosynē*), courage (*andreia*), temperance (*sophrosynē*), and wisdom (*phronēsis*, 1:6, 18). The temperate (*sophron*) Joseph was able to overcome "the frenzy of the passions" through reason (2:4). Moses controlled anger through reason (2:17–18). Jacob condemned the anger of the households of Simeon and Levi (2:19). When David's servants brought him the water that he craved, he poured it on the ground, confronting his desire with reason (3:7–16).

According to the theoretical analysis in chapters 1–3, the God who planted the passions in the body and the soul also provided the power to place them under control. Reason (*logismos*) is the sovereign (*autokratōr*, 1:7, 13, 30; 16:1; *autodespotēs*, 1:1; 13:1) and master (*despotēs*, 2:24; *kyrios*, 2:7) of the emotions, providing the means so that no one will give way to them (1:7). It bridles the impulses (1:29), and it rules (*kratei*, 2:6, 15, 20; *epikratei*, 3:1) and controls (*epikratei*, 1:33–35).[58]

This theoretical foundation lays the basis for the narrative of the martyrs in the second part (chs. 4–18). The martyrs demonstrated the cardinal virtues and a willingness to suffer and die for the law and virtue. The heroes have been educated in the law (5:21–25; 13:22). They fight for the ancestral law (6:21, 30; 9:15; 11:27; 13:13; 15:29, 32; 16:16) and die for it (6:27, 30; 13:9) and for piety (*eusebeia*, 7:15; 9:16–24, 29, 30; 11:20; 13:12; 14:13; 15:3, 14, 32; 16:13–14, 23; 18:3). Eleazar maintains his reason in the context of torture (5:31; 6:7), dies nobly because of reason (6:31–7:1, 4, 14, 16–17), and is followed in this by the sons (9:14–16; 15:1) and their mother (15:11, 23), all of whom exhibit the cardinal virtues. In response to the tyrant, Eleazar

56. Klauck, *4 Makkabäerbuch*, 659; deSilva, *Fourth Maccabees*, 44.

57. Klauck, "Die Bruderliebe bei Plutarch und im vierten Makkabäerbuch," 91.

58. Thompson, *Moral Formation according to Paul*, 23–24.

declares that the practice of the law teaches self-control, courage, justice, and piety (5:23–24). In observing the law, the martyrs become the exemplars of courage (*andreia*) and self-control (*sophrosynē*).[59]

Like Philo, the author appeals to the tenth commandment, "You shall not covet (*epithumēseis*) to elaborate on the general subject of *epithumia*, commonly rendered as "passion" or "desire." By omitting the direct object in Exod 20:17, he engages in the philosophical discussion of the control of the passions. The fact that Paul also alludes to the tenth commandment in a discourse on the control of the passions (Rom 7:7) suggests that the use of the commandment in discussions of the passions was common in Hellenistic Judaism.

The author of 4 Maccabees "cannot think about his own heritage apart from the master's categories"[60] but nevertheless engages in a critique of the dominant culture. Like Philo, he uses his education and rhetorical ability to demonstrate the congruence of the Jewish way of life with the highest ideals of Hellenistic culture. The portrayal of the heroes who died for the law is an encouragement to the readers, who also live as minorities in their own communities. The author concludes with the exhortation to the readers: "O Israelite children, offspring of the seed of Abraham, obey this law and exercise piety in every way, knowing that devout reason is master of all emotions, not only of suffering from within, but also those from without" (18:1–2). The readers can live comfortably within the Hellenistic culture and remain faithful to the law. Thus the author reinforces group commitment as they face the tensions of life in the diaspora.

Other documents from the Hellenistic age reflect the tendency toward the maintenance of Jewish identity and the adoption of Hellenistic culture. Many of them exist only in fragments. *Ezekiel the Tragedian* presents the story of the Hebrews as a Greek tragedy, adopting the Greek literary tradition while remaining faithful to Jewish identity. The presentation of Moses belongs to the tradition of the Greek seer.[61] Aristobulus preceded Philo of Alexandria in employing allegory to find a convergence between Scripture and philosophy.[62] The fragments of his exegetical work reflect his eclectic philosophical interests, including a familiarity with Stoic and Pythagorean traditions. His allegorical interpretation of Scripture corresponds to some

---

59. Thompson, *Moral Formation according to Paul*, 27.

60. DeSilva, *Fourth Maccabees*, 67.

61. Barclay, *Jews in the Mediterranean Diaspora*, 133. Holladay, "Paul and His Predecessors in the Diaspora," 447.

62. See Holladay, "Paul and His Predecessors," 448–51.

extent to the Stoic allegorical interpretation of Homer.[63] Artapanus retells the biblical story, demonstrating his Jewish commitments while reflecting his appreciation of Egyptian culture. He depicts Abraham as the one responsible for introducing astrology to Egypt (18.1). Joseph introduced enhanced Jewish life by introducing irrigation and the proper allocation of the land (23.2). Moses invented boats, weapons, and various machines (27.4).[64] He is the one whom the Greeks called Musaeus (27.3–4).

This literature reflects the extent of Jewish participation in Greek intellectual life. Jewish families apparently sent their children to the Greek gymnasia. The Jewish literature, according to Carl Holladay, represents both ethnic promotion and self-preservation. To varying degrees, these texts have missionary, apologetic, and propagandistic tendencies. Although they are conversant with Greek literature and interact with Greek philosophers and historians, they remain sympathetic to the Jewish tradition. This engagement with Greek culture indicates "not only that Greek culture was speaking to them but also that they were speaking to Hellenistic culture."[65]

CONCLUSION

The major challenge for Jews in both Palestine and the diaspora was to maintain their identity in a culture that discriminated against them, ridiculed them, and enticed them to abandon the traditional faith. No group was totally untouched by aspects of Greek culture although Jewish groups responded in a variety of ways. Some assimilated fully to Greek culture while our literature records the others who maintained their Jewish identity. Among these, some withdrew from the culture while others adopted various elements of Greek culture while maintaining Jewish practices.

These issues form the background for both the ministry of Jesus and the work of Paul. Jesus's table fellowship with sinners violated Pharisaic norms of separation. When Paul later formed communities of Christ-believers in the diaspora, he had models for community formation in the Jewish tradition. His controversies with those who insisted on circumcising converts also challenges the traditions of separation (see ch. 3). Nevertheless, he encouraged separation for his own converts, insisting on drawing boundaries between the community and the larger society (see ch. 3). He established communities that, like the diaspora counterparts, rejected

63. Holladay, "Jewish Responses to Hellenistic Culture in Early Ptolemaic Egypt," 142.

64. Barclay, *Jews in the Mediterranean Diaspora*, 128. See texts in Eusebius, *Preparation for the Gospel*, 23–24.

65. Holladay, "Jewish Responses to Hellenistic Culture in Early Ptolemaic Egypt," 144.

idolatry and activities associated with it. He also shaped communities that rejected the sexual practices of the society. Consequently, the communities established by Paul, like the communities of the diaspora, lived as minorities in their culture and faced the hostility of the populace. Paul provided them with a corporate identity that empowered them to resist the temptation to assimilation.

2

Jesus, the Kingdom of God, and Human Culture

When Jesus came into Galilee, preaching "The time is fulfilled; the kingdom of God is at hand" (Mark 1:15), he was evoking an image for the culmination of Israel's hopes, which would usher in a new society.[1] Although the phrase "kingdom of God" is rare in Jewish literature, the OT and Jewish literature declare that "God reigns" (Ps 93:1; 96:10; 97:1) and that God's kingdom is everlasting (Ps 145:13). In the midst of defeat and desolation after the exile, the reign of God is interpreted eschatologically. The prophets anticipate the time when "God will be king over all the earth" (Zech 14:9). The author of Daniel surveys the succession of kingdoms and announces the future "kingdom that will not be destroyed" (Dan 2:44). Deutero-Isaiah announces the return from exile, exclaiming "Your God reigns" (Isa 52:7). God will reign over Israel and all creation (Isa 40:3–4; 41:4; 43:3). Thus the OT reflects a tension between the present reign of God and the expectation of a future kingdom. The latter dimension dominates Jewish apocalyptic literature.[2]

While descriptions of the coming kingdom vary in Jewish literature, the common themes were the conquering of God's enemies (*1 QM* 1:9–10),

1. See Wright, *Jesus and the Victory of God*, 199.
2. Schnelle, *Theology of the New Testament*, 88.

the defeat of Satan/Beliar (*As. Mos.* 10:1; *1 QM* 1:5; *T. Dan* 5:10–13), vengeance on the nations (Isa 61:2; Ps. Sol. 17:30–31; *As. Mos.* 10:7), and the restoration of peace and justice in the land (Isa 52:7; 54:12, 14; 55:12; 57:2, 19; 60:17). This will be the time for the restoration of the monarchy, according to numerous sources. According to the Psalms of Solomon, God chose David to be king over Israel and swore that his descendants would be kings forever and that his kingdom would never fall (17:3; cf. 2 Sam 7:14). The author prays, "Raise up for them their king, the son of David, to rule over your servant Israel" (17:21). This descendant of David will destroy the enemies, purify Jerusalem, and gather a holy people, whom he will lead in righteousness (17:26). In addition, the proto-rabbinic texts show that the prayer for the coming of God's kingdom was a central element of Jewish hope at the time of Jesus.[3] In the prayer, the kaddish, they pray: "Magnified and sanctified be his great name in the world that he has created according to his will. May he establish his kingdom in your lifetime and in your days and in your lifetime of all the house of Israel, even speedily and at a near time."[4]

Jesus made his announcement in the context of political, religious, cultural, and social institutions that already existed and would be challenged by his message. Indeed, the signs of Greco-Roman culture and institutions were everywhere. As Martin Hengel observed, Greco-Roman culture was not limited to the Jewish diaspora but penetrated into Judea and Galilee.[5] Herod the Great and his son Herod Antipas had engaged in major building projects in Judea and Galilee. The Hellenistic cities of Tiberias and Sepphoris were not far away from Jesus's home in Nazareth. A Greek theater was built in Sepphoris, only a few miles from Jesus's home.[6] Jewish groups could not ignore the influence of Greek culture but defined themselves on a continuum between resistance and accommodation (see ch. 1). Thus while Jesus did not address the relationship between the kingdom and the culture, his message undoubtedly had implications for the existing society. Like his predecessor John the Baptist, he did not minister within the established institutions or affiliate with any of the parties within Galilee and Judea. He called all Israel to repent in anticipation of the coming of the kingdom.

Despite the proximity of the Greco-Roman culture to Jesus's home, the Gospels record no explicit engagement with it. Nor do they refer to Jesus's presence in the Hellenistic-Roman cities of Sepphoris and Tiberias. Jesus

---

3. Schnelle, *Theology of the New Testament*, 89–90.

4. Schnelle, *Theology of the New Testament*, 89–90.

5. Hengel, *Judaism and Hellenism*.

6. Batey, "Sepphoris and the Jesus Movement," 408–9.

makes no reference to the culture of the theater, the arts, or the philosophy of the day.

The dark cloud overshadowing the ministry of Jesus was the reality of Roman occupation.[7] One may be surprised, however, that the Gospel narratives contain few reports of Jesus's encounter with the signs of Roman power or of Rome's client in Galilee, Herod Antipas. In fact, "the ruling hand of Rome was fairly light."[8] Antipas is mentioned only rarely in the Gospel narratives (cf. Mark 6:14–22; Luke 23:7–15). This fact is especially surprising when one considers that Herod Antipas executed John the Baptist. When Jesus is told that Herod Antipas wants to kill him, he replied, "Go and tell that fox, 'Behold, I cast out demons and perform cures today and tomorrow'" (Luke 13:31–32). He speaks directly of Roman power only when he is asked about the payment of taxes (Mark 12:13–17 par.).

While Jesus does not speak of the high culture of literature and the arts, his language reflects his place in the ordinary village culture of Galilee. He speaks of weddings (Mark 2:19–20 par.), households (Mark 6:10 par.; 10:29), absentee landlords, tenant farmers, day laborers, fishermen, tax collectors, and village life. He assumes the existence of slavery (Matt 10:24; 18:23; 22:3; Luke 12:42) and life under Roman rule. The immediate culture among Jews in Galilee was dominated by the synagogue and the way of life based on the Torah. Jesus frequently encounters the Pharisees and scribes as well as the crowds in Galilee, the culture that he engages.

Jesus's message of the kingdom addressed the deep longings of an oppressed people. However, the Gospels contain no record of a confrontation with Roman rule. The kingdom was already "at hand" (Mark 1:15); indeed, Jesus claims that the prophetic hope for the "good news for the poor" was already fulfilled (Luke 4:21). While the "good news for the poor" was understood in Jewish tradition as the reversal of Israel's fortunes, Jesus demonstrated this good news in his ministry to the diseased and the outcasts within Israel. In his exorcisms, he declared that "the kingdom of God has come upon you" (Luke 11:20). Indeed, the defeat of Satan was not expressed in terms of an actual military confrontation, but in his healings and exorcisms (cf. Mark 3:23–27; Luke 10:18).

Although the Gospels indicate that Jesus attracted great crowds, his message was rejected by most of the listeners. His generation was "like children in the marketplace" who say, "We played the flute to you and you did not dance, we sang a dirge and you did not weep" (Matt 11:16; Luke

---

7. Dunn, "Thought World of Jesus," 342.

8. Dunn, "Thought World of Jesus," 342.

7:31).[9] He describes it as "an evil generation" that demands a sign (Luke 7:29), and he denounces the cities where his preaching did not lead to repentance, expressing woes on Chorazin, Bethsaida, and Capernaum (Matt 11:20–24). The response to his message is indicated in the parable of the banquet. Those who were first invited rejected the invitation (Luke 14:16–24; cf. Matt 22:1–14).

Because Jesus worked outside the established institutions, a conflict with the culture was inevitable. The Gospel writers record the conflict between Jesus and Jewish groups from the beginning (cf. Mark 2:1—3:6). While these conflicts reflect issues from the period when the Gospels were written, they also point back to the issues in Jesus's own time, for the message of the kingdom inevitably provoked conflict with the existing institutions; the "new wine" did not fit in the old "wineskins."

Although Jesus was faithful to the Torah, he challenged the Pharisaic fence around the law, as evidenced by his activities on the Sabbath (cf. Mark 2:1–12 par; Luke 13:14–15; 14:1). In his table fellowship with tax collectors and sinners, he violated the Pharisees' purity laws and undermined their insistence on separation (cf. Luke 15:1). Consequently, the conflict with the Jewish leaders was inevitable.

While the Gospels do not record a direct challenge to Roman power by Jesus, the message of the kingdom inevitably led to a conflict with Roman power, as the sign on the cross, "king of the Jews," recorded in all four Gospels (Matt 27:37; Mark 15:26; Luke 23:38; John 19:19), suggests. Thus the Gospels report a conflict between Jesus and both the Jewish leadership and the Roman rulers.

JESUS AND THE ALTERNATIVE COMMUNITY

Jesus's message of the kingdom was rejected by the leaders and most of the populace. However, he gathered disciples who followed him. Some followed his itinerant life, while others were sedentary disciples who remained in their villages. Those who followed him established a distinctive way of life and shared the rejection by society with him.

Jesus and the Family

While Jesus assumed the realities of family life, the message of the kingdom had an impact on his teaching about the family. When he was asked about

---

9. See Schnelle, *Die getrennten Wege von Römern, Juden und Christen,* 65.

divorce, he challenged the classic text on the topic, Deut 24:1–4, as well as its common interpretation. By appealing to the creation story as the basis for marriage (cf. Mark 10:7), he indicated that the reality of marriage has been transformed, for he maintained that the coming of the kingdom brought with it absolute obedience.

On the other hand, he relativized the importance of the family. The sons of Zebedee left their father to follow Jesus (Mark 1:20). When the would-be disciple said, "Let me first bury my father," Jesus said, "Follow me, and let the dead bury their own dead" (Matt 8:21–22). This demand was contrary to the heart of Jewish piety. Under Pharisaic influence, the last offices for the dead had gained primacy among all the good works.[10] When his disciples said, "We have left all to follow you," Jesus speaks of those who "have left house or brothers or sisters and mothers and children and lands" for his sake (Mark 10:29). When he describes the coming of the Son of Man, he says, "As in the days of Noah, they were eating and drinking and marrying and giving in marriage" (Luke 17:26–27). In the parable of the banquet, some of those who were invited said, "I have married a wife and cannot come" (Luke 14:20). When Jesus's mother and brothers come for him, he replies, "Who are my mother and brothers?" (Mark 3:31–35). Thus Jesus relativized the family and spoke of an alternative family composed of his disciples.

Jesus and the Structures of Domination

In the Synoptic tradition, the stratified society that includes the relationship between master (*kyrios*) and slave (*doulos*) is assumed. Jesus encounters a centurion whose slave is ill (Matt 8:11; Luke 7:2). The parables consistently portray the world of slave and master (Matt 13:27; 18:23; 21:34–36; 22:3–4, 6, 8, 10; 24:45–46, 48, 50; 25:14, 19, 21, 23, 26; Luke 12:41–48; 15:22). The high priest has a slave (Matt 26:51). Jesus comments that "a disciple is not above his teacher, nor a slave above his master" (Matt 20:24; cf. John 13:16).

Jesus also knew the political world of kings and subjects. His parables describe kings who go to war (Luke 14:31), a king who wished to settle accounts with his servants (Matt 18:23), and a king who gave a marriage feast for his son (Matt 22:7). He indicates that his disciples "will be dragged before kings" (Matt 10:18) for his sake. He speaks of those who "live in kings' houses" (Matt 11:8). He knew the story of John the Baptist, who was

---

10. Hengel, *Charismatic Leader and His Followers*, 8. On the wish of parents to be buried by their sons, see Gen 49:29–33; 50:1–3, 50:25–26; Tob 4:3–4.

beheaded by the king (Herod Antipas, Mark 6:14–27 par.). He knows of kings who receive tribute from their subjects (Matt 17:25).

While society recognized structures of domination, Jesus called for a community that rejected these values. When the disciples are tempted to adopt the values of their culture, Jesus responded that "the rulers of the gentiles lord it over them. But it shall not be so among you. But whoever would be great among you must be your servant, and whoever would be first among you must be slave of all" (Mark 10:42–43). Similarly, Jesus encouraged his disciples, "Neither be called masters, for you have one master, the Christ. He who is greatest among you shall be your servant; whoever exalts himself will be humbled, and whoever humbles himself will be exalted" (Matt 23:8–12).

This expectation had major political implications for subject peoples, as the revolts in AD 6, 66–70, and 132–35 indicate. Jesus's announcement of the kingdom, however, made no direct reference to the immediate political situation. Indeed, he consistently indicates that the kingdom is already present. As the agricultural parables indicate, the kingdom is growing secretly. The expectation of "good news for the poor" has already been fulfilled in his ministry. The parables describe a new world of values.

The Kingdom and the Reversal of Values

Jesus disassociates his message of the kingdom from the common expectations and announces the reversal of values that is already present among his disciples. Jesus presents an alternative world that is already present in his ministry. Whereas children are marginalized in ancient society, Jesus includes them among the examples of the humility required for the disciples (Matt 18:3). They, along with the poor, are the marginalized little ones to whom "the kingdom of God belongs" (Mark 10:14; cf. Luke 6:20). His statement, "How hard it will be for the rich to enter the kingdom of God" (Mark 10:25), also looks forward to a new reality.[11] Similarly, the Lukan beatitude "Blessed are the poor" and the pronouncement "woe to you rich" expresses the reversal in the kingdom of God in Jesus's alternative community (Luke 6:20, 24). The reversal is also evident in the sayings of Jesus, "The first will be last" (Mark 10:31) and "For all who exalt themselves will be humbled, and all those who are humbled will be exalted" (Luke 14:11). Similarly, the reversal of values is the consistent theme of the parables. Those who come to the eschatological banquet are not the ones who were first invited but "the poor, the crippled, the blind, and the lame" (Luke 14:11). In response to the

11. Schnelle, *Theology of the New Testament*, 95.

criticism that Jesus eats with tax collectors and sinners, Jesus tells the story of the one who is welcomed home after he has wasted his inheritance (Luke 15:11–32) while the dutiful son has excluded himself from the celebration. The one who goes to his home justified is not the Pharisee who has exceeded the commands of the law but the tax collector who says, "God, be merciful to me a sinner" (Luke 18:9–14).

The Sermon on the Mount and the Alternative Community

According to Joseph Klausner, Jesus "did not come to enlarge his nation's knowledge of art and culture, but to abolish such culture as it possessed, bound up with religion, a culture which the scribes and Pharisees . . . held tightly as though it were the single anchor of safety left to the nation."[12] Alluding to the Sermon on the Mount, Klausner argued that civil justice and state efforts at reform would be impossible when one must "resist not evil" and when one turned the other cheek. "How can the state endure if Jesus's request that a man not swear at all?"[13] He adds that "even family life breaks down for one who would be a true disciple of Christ."[14] Klausner asks, "What interest has he in labor, in culture, in economic or political achievements, who recommends us to be like 'lilies of the field?'"[15]

Klausner adds that "the nation as a whole could only see in such public ideas a dangerous fantasy" that stands outside civilization.[16] Thus as a summary of the teachings of Jesus, the Sermon on the Mount gives a clear indication of the relation to the existing culture. As a comparison with Luke indicates, Matthew has brought together sayings of Jesus from different contexts. According to Matthew the instructions in the Sermon on the Mount appear only after Jesus has announced the imminent arrival of the kingdom (Matt 4:17, 23). Thus this sermon presupposes the arrival of the kingdom of God, which is a challenge to the existing culture. As the introductory words indicate, the crowds are present, but Jesus addresses the disciples.[17]

12. Klausner, *Jesus of Nazareth*, 373.

13. Klausner, *Jesus of Nazareth*, 374.

14. Klausner, *Jesus of Nazareth*, 374.

15. Klausner, *Jesus of Nazareth*, 374.

16. Klausner, *Jesus of Nazareth*, 376.

17. See du Toit, "Revisiting the Sermon on the Mount," 62. "The intra-textual audience of the SM can be envisaged as two concentric circles: The disciples in the inner circle, sitting as pupils at the feet of their teacher (5:1–2) and the crowds (*hoi ochloi*) in the outer one (5:1; 7:28–29)." See also Lohfink, *Jesus and Community*, 35: "The moral teaching of Jesus was to be practiced within the circle of disciples, but it was at the same time instruction for all Israel."

The first four beatitudes indicate that Jesus addresses the marginalized in society, while the blessings on the merciful (5:7), the pure in heart (5:8), and the peacemakers (5:9) indicate the ethical responsibilities of the disciples. The beatitudes in 5:10–11 indicate that the disciples face a hostile environment; they will be persecuted and abused for righteousness's sake. These two beatitudes anticipate the later references to the persecution of the disciples (cf. 5:44; 10:23). While the beatitudes appear in the indicative, expressing future hope for the marginalized, they also imply an ethical dimension, signifying the manner of life that distinguishes this community from their society.[18]

The last of the beatitudes shifts from the third person to the second person (plural), anticipating the statements, "You are the salt of the earth" and "you are the light of the world" (5:14–16). Interpreters have debated the meaning of the metaphor of salt. Its meaning is most likely determined by the parallel statement, "You are the light of the world." The parallel of "earth/land" and "world" suggests both the disciples' separation from the world and their impact on it. The image of light was well known in Scripture, especially in Isaiah (cf. Isa 9:2), which had a special significance in the teachings of both Jesus and Paul. Both Israel (Isa 42:6) and the servant (Isa 49:6) are a "light to the nations." Isaiah 60 is built around the light metaphor. The community is encouraged, "Arise, shine; for your light has come" (60:1), affirming that "nations shall come to your light, and kings to the brightness of your dawn" (60:3). Prior to the Sermon on the Mount, Matthew has cited Isa 9:2 ("Those who go in darkness have seen a great light") and 58:10 ("your light will rise in the darkness"). The first imperative in the Sermon on the Mount, "Let your light so shine before men that they will glorify your father in heaven" (5:16) indicates that the separation from the culture is also the impact on the culture.[19]

The command to let the light shine before others forms the transition to the imperatives in the Sermon on the Mount. The disciples' relationship to existing institutions is evident in the statement, "Unless your righteousness exceeds that of the Scribes and Pharisees, you will not enter the kingdom of heaven" (5:20). In keeping with the Torah, the Pharisees had developed a way of life based on the interpretation of the Torah. With their fence around the law, the Pharisees had developed an extensive case law for the whole society. The remainder of the Sermon on the Mount defines the proper behavior of the disciples in contrast to the wrong type practiced by the hypocrites (6:2, 5, 16; 7:5). This demand for a countercultural existence

18. Esler, *First Christians in Their Social Worlds*, 8.

19. See Pennington, *Sermon on the Mount and Human Flourishing*, 163.

is particularly evident in the final and climactic antithesis (5:43–48) where the conduct of the disciples is contrasted to that of the tax collectors and the gentiles. The question, "What more are you doing than others" (*ti perisson poieite*, 5:47a), recalling Jesus's statement in 5:20, "Unless your righteousness exceeds that of the scribes and Pharisees, you will not enter into heaven," is to be understood in a *qualitative* sense; BDAG renders the Greek as "What are you doing *that is remarkable*?"[20]

As the antitheses indicate, the rigorous commands cannot be instituted for the entire society but only for the disciples. Laws against anger (5:21–26) and lust (5:27–30) cannot be instituted as civil law or enforced. Similarly, the prohibition of resistance (5:38–42), the command to love one's enemies (5:43–48), cannot be the basis of civil law. As the Sermon on the Mount indicates, the disciples follow the interpretation of the Torah as Jesus has interpreted it. As Gerhard Lohfink has indicated, Jesus understands the gathered community as a contrast society.[21] The radical ethos of the Sermon on the Mount is not for society but for the people who are shaped by the good news.

Jesus stood outside the dominant culture of Jewish leadership, as their consistent criticisms of Jesus indicate. Over against the Pharisaic demands for observance of the purity regulations, Jesus is remembered for his friendship with "sinners." In numerous instances "tax collectors and sinners" are grouped together. The Pharisees criticize him because he eats with "tax collectors and sinners" (Mark 2:15–17 par.). He is accused of being "a friend of tax collectors and sinners" (Matt 11:19). The Pharisees and scribes complain that "he receives tax collectors and sinners and eats with them" (Luke 15:1–2). In other instances, tax collectors appear alone as the antithesis of the righteous, apparently because they were considered the prototypical sinners.[22] The tax collector appears as the antithesis of the righteous Pharisee in the parable (Luke 18:9–14). Jesus addresses the sinner within the community, saying "Let him be as a gentile and a tax collector" (Matt 18:17). When Jesus speaks of loving those who love in return, he asks, "Do the gentiles and tax collectors not do the same?" (Matt 5:46).

The sinners were those who either disregarded or disputed the interpretation of the Torah established by the Pharisees.[23] The tax collectors are commonly associated with sinners because of their reputation for enriching themselves and exploiting others. This view of tax collectors is reflected in

20. BDAG 805; du Toit, "Revisiting the Sermon on the Mount," 76.
21. Lohfink, *Jesus and Community*, 50, 56, 122–25.
22. See Dunn, *Jesus Remembered*, 1:533.
23. Dunn, *Jesus Remembered*, 1:531.

the encounter of John the Baptist and the tax collectors; John indicated that repentance involved collecting "no more than you are authorized to do" (Luke 3:12–13). Indeed, tax collectors are grouped with gentiles in Matthew's admonition to expel the unrepentant member of the community, "Let him be to you as a gentile and a tax collector." Thus tax collectors and sinners were outside the boundaries of Jewish purity laws. Jesus's message of the kingdom challenged those who drew sharp boundaries between the sinners—those who did not maintain the Pharisaic purity laws—and the righteous. Consequently, by crossing the traditional boundaries, Jesus stood outside the dominant culture in Galilee.

JESUS AND CAESAR

As Jesus's only direct statement about the disciples' relationship to the Caesar or Roman rule, his response to his interrogators, "Render to Caesar the things that belong to Caesar, and to God the things that belong to God" (Mark 12:17; cf. Matt 22:21; Luke 20:25), has been the center of attention in recent years, especially since the emergence of liberation theology and empire studies. The statement seems to encapsulate, if any specific passage can, Jesus's political outlook.[24] Because Jesus's statement does not unambiguously answer the question of tribute with a "yes" or "no," this passage is the central focus for interpreters who have debated Jesus's relationship to Roman rule.

Jesus's response must be seen in the larger context of the Jewish struggle over its relation to the Roman occupiers and his own message of the kingdom. Undoubtedly, Jesus was well aware of the Jewish revolt led by the Zealots that was crushed by the Romans in AD 6. The relationship to the state had been a major issue in Jewish circles. Judaism itself had a tenuous relationship to Roman rule, as the revolt in AD 6 indicates. This revolt was the result of the direct imposition of Roman rule after Archelaus was deposed and taxes on the populace were instituted. The imposition of taxes stood in direct conflict with the Jewish view of the sovereignty of God over the land.[25] According to Josephus, "a Galilean named Judas incited his countrymen to revolt, upbraiding them as cowards for consenting to pay tribute to the Romans and tolerating mortal masters, after having God for their lord" (*B.J.* 2.118). Judas the Galilean apparently considered the census and the taxes levied by the Romans as a form of slavery. The use of coins with the divine claims of the Caesar evoked the resistance of Judas and those who followed him.

---

24. Croy, "'Show Me the Money'," 191.

25. See Förster, *Jesus und die Steuerfrage*, 135.

Although Judas's revolt was quickly suppressed and Judas himself executed, his teaching lived on. Josephus (*Ant.* 18.6–8) traced the later Jewish revolt that led to disaster in AD 70 to his teaching.[26] By the time of Jesus's public ministry, the tribute had become a controversial issue, as Jews struggled with the reality of Roman occupation. Jesus was aware of the Galileans, whose blood Pilate had mingled with their sacrifices (Luke 13:1), and the fate of John the Baptist (cf. Mark 6:17–29), who had been put into prison prior to the beginning of Jesus's ministry and was later executed (Mark 1:14; 6:17–20). However, he says little about Roman rule or the rule of their clients, the Herods,[27] although his encounter with a Roman centurion (Matt 8:5) suggests that Jesus sometimes interacted with Roman representatives. Herod Antipas hears about him and concludes that he is John the Baptist risen from the dead (Mark 6:14). According to Luke the disciples warn him that Herod wants to kill him (13:31).

Despite the absence of direct references to Roman occupation in the Gospels, scholars from the eighteenth century until now have maintained that Jesus was involved in anti-Roman activity. In the eighteenth century, Hermann S. Reimarus argued that Jesus was engaged in revolutionary activity, as the message of the kingdom indicates. Similar arguments were made by Karl Kautsky, Robert Eisler, S. G. F. Brandon, Joel Carmichael, and Hyam Maccoby. The arguments have been summarized by Fernando Bermejo-Rubio. These include Jesus's instruction to the disciples to buy a sword (Luke 22:36), the apparent violence in the cleansing of the temple, the presence of armed troops in Gethsemane, and the execution by the Romans. In several publications, Richard Horsley has argued that Jesus made a direct challenge to Roman power. He maintains that the Gospel writers have minimized any anti-Roman activity. The coming of the kingdom is the judgment on all oppressive rulers. The crucifixion by the Romans is the evidence of Jesus's anti-Roman activity.

> Once we "take the Gospel whole," it is clear not only that Jesus spearheaded a program of renewal of the people. He also pronounces judgment on the people's rulers, on the Romans themselves as well as on their Jerusalem rulers, the face that the Roman imperial order presented to the people of Palestine.[28]

All contrary evidence, according to Rubio, is the result of the Gospels' attempts to cover up the seditious nature of Jesus's ministry.

---

26. Ukpong, "Tribute to Caesar, Mark 12:13–17 (Mt 22:15–22, Luke 20:20–26)," 436.

27. Bermejo-Rubio, "Jesus and the Anti-Roman Resistance," 2.

28. Horsley, *Jesus and the Powers*, 78–79.

The Synoptic Gospels record a series of questions from Jewish leaders in the days prior to the arrest and trial of Jesus, all of which reflect their growing hostility to Jesus and the desire to "trap him in his talk" (Mark 12:13). This conversation occurred in the temple precincts (Mark 11:27) with the "chief priests and the scribes and the elders" (11:27).

The passage in Mark 12:13–17 par. is one of the many pronouncement stories in which the brief controversy ends with a decisive statement from Jesus (cf. Mark 2:17, 21–22, 27–28), often challenging the common interpretations of Jewish law (cf. Mark 2:21–22; 10:2–9). Those who sent the Pharisees and the Herodians to entrap Jesus by his words are apparently the chief priests, scribes, and elders (Mark 11:27) who ask Jesus to comment on questions of Jewish law. In Mark's Gospel the passage comes after the parable of the tenants in the vineyard (12:1–11), which presented the Jewish leaders as the tenants who killed the vinedresser's son. "They"—apparently the chief priests, scribes, and elders (11:27)—thus expressed their hostility to Jesus when the Pharisees and Herodians sought to catch him in a word (Mark 12:13). According to all four Gospels, the initial hostility to Jesus and his movement came not from Rome but from the Jewish leadership.

Pharisees and Herodians had previously conspired against Jesus at the conclusion of an earlier conflict story (Mark 3:6).[29] The alliance of the Pharisees and Herodians in these two instances cannot easily be explained.[30] We know little about the Herodians, although we may assume that they were followers of Herod Antipas and thus favorable to Rome.[31] The Pharisees had been the major opposition throughout Mark's Gospel, but they are not presented in the Gospels as politically engaged. Most likely a range of views with respect to Rome and taxation existed among the Pharisees.

---

29. The Herodians do not appear in the Matthean and Lukan parallels (cf. Matt 12:14; Luke 11).

30. Gnilka, *Das Evangelium nach Markus (Mk 8,26–16,20)*, 151. See the discussion by Taylor, "Herodians and Pharisees," 299–310. Taylor suggests that the most likely period for an alliance of Pharisees and Herodians was during the reign of Herod Agrippa 1 (AD 41–44).

31. Plümacher, "Die Rätsel der Ἡρωδιανοί im Markusevangelium," 124, maintains that, within the world of the Markan narrative, the Herodians are the representatives of Herod Antipas, who now continue the latter's work of execution, leading to the execution of Jesus. While the Pharisees represent religious leadership, the Herodians represent political power. He argues that the Herodians are not historical figures, but a literary creation of Mark. Förster argues that they were the slaves and freedmen of Herod Antipas, who possessed considerable authority in the financial and administrative tasks on behalf of the tetrarch (Förster, *Jesus und die Steuerfrage*, 148–49). According to Josephus, in the events that led up to the Jewish war, the Zealots engaged in murderous attacks on Herodian nobles (*B. J.* 4.139–41).

Although the interlocutors ask Jesus the question in order to "catch him" in an unguarded statement (12:13), they begin with a *captatio benevolentiae*: "We know that you are true and do not care for anyone's opinion." This is followed by the question, "Is it lawful (*exestin*) to give tribute (*dounai kēnson*) to Caesar?" *Exestin* recalls previous conversations on controversial questions of Jewish law in the Synoptic Gospels. The Pharisees had accused Jesus of doing what is not lawful (*ouk exestin*) to do (Mark 2:24 par.) on the Sabbath. In a healing controversy, Jesus asks, "Is it lawful (*exestin*) to do good or to do evil?" (Mark 3:4). John the Baptist had told Herod Antipas that it is not lawful (*ouk exestin*) to have his brother's wife (Mark 6:18). The questions about the Sabbath and divorce were matters of halakic debate, according to the Mishnah. The issue of paying taxes is not treated in the Mishnah, but it had been a matter of debate since the Jewish uprising in AD 6–7. The questioners thus place before Jesus the life-threatening alternative. Jesus would either acknowledge his loyalty to Rome, alienating the crowds, or lay the basis for the accusation that he is inciting rebellion.[32]

Kēnsos is a technical term of Roman taxation, a loan word from the Latin *census*. Like *phoros* in the Lukan parallel (20:22), it designates the tribute associated with Roman rule.[33] According to Matt 17:25, Jesus responds to those who ask, "Does your teacher not pay (*ou telei*) the tax (*didrachma*)?" He replies, asking Peter, "From whom do the kings of the earth take toll (*telē*) or tribute (*kēnson*)?" Do they receive from their own or from others? Peter responds, "From others," indicating the situation of the Jews in an occupied land. The story of the coin in the fish's mouth (Matt 17:27) may reflect the memory that Jesus paid taxes.

While rabbinic sources do not comment extensively on the question of the payment of taxes, the issue was debated in Jewish circles. "After the first authenticated provincial census of Judea (with Samaria and Idumea) in AD 6 under the Syrian governor P. Sulpicius Quirinius, the Roman procurators were responsible for the census. They were assisted by local Jewish authorities who were authorized to collect taxes (Josephus, *B.J.* 2.)." An embittered resistance rose up simultaneously with the tax, which was led by Judas the Galilean (cf. Acts 5:37; Josephus, *Ant.* 18.1f.; *B.J.* 2.118). In the events leading to the Jewish revolt, the payment of taxes was the major issue (*B.J.*

32. Förster, *Jesus und die Steuerfrage*, 148–49.

33. Cf. Matthew's term, *nomisma tou kēnsou* ("the coin used for tax," Matt 22:19). At the time of Jesus, the Jews in Judaea had to pay three main types of tax: the temple tax and the annual half-shekel poll tax, direct imperial taxes on landed property (*tributum agri/tributum soli*) and on personal property (*tributum capitis*), and indirect imperial taxes such as customs dues. See Ukpong, "Tribute," 436.

2.403).[34] The fact that the emperor was the foreign master of the land and the people was the basis for the taxation, and this brought lasting conflict with faith in God as the only master (*Ant.* 28.23; *B.J.* 2.433).[35]

Jesus's response is not typical in the pronouncement stories. Before he gives the definitive answer, as in the other pronouncement stories, he asks the interlocutors to bring a denarius, the common coinage in the Roman Empire. The fact that the interlocutors have the denarius indicates their own response to the question: they are using Caesar's coinage with Caesar's image. The image would be that of Tiberius with the inscription "Tiberius Caesar, son of the divine Augustus" on one side and "Pontifex Maximus" with the image of the mother of the Caesar sitting on the heavenly throne with the Olympic scepter in the right hand and the olive branch symbolizing the earthly incarnation of the heavenly peace on the other side.[36]

The meaning of Jesus's answer, "Give (*apodote*) to the emperor the things that are the emperor's, and to God what belongs to God," has been a matter of debate; the interpretation has frequently been influenced by political conditions in the last two centuries and the political position of the interpreter. Some, having seen the misuse of power by the state, have regarded with suspicion any claim that acknowledges anything belongs to Caesar.[37] Consequently, they interpret the passage as a message of resistance; that is, nothing belongs to Caesar. This interpretation is commonly understood as part of a pattern of resistance throughout Jesus's ministry.[38] Others interpret the passage as a rejection of the Zealot resistance to the payment of taxes. Another interpretation places the passage within an eschatological context,

34. See Josephus, *B.J.* 2.403: "Still they began to cry out that they were not taking up arms against the Romans, but against Florus, because of all the wrong that he had done them. To this king Agrippa replied: 'But your actions are already acts of war against Rome: you have not paid your tribute to Caesar, and you have cut down the porticoes communicating with Antonia. If you wish to clear yourselves of the charge of insurrection, re-establish the porticoes and pay the tax; for assuredly the fortress does not belong to Florus, and it is not Florus to whom your money will go.'"

35. Balz, κῆνσος, EDNT 2.287.

36. Pesch, *Das Markusevangelium*, 227.

37. Burke, "'Render to Caesar the Things of Caesar and to God the Things of God': Recent Perspectives on a Puzzling Command (1945–Present)," 58. "There are, for instance, the rather worrying examples of New Testament scholars with affinities to German National Socialism attempting to shore up the authority of the state through the 'render' command and Romans 13." Burke adds that "geopolitical events continue to shape the history of interpretation of this command (as with a good many biblical texts), despite protestations to the contrary" (159).

38. See Bermejo-Rubio, "Jesus and the Anti-Roman Resistance: A Reassessment of the Arguments," 100–105. Rubio provides an extended portrait of the seditious Jesus, whose revolutionary intentions are obscured by the Gospels.

maintaining that the imminence of the kingdom has relativized the claims of the state. Finally, the passage has been interpreted within the framework of the two kingdoms, according to which political and religious matters are demarcated and the state has its legitimate role.[39]

The coin—and presumably the authority to tax—belongs to Caesar. *Apodote* is a *terminus technicus* for any debt or payment for services, including taxes, and it also has the meaning "to give back" or "return to the owner."[40] That Jesus uses *apodidomi* (give back) rather than *didomi* (give) as used by the interlocutors is significant. While the interlocutors have asked if it is lawful to "give" (*dounai*) to Caesar, Jesus responds, "Give back" (*apodote*) to Caesar. Thus the meaning is probably "Give back the things that belong to Caesar." The things that are Caesar's (*ta Kaisaros*) is an immediate reference to the coin that the interlocutors possess, but it also suggests the more expanded meaning of anything that belongs to Caesar.[41] To pay taxes is merely to give back the coinage that Caesar has given. This response is consistent with the comment in Matthew that "the kings of the earth receive tribute," not from their own people but from others (Matt 17:25). Thus Jesus is not a Zealot. Indeed, nothing in the Gospel tradition suggests that Jesus is a Zealot. One gives back to Caesar what is already Caesar's. At the present, taxation, like the other institutions of society, is a reality.

Jesus's response does not suggest an equivalent between the "things that are Caesar's" and the "things that are God's," for the "things that are Caesar's" are limited. As Förster maintains, Jesus's response to the question of taxation must be seen within his message of the kingdom. Jesus describes the reign of God that is already "at hand" (Mark 1:14) in his outreach to the outcasts and table fellowship with sinners (cf. Mark 12:13–17; Luke 11:20; 15:1). Unlike the apocalyptic writers, he does not speak of the downfall of Roman power (cf. Dan 2:44) or a war against the enemies, as in the Qumran texts (e.g., 1 QM). He envisions the time when people from east and west sit down at the table in the kingdom of God (Matt 8:11; Luke 13:29). Jesus's message of the kingdom suggests that the authority of Caesar is only temporary, while God's rule is eternal.[42] As Jesus's apocalyptic message in Mark 13 indicates, the disciples live in the interim before the manifestation of God's rule. They will demonstrate their absolute loyalty to "the things that belong to God" as they suffer for Christ and anticipate his coming.[43] The ultimate

39. See Burke, "'Render to Caesar,'" 159.

40. BDAG, 110.

41. Ukpong, "Tribute," 446.

42. Joachim Gnilka, *Das Evangelium nach Markus*, 154.

43. On "the things that belong to God," see the extended discussion in Förster, *Jesus*

loyalty, as the entire narrative suggests, consists of the "things that belong to God." Disciples leave their occupations to follow Jesus, who challenges people to leave everything and give up possessions to follow him. Jesus calls on disciples to take up a cross to follow him. Thus Jesus acknowledges "the things that belong to Caesar" but relativizes their significance, knowing that God will ultimately triumph over all of the world's powers.[44]

The political implications are evident, however, in the proclamation of the future kingdom. As the arrest and execution of Jesus indicate, his message of the kingdom was nevertheless subversive, for it relativized political affiliation and undermined the absolute loyalty that Rome demanded. Just as Jesus spoke of other institutions, including marriage and family, from an eschatological perspective (cf. Mark 12:18–27), he also regarded political power as one of the institutions that would ultimately pass away. Jesus holds that God will soon bring to an end the entire cosmos, including the Roman Empire.

CONCLUSION

Living in the interim between the inauguration of the kingdom and God's ultimate reign, Jesus called together an alternative community that lived between these two worlds. Although some left everything to follow Jesus, others lived in the villages, had families, labored in various trades, and encountered Roman authorities regularly. Unlike the Qumran community, they did not retreat from the world. Jesus formed an alternative society in anticipation of the time when God's kingdom would "come with power" (cf. Mark 9:1), in part living as if that day were already present. While Jesus recognized society's institutions, he relativized them, refusing to give ultimate significance to the family, work, commercial activity, and politics. As the Sermon on the Mount indicates, the message of the kingdom created a new situation in which the disciples would surpass the ethic of their peers, the scribes and the Pharisees (Matt 5:20). This ethic was not intended for the entire society, but those who practiced it were "the light of the world" (Matt 5:16). Jesus did not call for them to retreat from the world but to "let [their] light shine" so that others would see their good works and glorify God. Those who separated from the values of the culture would then have an impact on the culture.

---

und die Steuerfrage, 178–220. In the Old Testament, the whole world belongs to God. In apocalyptic literature, the wealth of the nations will ultimately be Israel's (and God's) possession when Rome is destroyed (Förster, *Jesus und die Steuerfrage,* 212).

44. See Ukpong, "Tribute," 442.

3

Having as Not Having

Paul and Culture

A major point of continuity between the teachings of Jesus and Paul is the tension between the "now" and the "not yet." Jesus declares that the kingdom "has come upon you" (Luke 11:20 par; cf. Matt 11:2–6; Mark 1:15; Luke 17:21) but is still to come (Mark 9:1; cf. Matt 6:10; 11:2–6; Luke 22:16), while in Romans Paul announces that the eschatological revelation of God's righteousness "has [now] been made known" in the death of Christ (Rom 3:21; cf. 1:17; 8:1) but that "salvation is nearer to us than when we first became believers" (Rom 13:11), who wait for the glory to be revealed (Rom 8:16, 23–25). Paul indicates to the Corinthians that "the end of the ages has come" for believers (1 Cor 10:11) but gives an extended treatment of the general resurrection and the return of Christ (15:1–58).

Paul describes the arrival of the new age in a variety of ways. He reminds the Galatians that they have been "rescued from this present evil age" (Gal 1:4) inasmuch as God sent his son "in the fullness of time" (Gal 4:4). The new creation promised by the prophets (Isa 65:17; 66:2) has become a reality (2 Cor 5:17; Gal 6:15). Paul is a minister of the new covenant (2 Cor 3:6) promised by Jeremiah (31:31–34). In the death of Jesus Christ the mystery that was long hidden has now been made known (1 Cor 2:8–10). Nevertheless, Paul consistently speaks of the day of Christ (or "day of the Lord"; cf. 1 Cor 1:8; 2 Cor 1:14; Phil 1:6, 10; 1 Thess 5:2), the parousia (1 Cor 15:23; 1 Thess 2:19; 3:13; 4:15; 5:23), the future kingdom (1 Cor 6:9; 15:50),

47

and the final righteousness of God for which believers wait (cf. Gal 5:5). Believers, therefore, live in the interim between their rescue from "the present evil age" and the final day. Consequently, they live in the world while they also belong to the new world. This situation creates distance from the existing culture.

Paul's task is to build communities that reflect their existence in the interim between this age and the age to come. On the one hand, in this new age believers possess the Spirit that the prophets had promised (Rom 5:5; 8:2–8; 1 Cor 2:10–17; Gal 3:1–5; 5:22–29; cf. Ezek 36:22–32; Joel 2:28–29), which now enables them to overcome the power of sin (Rom 8:2–4; Gal 3:1–5; 5:22–26) and no longer be "conformed to this age" (Rom 12:2). In this new aeon the old distinctions of this age are removed. "There is neither Jew nor Greek, slave or free, male and female" (Gal 3:28; cf. 1 Cor 12:13; Col 3:11). On the other hand, Paul speaks of his anxiety over his churches (2 Cor 11:28), describing himself as being in the pangs of childbirth "until Christ is formed" among his churches (Gal 4:19). Indeed, he indicates to the Corinthians that "we are being transformed into the same image" (2 Cor 3:18) and appeals to the Romans not to be conformed to this age but to "be transformed" by the renewing of their minds (Rom 12:2). His exhortations indicate that they are not yet transformed into the image of Christ. This transformation will occur only at the end (Rom 8:29; Phil 3:21).

BOUNDARIES BETWEEN THE CHURCH AND THE WORLD

The existence of the church as a new creation establishes a sharp distinction between the community and the society, for the process of identity formation requires a demarcation from all others.[1] Because Paul is building communities of the new age, he writes to ensure their moral transformation rather than address matters for the larger society. He does not use the language of Christ and culture but of the church and the world (*kosmos*). For Paul, the world is not the creation (*ktisis*) but the sphere of the evil powers that tempt humankind. It is the equivalent of "this age" (cf. 1 Cor 1:20; 3:18–19). Although God is the Creator of the world (Rom 1:20; cf. 1 Cor 10:26), it is nevertheless dominated by the power of sin (Rom 5:12; cf. Rom 6:12) and the god of this world (2 Cor 4:4), which will ultimately be judged (Rom 3:6; 1 Cor 6:2; 11:32).[2] Because this age is under the power of sin, God was in Christ "reconciling the world to himself" (2 Cor 5:19).

---

1. Rabens, "Paul's Rhetoric of Demarcation," 229.
2. Schrage, "Die Stellung zur Welt bei Paulus, Epiktet und in der Apokalyptik," 60.

The Christian message of the cross stands in sharp contrast to the "wisdom of the world" (1 Cor 1:20-21; 3:19; 6:9), for God has made both the "wisdom of this age" (1 Cor 2:6) and the "wisdom of the world" foolishness (1 Cor 1:20; 3:19). Inasmuch as the church is composed primarily of those who were not wise, powerful, or of noble birth according to the standards of the world (1 Cor 1:26-29), it reflects the divine wisdom of the one who chooses the weak things of the world in order to shame the strong and the foolish things of the world to shame the wise (1:27). Paul himself is a "spectacle to the world" (1 Cor 4:9) and "the rubbish of the world" (1 Cor 4:13).

Although believers have been rescued from the present evil age, they still live in the world (*kosmos*, cf. Rom 5:12; 1 Cor 1:20, 21, 27-28; 2:12; 3:19; 4:9; 5:10; 7:31; Phil 2:15), but Paul urges them not "to be conformed to this world" (Rom 12:1), and he declares that he has "been crucified to the world" (Gal 6:14). The world is thus the equivalent of "this age" as the place of unredeemed humanity, from which believers have been rescued (cf. Gal 1:4) although they still live in it.

In other instances he speaks of unredeemed humanity—the "natural person" (NRSV "unspiritual," 1 Cor 2:14) in contrast to the spiritual person (1 Cor 2:13-15). When believers do not conduct themselves according to the standards of the new age, as in Corinth, they are behaving "according to human limitations" (*kata anthrōpon* in 1 Cor 3:3), that is, according to the standards of the culture.

The sharp distinction between the church and the world corresponds to the distinction between insiders and outsiders. Paul consistently distinguishes between believers (*hoi pisteuontes*) and unbelievers (*apistoi*), especially in 1 Corinthians (6:6; 7:12-14; 10:27; 14:22-23; 2 Cor 4:4; 6:14). The self-designation of the community as "believers" (cf. 1 Thess 1:7; 2:10, 13) leads to the logical opposite term—unbelievers—to describe outsiders.[3] In 1 Corinthians, *hoi pisteuontes* is used three times (1:21; 14:22 [twice]), and *hoi apistoi* is used eleven times (6:6; 7:12, 13, 14 [twice], 15; 10:27; 14:22 [twice], 23, 24) to designate the boundaries between the community and outsiders. Believers should handle their own disputes rather than take them before unbelievers (1 Cor 6:1, 6).[4] Living in a society where contact with unbelievers is inevitable—in marriage (7:12-14), in social relationships (10:27), in the assemblies (14:22-24)—believers must decide about their relationship with the outside world as they establish boundaries.

---

3. Trebilco, *Outsider Designations and Boundary Construction in the New Testament,* 48.

4. In 1 Cor 6:1, "the righteous" are contrasted with the unbelievers.

Paul uses other terms to distinguish insiders from outsiders in 1 Corinthians. Indeed, He insists that believers refuse to associate with immoral believers but leave to God the task of judging "those outside" (1 Cor 5:12–13). He speaks also of "those who are perishing" (1:18), the immoral (*pornoi*, 5:9–11; 6:9), and those who are engaged in the vices that prevent them from entering the kingdom of God (1 Cor 6:9–10). He speaks also of "outsiders" (*idiōtai*) who come into their assemblies (14:16, 23–24).

While Paul faces a separate set of issues in 2 Corinthians, including the need for boundaries against the opponents who undermine his work of community formation, he maintains his focus on the boundaries between the community and the world. As in 1 Corinthians, he argues that his preaching results in the division of the world into "those who are being saved" and "those who are perishing" (2 Cor 2:17). His ministry is more glorious than that of Moses (3:7–11), but the minds of many listeners have been hardened (3:14), and a veil still covers them as they read the Scripture (3:15). Indeed, if his gospel is veiled, it is veiled only among the perishing (4:3), that is, the unbelievers (*apistoi*) whose minds the God of this world has blinded "to keep them from seeing the light of the gospel of the glory of Christ, who is the image of God" (4:4). Thus Paul divided the world into two groups: those who are being saved and those who are perishing (2:15; cf. 4:3), that is, the unbelievers (*apistoi*, 4:4). He insists on boundaries between believers and unbelievers.

Paul's most vivid and extended appeal for boundaries between the community and the unbelievers (*apistoi*) appears in 2 Cor 6:14—7:1. He appeals to the listeners not to "be mismatched with unbelievers" (6:14), supporting his demand with an argument based on Scripture (6:14b—7:1). The passage is widely regarded as an interpolation, either by Paul or by someone else.[5] Scholars have maintained that 6:13 fits easily with 7:2, indicating that 6:14—7:1 is an interpolation. They have also argued that the numerous hapax legomena suggest that 6:14—7:1 is not a part of the original composition. Furthermore, some have argued that the radical separation reflects a conflict with Pauline theology.[6]

The argument that 2 Cor 6:14—7:1 is an interpolation is not convincing. One may observe that 6:13 and 7:2 do not fit together well. "Make room for us in your hearts" (*platunthēte*, literally "make room for us") in 6:13 followed by "make room for us in your hearts" (*chōrēsate*, 7:2) would

---

5. Betz, "2 Cor 6:14–71," 88–108. Betz argues that the passage is an anti-Pauline fragment. "Paul must have been the very embodiment of everything that the Christians speaking in 2 Cor 6:14–71 warned against (108)."

6. See Heil, "Die Sprache der Absonderung in 2 Kor 6,17 und bei Paulus," 717–29.

be an awkward redundancy.[7] Furthermore, 6:14—7:1 fits within a series of imperatives that begin in 6:11–13 as Paul appeals to the Corinthians to reciprocate his affections for him (6:11–13). To "make room" (6:11, 13) for him is to "not be mismatched (*heterozygountes*) with the *apistoi*" (6:14). The rhetorical questions that follow in 6:14b–16a ("what partnership is there between righteousness and lawlessness . . . between light and darkness, . . . Christ and Beliar . . . believer with an unbeliever . . . the temple of God and idols") indicate the binary choice they face between opening their hearts to Paul and engaging in relationships with the *apistoi*.

The focus of the rhetorical questions is the last question, "What agreement does the temple of God have with idols" (6:16)? As Paul's affirmation "we are the temple of the living God" indicates, the claim that the church is the temple of God is consistent with Paul's ecclesiology in 1 Cor 3:16 (cf. 6:19). As the Scripture citations indicate, because God dwells in the temple (6:16; cf. Lev 26:11–12), the Corinthians must "come out from among them" 6:17; cf. Isa 52:11) and "cleanse themselves from every defilement of body and spirit, making holiness perfect in the fear of the Lord" (7:1). When they understand their identity as God's temple, they will separate themselves from all impurity, including the surrounding society.

This challenge is not inconsistent with what Paul has said in other letters but is the continuation of the boundaries that Paul established in 1 Corinthians (cf. 5:9–11; 6:9–11).[8] Indeed, Paul's designation of the members as saints and his call for holiness (cf. 1 Cor 1:1–2; 6:11; 1 Thess 3:11–14) are regular features in his letters (cf. 1 Thess 4:3, 8). He establishes boundaries between the community and the world, knowing that the Corinthians have been too engaged with the wider society and those who demonstrate their existence in the old creation (cf. 5:16–7).[9] Their openness to him (6:11–13) is the rejection of the values of the world (6:14–7:1).

Who are the unbelievers (*apistoi*) in 2 Corinthians? Elsewhere the term is employed for the outsiders who have not accepted the Christian message (cf. 2 Cor 4:4; cf. 1 Cor 6:6; 7:12; 10:27; 14:22–23). Within the context of the *apologia* in 2:14—7:4, however, the primary issue is posed, not by outsiders, but by the opponents, who have undermined Paul's ministry (cf. 2:17; 3:1–2; 5:12; 6:4) and strained the affections of the Corinthians for Paul (6:11–13). The *apistoi* here probably include not only outsiders, but

---

7. See Starling, "ἄπιστοι of 2 Cor 6:14," 48–49. The NRSV "in your hearts" is not in the Greek in 6:13 and 7:2.

8. Trebilco, *Outsider Designations*, 66–68; Starling, "ἄπιστοι of 2 Cor 6:14," 48.

9. Trebilco, *Outsider Designations*, 70.

all who live within the standards of the old age (cf. 5:16–18).[10] Those who question the legitimacy of Paul's ministry share the "earthly wisdom" with the surrounding culture (cf. 1:12; cf. 5:16). Paul's concluding challenge for believers to pursue sanctification (6:14) is the alternative to the separation from all defilements.[11]

Similarly, community formation in 1 Thessalonians involves the establishment of boundaries from the existing culture. The sexual morality of believers should differ from that of "the Gentiles who do not know God" (4:5). Believers live in hope, in contrast to "the others" (*hoi loipoi*) who have no hope (4:13). They work with their hands in order to behave properly toward outsiders (4:12). The insider/outsider terminology "implies a negative perception of society and the "qualitative difference" between outsiders and insiders.[12] This language communicates to the believers that there are only two classes of humanity: "the sect and outsiders."[13]

These boundaries exist because believers have entered the new age. The "rescue" from the present age (Gal 1:4) necessarily requires separation from the old age and its culture. Paul employs the language of sanctification, derived from the Levitical code, to describe the separation of his communities from the society. Just as the Israelites were instructed to "be holy" as God is holy (Lev 19:2), separating themselves from the practices of their neighbors (Lev 18:2–5), Paul consistently describes his converts as saints—the separated ones—and reminds them of their radical separation from their past (Rom 6:17–22; 7:5–6; 1 Cor 6:9–11; cf. Col 3:8) and their current environment. He addresses the Corinthians as people "who are sanctified" and "called to be saints (*hagioi*)" (1 Cor 1:2). In 1 Thessalonians, he encourages the gentile converts not to engage in inappropriate sexual behavior, reminding them that this is "their sanctification" (1 Thess 4:3; cf.

10. Starling, "ἄπιστοι of 2 Cor 6:14," 59–60. See also Rabens, "Paul's Rhetoric of Demarcation," 232–33, who concludes that 2 Cor 6:14—7:1 "should be/can be understood on a first and primary reading/hearing as a selective removal from covenant-forming relationships with idolatrous people outside the church (=unbelievers). However, the text appears to transport deliberate ambiguity through the rhetorical device of double entendre (lit. 'double hearing/understanding')." He adds, "The readers/hearers of Paul's letter are thus in a position to interpret the imperative not to be mismatched with ἄπιστοι upon a second and secondary reading/hearing as a reference to Paul's opponents, the 'false apostles.'"

11. Against the charges of his opponents, Paul denies that he conducts himself with "earthly wisdom" (1:12) or conducts himself "according to human standards" (*kata sarka*, 10:2), but insists that he has abandoned a "human point of view" (*kata sarka*, 5:16) while claiming that his opponents engage in boasting by "human standards" (*kata sarka*, 11:18).

12. Constantineanu, "Bible and the Public Arena," 142.

13. Meeks, *First Urban Christians*, 86.

4:7). Indeed, he prays that God will continue to strengthen the community in holiness (*hagisasmos*, 3:13) until the end.

Because Paul's major concern is the moral formation of his communities, his ethical exhortations focus primarily on the relationships within the community. Indeed, his internal focus is evident in his pervasive use of "one another" (*allēlōn*). His communities are "members of one another" (Rom 12:5; cf. Eph. 4:25) who "love one another" (Rom 12:10; 1 Thess 3:12), "live in harmony with one another" (Rom 12:16; 15:5), build one another up (Rom 14:19; 1 Thess 5:11), encourage one another (1 Thess 5:11), bear one another's burdens (Gal 6:2), and through love serve one another (Gal 5:14). Indeed, the term *philadelphia*, used for actual siblings in antiquity, is used by both Paul and other NT writers for the love among members of the community (Rom 12:9; 1 Thess 4:9; cf. Heb 13:1; 1 Pet 3:8). The most pervasive moral advice in the Pauline letters is expressed in the noun *agape* and the verb *agapan*, both of which are employed primarily for love within the community as it supplies the social safety net that believers have lost as they separated from familial networks at their conversion.

CONFLICT WITH THE OLD AGE AND THE EXISTING CULTURE

The separation from the people of the old age brings about inevitable conflict with the world. Gentile believers break with ancestral customs and fracture the familial practices that unite the household. The confession that "Jesus is Lord" (cf. 2 Cor 4:5; Phil 2:11) inevitably provokes the hostility of Roman authorities as well as the general populace, for whom "Caesar is Lord." Consequently, outsiders persecute believers (Rom 12:14) in a variety of ways. Paul's affirmation that "our citizenship is in heaven" (Phil 3:20) undoubtedly evoked the hostility of the populace in Philippi, a Roman colony that took pride in its Roman citizenship. Consequently, the Philippians face adversaries (1:28), but Paul encourages the believers not to be intimidated by them, but to struggle together in harmony. He declares that suffering is actually a privilege; the Philippians suffer in imitation of the apostle himself (Phil 1:29). Believers struggle together, knowing that they face an adversary in unity with each other (Phil 1:28).

When Paul's converts in Thessalonica receive the gospel in much affliction (1 Thess 1:6), they suffer the same fate as the believers in Judea (1 Thess 2:14). Paul declares that suffering is to be their destiny (1 Thess 3:2). In describing his own sufferings for Christ (2 Cor 1:3–11; cf. 4:10–11), he adds that the sufferings of Christ overflow not only to him (2 Cor 1:5) but to all believers (2 Cor 1:6).

The conflict of cultures is most evident in the Corinthian correspondence, as Paul attempts to build a community of the new age among those who have brought into the community the values of the old age of Greco-Roman culture. The multiple issues in Corinth reflect the conflict between Christ and culture. The Corinthians have brought with them the values of competitiveness among teachers,[14] political intrigue,[15] the celebration of human wisdom and rhetoric, social status,[16] and the emphasis on individual rights, expressed in the slogan "all things are lawful" (1 Cor 6:12; 10:23).[17] Those who claim "I am of Apollos" apparently measure their leaders according to the standard of human eloquence, which Apollos exemplifies. The Corinthian abuses at the Lord's Supper also reflect the Greco-Roman values of social status, especially at meals.[18]

Paul's task of shaping a new kind of community begins with the theological foundation in 1 Cor 1–4, where he draws a sharp dichotomy between the values of Christ and culture—between the old age and the new age. One may observe the sharp dichotomies in Paul's presentation between the word of the cross and human wisdom and rhetoric. His focus on the word of the cross (1:17–18) is probably a response to the Corinthians' interpretation of the event through the lenses of their culture. According to Jürgen Becker:

> This Corinthian development took place under the conditions of a newly arisen Gentile-Christian church, which did not simply lay aside its former culture, understanding of religion, and interpretation of the world, nor did it adapt itself fully to the apostle's understanding during Paul's stay in Corinth. Thus the problem of the Corinthian church was, first, how the Paulinism known to it stood in contrast to the old ways or to what extent the old ways could also be a help in giving life to the new.[19]

14. See Winter, *After Paul Left Corinth*, 36; Barton, "Sanctification and Oneness in 1 Corinthians with Implications for the Case of 'Mixed Marriages' (1 Corinthians 7:12–16," 39.

15. See Welborn, *Politics and Rhetoric in the Corinthian Epistles*, 1–42. The slogans "I belong to Paul" and "I belong to Cephas" and "I belong to Apollos," echo political debates and suggest that the Corinthians envision the church as a political entity.

16. Pogoloff, *Logos and Sophia*, 129–37.

17. Cf. Epictetus, *Diatr.* 4.1.1., "He is free who lives as he wills." See Marshall, *Enmity at Corinth*, 287.

18. See Lampe, "Das korinthische Herrenmahl im Schnittpunkt hellenistisch-römischer Mahlpraxis und paulinischer Theologia Crucis (IKor 11,17–34)," 86–87; Pogoloff, *Logos and Sophia*, 237–71.

19. Becker, *Paul*, 199.

The dichotomies in the argument reflect the issues of Christ and culture.

1:17 eloquent wisdom	cross
1:18 foolishness	power
1:20 wisdom of the world	(God's) foolishness
1:21 (human wisdom)	wisdom of God
1:22 signs/wisdom	Christ crucified
1:23–24 foolishness to Greeks	God's power
2:1–12 lofty speech or wisdom	Christ crucified
2:5 human wisdom	power of God
2:12 spirit of the world	Spirit of God
2:13 human wisdom	the Spirit
2:14 the natural person	the spiritual person

The distinction between this age (1:20; 2:6, 8) and the message that is "not of this age" (2:6) indicates that the cross is the manifestation of the new age and that it confounds the wisdom of this age. This message divides the world between those who are perishing and those who are being saved (1:18). Indeed, those who receive the message also have a new epistemology by which they understand the deep things of God—those things that the world does not understand (cf. 2:8). Therefore, humankind is divided between the "natural" (*psychikos*) person and the spiritual person (2:14–15). The community consists of those who share in the divine wisdom that the culture does not know; only members of the community have the mind of Christ (2:16).

The challenge in 1 Corinthians is to ensure that it lives up to its calling—that the message of the new age determines the way that they live. Indeed, Paul chastises the Corinthians for their divisiveness, which indicates that they are living by the values of the culture of competition (3:1–5). He wants to ensure that they are not "wise in this age" (3:18) and that they reject the wisdom of this world (3:18–20).

A community that lives in the new age needs to have boundaries from those who live in the old age, as Paul indicates in 5:1–11:1.[20] The Corinthians have been set apart—"sanctified in Christ" (1:2). They once were among the sinners named in 6:9–10 but were "washed," "sanctified," and "justified" (6:11). Now they are a holy (*hagios*) temple (3:17) who greet one another with a holy (*hagios*) kiss (1 Cor 16:20). Paul instructs believers to avoid pagan courts in 1 Cor 6:1–11, distinguishing between the "saints" (*hagioi*) and the unrighteous (*adikoi*). The latter are those who "have no standing"

20. Cf. Mitchell, *Paul and the Rhetoric of Reconciliation*, 225.

(*exouthenēmenous*) in the church (6:4).[21] They will not enter the kingdom of God (6:9). The language of sanctification that runs throughout the letter leaves no doubt that Paul is in the process of identity formation,[22] which requires a distinction between insiders and outsiders.[23] Thus Paul instructs the community to expel one who lives with his father's wife in violation of the principle of sanctification (5:5–6), instructs believers to avoid pagan courts (6:1–11), encourages the unmarried to marry only "in the Lord" (7:39) if they choose to marry, and to flee the idolatry of their fellow citizens (10:14).

Similar issues are at the center of the debate in 2 Corinthians. Although interpreters debate the integrity of this letter, a singular issue dominates all parts: Paul's response to opponents who question the legitimacy of his ministry. Here Paul faces the challenge of those who judge his ministry "in a secular way" (*kata sarka*).[24] When he does not make the visit he has promised, the opponents evidently accuse him of making his plans "according to ordinary human standards" (*kata sarka*, 1:17), but he insists that he has not conducted himself with "earthly wisdom" (*sophia sarkikē*, 1:12). His opponents "commend themselves" (10:12; cf. 10:18), compare themselves with others (10:12), and boast of their achievements "according to human standards" (*kata sarka*, 11:18),[25] forcing Paul to boast also (11:23–33; cf. 12:11). While the opponents boast of the adversities they have overcome, Paul boasts of his weaknesses (11:29–30; 12:5).

The opponents of Paul judge the apostle by the standards of their own culture. Their charge that he is humble (*tapeinos*, 10:1) and the suggestion that he "humbled" himself by working with his hands (11:7) reflects the ancient cultural disdain for humility.[26] Their charge that "his bodily presence is weak and his speech of no account" (10:10) also reflects the value placed on physical strength and rhetorical ability in antiquity. Paul's entire defense

---

21. *Exouthenēmenos* has the connotation of something to be disdained. Cf. BDAG 552.

22. Barton, "Sanctification and Oneness in Christ," 39.

23. See Hogg, "Social Categorization, Depersonalization, and Group Behavior," 56: "Groups exist by virtue of there being out-groups. For a collection of people to be a group there must, logically, be other people, who are not in the group."

24. Literally "according to the flesh." Cf. NRSV "from a human point of view."

25. On the Greco-Roman catalogues of sufferings, see Fitzgerald, *Cracks in an Earthen Vessel*. On boasting and Paul's contemporaries, see Judge, "Paul's Boasting and Contemporary Professional Practice," 37–50; Christopher Forbes, "Comparison, Self-Praise and Irony," 1–30.

26. Aristotle does not present *tapein-* as a desirable attitude, but speaks instead of *praotes* or *prautes* (meekness) as an ethical virtue (*Eth. nic.* 2.7.1107b). In early Christianity humility was regarded as a virtue that was unknown in the ancient world and was thus an identity marker. See Becker, *Paul on Humility*, 24, 28.

is intended to demonstrate that his criteria for ministry is shaped by the cross—that he shares in the sufferings of Christ.

Paul's major apologia appears in 2:14—7:4. At the heart of Paul's defense is the section in 2 Cor 5:11—6:2. Paul introduces his defense—his boast—in order that his listeners can boast about him (5:12). The foundation of his defense is the creed "One died for all" (5:14–15), to which he adds the interpretation "therefore all died" (5:14) and "so that those living will no longer live for themselves" (5:15) but for the one who died and was raised. The *hōste* ("so that") clause indicates Paul's new epistemology. He once knew Christ "in a worldly way" (*kata sarka*), but no longer. In the second *hōste* clause he adds, "If anyone is in Christ, there is a new creation" (5:17). The new creation promised in Isaiah (65:17; 66:22) has become a reality. The Christ event establishes a new epistemology and a new understanding of ministry. Paul's ministry, therefore, is countercultural because it is founded on the cross of Christ.

Similarly, in Galatians Paul describes the community that has been "rescued from the present evil age" (1:4) and now lives in the "new creation" (6:15). A consistent feature is that this is a new kind of community. Among those rescued from the present evil age, there is no longer "Jew or Greek, slave or free, male and female." One may compare 1 Cor 12:13, which describes a new community in which "all were baptized into one body—Jews or Greeks, slaves or free." He expresses the same understanding in Colossians, according to which there is no longer "Greek or Jew, circumcised or uncircumcised, barbarian, Scythian, slave, free" (Col 3:11). The church is the new humanity in which the cultural distinctions of this age have been removed.

Paul's major task is to build communities that exhibit the values of the new age. His letters involve community formation and the development of a *habitus* of norms that separate it from the surrounding culture. In some instances the *habitus* is drawn from the Jewish tradition, especially as it had been developed in the diaspora (cf. 1 Cor 6:12–21; 1 Thess 4:5) without adopting the practices of Sabbath, circumcision, and Jewish food laws.[27] For Paul, this *habitus* grew out of the story of Christ. Believers die with the crucified Christ, no longer living for themselves but for the one who died for them (cf. 2 Cor 5:14–15; Phil 1:17–2:11). Thus the ethic is ecclesial rather than public. Nevertheless, his communities still live in the world and must determine how they will relate to the culture.[28]

27. See Thompson, *Moral Formation according to Paul*, 208. See also Barclay, *Pauline Churches and Diaspora Jews*, 27.

28. Although Paul insisted that believers abandon the practices that had previously defined their existence (cf. 1 Cor 6:9–11), the Christian *habitus* inevitably overlapped

ENGAGEMENT WITH THE CULTURE

Although Paul insists on boundaries between the church and culture, he does not commend a withdrawal from the society. As a diaspora Jew, Paul knew that, while communities maintained various boundary markers that differentiated the Jews from the larger society, the Jews did relate in various ways to the wider society in which they lived.[29] When Paul instructs his communities not to associate with the immoral people in his first (apparently lost) letter to the Corinthians (1 Cor 5:9), he qualifies the statement, indicating that he was not referring to "the immoral in the world," for then they would have to "go out of the world" (1 Cor 5:10). Consequently, believers cannot withdraw fully from the sexually immoral persons, the greedy, robbers, or idolaters without going out of the world. That some of them (presumably the wealthy) take their disputes to court (6:1–16) suggests that they have confidence in the legal system.[30] While believers are married to unbelieving spouses, Paul does not advise them to separate (1 Cor 7:12–16). Some are invited by unbelievers (*apistoi*) to banquets (1 Cor 10:27), and Paul does not forbid them from going. He anticipates that unbelievers may come to the assemblies (14:23), and he is concerned about the impression that the assembly will make on them. One of the members, Erastus, is "city treasurer" (*oikonomos tēs poleōs*, Rom 16:23).[31] Nevertheless, while Paul assumes Christian engagement with the world, he insists that believers separate from the world, including its law courts and sexual practices.

Although Paul's moral advice focuses primarily on relationships within the community, he also instructs believers to behave appropriately toward outsiders. He encourages the Romans to "bless those who persecute you" (12:14), to "take thought of what is noble in the sight of all" (12:17), and to "live peaceably with all" (12:18). He encourages the Galatians to "do good to all, especially those of the household of faith" (Gal 6:10). He prays that the Thessalonians will increase in love to one another and to all (1 Thess 3:12).

As Paul has indicated earlier, the withdrawal from immoral people is not absolute, for then believers would need to "go out of the world" (1 Cor 5:9). The Corinthians, recalling Paul's demand for separation from the world, have probably asked Paul if husbands and wives should divorce

---

with that of Greco-Roman society. Paul's lists of vices and virtues (cf. Gal 5:19–26) contain both common Greek virtues and vices as well as distinctively Christian practices.

29. See ch. 1. See also Constantineanu, "The Bible and the Public Arena," 141.

30. Barclay, *Pauline Churches*, 189.

31. According to a Latin inscription in Corinth, someone named Erastus paid the expense for the paving of a street. Scholars debate whether this influential person is the same as the Erastus in Rom 16:23.

their unbelieving spouses (cf. 7:12–13). Paul's reminder that their bodies are "members of Christ" (6:15) that should not be joined to a prostitute has raised the question of sexual relations with spouses who do not conform to the expectations of the believing community regarding sexual relationships.[32] In this instance, Paul interprets Jesus's prohibition of divorce casuistically for the sake of believers who are married to unbelievers, encouraging husbands and wives to remain with their unbelieving spouses who consent to live with them (7:12–13).[33] He also extends his comments about the mutuality of sexual relationships that he advised in 7:1–7. The mutuality that Paul describes in 7:1–7 applies also to the mixed marriages, for Paul applies the same standard to both husbands and wives who have unbelieving spouses. This advice was particularly challenging in a culture that expected subordinates, including wives, to observe the ritual activities of the household, which was sacred space where religious rituals were a part of the daily activities.[34] What were the implications for a subordinate member of the household who refuses to honor the gods of her husband and honors her own in their place?[35] Just as husbands and wives act with the consent (*symphōnos*) of the other in sexual matters (7:5), believing husbands and wives remain with their unbelieving spouses when the other agrees (*syneudokei*, 7:12).[36]

Paul offers the reason: "For the unbelieving husband is made holy (*hēgiastai*) through his wife, and the unbelieving wife is made holy (*hēgiastai*) through her husband" (7:14). Since the husband is "made holy,"

32. For the challenges for Christians married to unbelievers, see Johnson Hodge, "Married to an Unbeliever," 1–25. In view of Paul's portrayal of gentile immorality (cf. 1 Cor 6:9–11; cf. Rom 1:18–32; 1 Thess 4:5), marriage to an unbeliever placed a special burden on believers. Moreover, the ancient Roman household was commonly a place of veneration of the gods, whose images would be present in the household. Johnson Hodge asks what options were present for women in this situation if they did not leave their husbands. Did they practice their faith in secret? Or did they incorporate idolatrous practices into the traditional pagan customs?

33. Paul is applying traditional halakhic practice, distinguishing between the revealed commandment, which he identifies as coming from the Lord (7:10–11), and his interpretation, which he introduces with "I say, not the Lord." (7:12). See Gillihan, "Jewish Laws on Illicit Marriage, the Defilement of Offspring, and the Holiness of the Temple," 715.

34. Cf. Plutarch, *Conj. praec.* 140D: "A married woman should therefore worship and recognize the gods whom her husband holds dear, and these alone. The door must be closed to strange cults and foreign superstitions. No god takes pleasure in secret rites performed by a woman."

35. Johnson Hodge, "Married to an Unbeliever," 4. See also Hurtado, *Destroyer of the Gods*, 54.

36. See Thiselton, *First Epistle to the Corinthians*, 527.

the children are also holy (*hagia*). Although the logic of Paul's argument in 6:12–20 might lead to the conclusion that in mixed marriages the believer would be defiled by a sexual relationship with an unbelieving spouse, Paul affirms that holiness extends to the unbelieving spouse.

Inasmuch as holiness is consistently used for believers who have been separated from the behavior of the surrounding culture (Lev 18:1–3; 19:2), this statement is one of the most puzzling in Pauline literature. Since sanctification signifies the separation of believers from unbelievers, one may ask how unbelieving spouses can be "made holy" (*hēgiastai*).[37] Indeed, Paul has earlier described the Corinthians' own experience. Although they had once been numbered among the immoral people described in 1 Cor 6:9–11, they were "washed," "sanctified" (*hēgiasthēte*), and "justified."

The holiness of believers is especially evident in their separation from the sexual practices of their neighbors (cf. Rom 6:12–20; 1 Cor 1:2; 6:9–11; 1 Thess 4:1–8). The church is not a mixed body but the realm of purity and holiness, separated from the power of sin (cf. 1:1–3; 6:11). Thus the nature of the church as a holy community, set apart from the society, makes Paul's reasoning anomalous. The nonbeliever is made holy; the believer is not made unholy. The unbeliever comes into the sphere and aura of the spirit.

The rhetorical effect of Paul's reasoning undoubtedly plays a role in this passage. Paul's intent is to offer assurance to those who are uncertain of their status in a mixed marriage. Anthony Thiselton convincingly argues that holiness is not a contagion that spreads apart from faith, as some have suggested,[38] but the *"willingness of the unbeliever to continue the relationship"* which *"has had a decisive influence on his or her behavior"* (Thiselton's emphasis).[39] The lifestyle of the Christian may affect the conduct of the unbelieving spouse, who then belongs to the wider circle of the holy people (cf. 1 Pet 3:1–2) and ultimately becomes a believer (7:16).

The logical consequence of the holiness of the unbelieving spouse is the holiness of the children (7:14).[40] If the unbelieving husband or wife is

37. The perfect passive form *hēgiastai* indicates a past event that is a continuing reality. Thiselton, *First Corinthians*, 528.

38. Thiselton, *First Corinthians*, 530.

39. Thiselton, *First Corinthians*, 530.

40. The status of the offspring from illicit marriages was a major issue in rabbinic sources. Cf. *M.Qiddushin* 3:12, "And in the case of any woman whose marriage to such is not holiness, but with others would be holy, the offspring is a *mamzer*. And which is such? In the case of a man who has sexual intercourse with one of the prohibited degrees of marriage in the Law. . . ." "*Mamzerim* were impure and posed a threat to the holiness of the land of Israel, especially to the temple. Biblical and postbiblical Jewish legislators emphatically stressed their exclusion: Deut 23:3 forbids them and their descendants, to the tenth generation, from entering the holy assembly of Yahweh." Thus

influenced by the holy lifestyle of the spouse, the children will also belong to the sphere of the holy. Influenced by the parents' separation from the vices of pagan culture, the child also becomes holy. Thus Paul does not have a "bunker mentality" regarding the believers' relationship to the world but trusts in the saving power of Christ.[41] He is convinced that God's power cannot be held in an enclosed ghetto but extends beyond the community into the secular world.[42] Furthermore, the unbelieving spouse may become a believer (7:16).

The believers' engagement with the world is also evident in the exhortations to extend love beyond the community. While believers care primarily for one another, their love extends not only to fellow believers but to outsiders as well. Paul prays that the Thessalonians will "abound in love to one another and to all" (1 Thess 3:12) and instructs them "to pursue the good to one another and to all" (1 Thess 5:15). In Galatians, he says to do good to all people, especially those of the household of faith (6:10).

In the hostile climate of believers in Philippi (cf. Phil 1:28), Paul insists that the community struggle together against an adversary, having the mindset that is in Christ Jesus. Indeed, the Philippian hymn is a counternarrative to the dominant narrative of the culture. To claim that "Jesus is Lord" and to insist that "our citizenship is in heaven" necessarily separated the community from the larger society. Here also, the community does not retreat from the larger society. As it lives in harmony, it is a light shining in the darkness (Phil 2:15).

As apostle to the gentiles, Paul engages in a mission to proclaim Christ to the world, challenging listeners to "turn to God from idols" (1 Thess 1:9). He adapts himself to others that he might "win some" (1 Cor 9:19). While he does not assume that his converts will engage directly in his missionary project, he intends that their existence will have an evangelistic impact. Husbands and wives who are married to unbelieving spouses may save them (1 Cor 7:16; cf. 1 Pet 3:1). Indeed, Paul's suggestion offers a window into the growth of the early church as the gospel spread among family members and other networks.[43] He instructs the Corinthians to "give no offense to Jews or to Greeks or to the church of God" (1 Cor 10:32). He envisions occasions when the outsider enters the assembly (1 Cor 14:20–25), and he suggests that it may not only build up the believer but have a positive impact on the unbeliever.

Paul is reassuring the readers that the children are not *mamzerim*. Gillihan, "Jewish Laws," 720.

41. Schrage, *Der erste Brief an die Korinther*, 2.104.

42. Schrage, *Der erste Brief an die Korinther*, 2.105.

43. See Sandnes, *New Family*, 93–111; Reinbold, *Propaganda und Mission im ältesten Christentum*, 299–310; Thompson, *The Church according to Paul*, 166.

A DIALECTICAL RELATIONSHIP TO CULTURE

Paul interrupts the advice on marriage in 7:17–24 to offer the guiding principle that extends beyond the issues of marriage: "Let each of you (*hekastos*) lead the life (*peripateite*) that the Lord has assigned, to which God has called you" (7:14), which reiterates the earlier advice to the unmarried (7:8, 11) and those involved in a mixed marriage (7:12–26). The advice in 7:17 forms an *inclusio* with the instruction in 7:24, "Let each of you remain (*menetō*) in the condition in which you were called." The latter imperative repeats the same instruction in 7:20. Thus the advice to remain in one's calling is a refrain that appears three times in 7:17–24 (vv. 17, 20, 24). The transitional *ei mē* (NRSV "however that may be") in 7:17 may refer to the exceptions in 7:15; that is, whatever the exceptions, the general principle stands: "let each of you live the life that the Lord has assigned, to which God called you" (7:17).

Paul's general principle of remaining in one's status extends to others in 7:17–24—the circumcised, the uncircumcised (7:18), and slaves (7:21–24). "Each of you" refers not only to the categories mentioned in 7:8–16 but also to others. That is, the advice covers the categories of marriage, ethnicity, and slavery, the major marks of individual identity (cf. Gal 3:28).

In the first place, neither the circumcised nor the uncircumcised should change their status (7:18). Paul offers a rationale for his advice: "circumcision is nothing and uncircumcision is nothing," but the keeping of the commandments (7:19). The declaration corresponds to Paul's statements in Galatians. According to Gal 5:6 and 6:15, "neither circumcision nor uncircumcision count for anything." What matters is "faith working through love" (5:6) and the new creation (6:15). That is, for those who live in the new creation, rescued from the present evil world (1:4), ethnic status counts for nothing.

Circumcision, one of the three major boundary markers of Jewish identity, is now *adiaphora* in the new aeon. As Paul says later, the "end of the ages has come" for the believing community (1 Cor 10:11). Similarly, Paul counsels slaves to remain as they are, and he offers a reason (7:22–24): "In the Lord"—the new eschatological reality—the slave is already free (7:22), and the free person is a slave of Christ. Thus both slaves and free persons are "bought with a price" (6:23), and their earthly status is irrelevant.

Before Paul offers the reasons for slaves to remain as they are, he inserts a statement, "If you are able to be free, 'make use'" (*chrēsai*). Since the verb *chrēsai* is ambiguous, interpreters have debated whether Paul is suggesting that slaves "make use of their freedom" or "make use of their present condition." The exception in 7:21 recalls the exceptions to the instructions on divorce in 7:11, 15. In view of the exceptions in 7:15, Paul is most likely suggesting that slaves make use of the opportunity for freedom.[44]

Paul gives further insight into the reasons for believers to remain in their present status in his advice to virgins to remain as they are (7:25): "because of the present distress" (*henestōsan anagkēn*), resuming the advice for married and unmarried to remain in whatever state they are in (7:25–28), but acknowledging that marriage is not a sin (7:28). While some interpreters have maintained that "the current distress" (*henestosan anagkēn*, 7:26) is a reference to dislocation caused by famine or social unrest,[45] the eschatological references in 7:29, 31 suggest that the "distress" is the eschatological situation. *Anagkē* is a common term in apocalyptic literature for the great distress that signals the imminence of the end (cf. Luke 21:23).[46] The term appears in the Pauline catalog of sufferings to describe Paul's eschatological existence (cf. 2 Cor 6:4; 10:10). *Henestōs* can refer to something that is either present or future.[47] Inasmuch as Paul understands that the end of the age has already come (1 Cor 10:11), the "current distress" is evidently the interim between the end of the age that has come and is yet to come.[48] The "affliction in the flesh" (*thlipsis*, 7:28) also points to the eschatological suffering that precedes the end (cf. Rom 5:3; 8:35; 1 Thess 1:6; 3:3, 7).

Paul offers further reflections on eschatology and cultural institutions in 7:29–32, extending his argument beyond the specific issues in the Corinthian situation to add a general principle that applies to other institutions, as in 7:17–24. He begins with the announcement, "This I say" (*touto de phēmi*), using a grammatical construction to alert his readers to the importance of what he is about to say."[49] This solemn pronouncement appears later in 15:50. Paul offers the reason for his advice for believers to remain in their calling in the *inclusio*, marked by "the appointed time has grown short" (7:29) and "the form of this world is passing away" (7:31), which suggests that believers live in the interim between the resurrection of Christ and the end (cf. 15:50–58). The "ends (*telē*) of the ages have come" (1 Cor 10:11), but believers still anticipate the end (*telos*, 15:24). This interim determines the believers' motivation for ethics (cf. Rom 13:11–13; 1 Thess 5:1–11) and their recognition of the provisional nature of human institutions. *Kairos* (time) is

---

44. On the caveats to Paul's advice in 7:1–2, 9, 11, 15 and the limited options for the liberated slave, see the discussion of slavery in ch. 4.

45. See Winter, "Seasons of This Life and Eschatology," 331.

46. Schrage, *Der erste Brief an die Korinther*, 2:156. See also Zeph 1:15, "a day of distress (*thlipsis*) and anguish (*anagkē*)."

47. BDAG, 337.

48. Schrage, *Der erste Brief an die Korinther*, 2:157.

49. Winter, "Seasons of This Life and Eschatology," 329.

frequently used in reference to the end time (cf. Rom 9:9; 13:11; 1 Cor 4:5; 2 Cor 6:2;). The fact that it has been "shortened" is the equivalent of "the world is passing away." The ESV and NRSV reading, "the appointed time has grown short," captures the meaning of *ho kairos synestalmenos,* and it corresponds to Rom 13:11, "Salvation is nearer than when we first believed."[50]

The eschatological focus shapes the believers' daily lives and places their relationship to human institutions in perspective. Paul challenges Christians to bring their ethical conduct into line with the eschatological turn of the ages. The institutions of the world, which is passing away, must still be acknowledged.[51] The consequence of the transience of the created order is introduced with *hina,* which points to the purpose for Paul's advice. In five *hōs mē* phrases Paul indicates the believers' response to the critical moment. All situations are governed by the *hōs mē*—to live "as though they were not."[52] *Hōs mē* does not mean that a believer should not be involved with the world although the believer will not be deeply invested in it,[53] The *hōs mē* existence is also a theme in 4 Ezra:

> Let him that sells be like one who will flee; let him that buys be like one who will lose; let him that does business be like one who will not make a profit; and let him that builds a house be like one who will not live in it; let him that sows be like the one who will not reap; so also him that prunes the vines, like one who will not gather the grapes; them that marry, like those who will have no children; and them that do marry, like those that are widowed. (OTP 16:40–45)

The concern is neither a passive waiting nor a radical separation from the world but a life that is "as though it was not."[54]

In keeping with the subject at hand, Paul speaks to married men, whom he has already acknowledged; indeed, he has instructed them to fulfill conjugal obligations and to remain married (7:1–7) although he has recommended that the unmarried remain unmarried. Paul assumes that believers marry but that they regard marriage from an eschatological point of view. Thus Paul relativizes marriage. Similarly, although Paul elsewhere encourages believers to "rejoice with those who rejoice and weep with those who weep" (Rom 12:15), both weeping and rejoicing are penultimate—"rejoicing

---

50. On the topos of the shortening of the time, see Mark 13:20; Barn. 4:3.

51. Schnelle, *Apostle Paul,* 541.

52. BDAG, 1105.

53. For the parallel with the Stoic disengagement from outward things, see Schrage, "Stellung," 67.

54. Schrage, *Der erste Brief an die Korinther,* 2.169.

as though not rejoicing." Those who weep should recognize that the eschatological hope diminishes their sense of loss since those circumstances in
which we weep or rejoice are penultimate.[55]

The same principle applies to commerce. Believers continue to buy
and sell, but possessions are penultimate. Those who buy should be as "not
possessing" (*mē katechontes*). *Katechō* is literally "keep in one's possession"
or "hold fast."[56] One may compare Paul's description of himself as "having
nothing, and yet possessing everything" (2 Cor 6:10). That is, in the new
aeon, one is indifferent to the things that occupy the world. Paul challenges
readers to bring their ethical commitments into line with the eschatological
turn of the ages.[57] His statements are reminiscent of Jesus's description of
the eschatological significance of both marriage and possessions when he
mentions those who were marrying and buying and selling but ignoring the
coming of the kingdom (Luke 14:18–19; 17:28; cf. Heb 10:32–34).

The dialectical relationship to the institutions of this world described
in 7:29–30 is summarized in 7:31 in Paul's reference to those who "use
the world (*hoi chrōmenoi*) as though they had no dealings with it (*hos mē
katachrōmenoi*)."[58] *Chrasthai* refers to one's total interaction with the world;
that is, "the earth and its fulness are the Lord's" (1 Cor 10:26). Believers eat
and drink and share in the world's blessings because they remain in the
world (5:9). However, the intensified *hōs mē katachrōmenoi* indicates that
they are not too heavily invested in the world,[59] knowing that "the form of
this world is passing away" (7:31).[60] This eschatological vision thus provides
the insight for believers' relationship to the world, especially to their understanding of marriage. Indeed, Paul's advice for believers to remain where
they are is based on his concern that believes not become too engaged in
"the cares of the world" (cf. 7:33) rather than "the concerns of the Lord"
(7:34). The eschatological vision relativizes the believers' relationship to the
institutions of this world. Slavery, marriage, and business relations are the

---

55. Winter, "Seasons of Life and Eschatology," 333.

56. BDAG, 533.

57. Schnelle, *Apostle Paul*, 541.

58. Cf. the alternate translations. NEB: "Buyers must not count on keeping what
they buy, nor those who use the world's wealth on using it to the full." Giorgio Agamben
renders the phrase, "those using the world as not using it up" (*Time That Remains*, 26).

59. BDAG, 530, "To use the world as if one had no use for it."

60. Agamben (*Time That Remains*, 26) indicates that Paul is employing Roman
legal terminology, distinguishing between *usus* and *dominium*—between making use
of property and owning it:"To remain in the calling in the form of *as not* means to not
ever make the calling an object of ownership, only of use."

continuing realities for Christians, who now acknowledge these institutions but maintain distance from them.

CONCLUSION

Niebuhr's portrayal of Paul's view as "Christ and culture in paradox" does not reflect the apostle's understanding of the relationship between the church and the world. Paul is neither an antagonist toward the world nor a conformist to it but holds a dialectical position. While he consistently affirms that believers live in the new creation, rescued from the "present evil age" (Gal 1:4), he acknowledges that believers continue to live in the world and interact with the people in it, recognizing the legitimacy of the institutions of family, government, commerce, and even engaging in the social life of unbelievers (cf. 1 Cor 10:27).

Although Paul advises believers not to marry unbelievers, he accepts the marriages between believers and nonbelievers that have already taken place. Nevertheless, he demands boundaries of believers from the world, which create hostility from the society and the authorities. Thus the letters consistently reflect the tenuous relationship between the believers and their culture.

Paul acknowledges the institutions of society, but the knowledge of the passing away of the world and its provisional nature leads to a distance from the world but not to escapism or nonengagement with the world. Because this world is passing away, it cannot claim ultimate loyalty from believers. Politics, economic activity, and the family are natural to Christian existence but are not ultimate values. The *hos mē*—"as though it were not"—that Paul encourages has continuing relevance for Christians, for believers have eyes to see beyond the present situation. Their vision of the ultimate reality determines their moral commitments in the present.

4

Neither Jew nor Greek, Slave or Free, Male and Female?

Paul and Multiculturalism

At the climax of the argument in Galatians for the full membership of gentiles in the people of God, Paul exclaims, "There is no longer Jew or Greek, there is no longer slave or free, there is no longer male and female" (3:28). This confessional statement closely resembles the claim in 1 Corinthians 12:13 that "we were all baptized into one body, whether Jew or Greek, slave or free" and the declaration in Col 3:11 that in the new humanity there is no longer "Greek and Jew, Greek, circumcised and uncircumcised, barbarian, Scythian, slave and free." Numerous scholars have maintained that Paul is appealing to a baptismal confessional statement of the believing community.[1] This claim portrays a Christian community that no longer recognizes the social and ethnic categories recognized by society, thus becoming a counterculture.

Later in Galatians, Paul reaffirms the claim made in 3:28. "For in Christ Jesus neither circumcision nor uncircumcision counts for anything; the only thing that counts is faith working through love" (5:6). At the conclusion of the letter, he declares, "For neither circumcision nor uncircumcision is anything, but a new creation is everything" (6:15). Similarly, Paul

---

1. See Betz, *Galatians*, 184; Martyn, *Galatians*, 374. See also Lategan, "Reconsidering the Origin and Function of Galatians 3:28," 274, for a persuasive critique of the view that Paul is quoting a liturgical baptismal tradition.

says, "Circumcision is nothing, and uncircumcision is nothing; but obeying the commandments of God is everything" (1 Cor 7:19). These passages also describe the new situation in Christ and a new understanding of one of the boundary markers separating Jews and gentiles.

Galatians 3:26–29 has become a central focus of discussion on the issues in contemporary discussion over inclusion, gender relationships, and multiculturalism.[2] Some interpreters have appealed to the passage in support of egalitarian universalism.[3] More than any other passage in Paul's corpus, Gal 3:28 is cited to support the contention that baptism into Christ erases social distinctions.[4] However, as the contemporary focus on multiculturalism has emerged, with its focus on preserving the unique features of specific groups, interpreters have also appealed to Paul's claim that there is "neither Jew nor Greek."[5]

Paul associates this new kind of community with existence in the new age. As he indicates in Galatians, believers have "been rescued from the present evil age" (Gal 1:4) and live in the new creation (Gal 6:15; cf. 2 Cor 5:17). J. Louis Martyn has observed that this confession is not stated in the imperative but is an apocalyptic pronouncement describing existence at the turn of the ages.[6] It describes a new humanity that has left behind the distinctions recognized throughout the Mediterranean world.

While Paul's communities live in the new age, they also inhabit the old age. To what extent did Paul's communities implement this bold declaration of unity in Christ? What role did ethnicity, slavery, and gender play in actual practice? Writing to churches that continue to live in the existing social environment, Paul regularly instructs his communities who live within the existing social institutions.

2. See Lategan, "Reconsidering the Origin," 274.

3. See Badiou, *Saint Paul*.

4. Buell and Johnson Hodge, "Rhetoric of Race and Ethnicity in Paul," 247. In a history of the research on Galatians, D. Francois Tolmie discovered that more attention had been given to Gal 3:28 from 2000 to 2010 than to any other passage in the epistle. The most attention by far was to "no longer male and female." See "Research on the Letter to the Galatians: 2000–2010," 118–57.

5. Barclay, "'Neither Jew nor Greek,'" 205. "Within the Christian community, the bad conscience of Western churches in assessing their mission history, the development of non-Western theologies and the sanctioning of 'inculturation' have induced a new awareness of the value of 'difference.'"

6. Martyn, "Galatians 3:28, Faculty Appointments, and Overcoming Christological Amnesia," 41.

PAUL AND ETHNICITY

Although Paul declares that "there is no longer slave or free" or "male and female" in Gal 3:28, the actual issue in Galatians is the claim that "there is no longer Jew or Greek," which is the focal point of Paul's gospel in Galatians. Indeed, to deny this principle by insisting on the circumcision of gentiles is to "pervert the gospel of Christ" (1:7). When Paul presented his gospel to the pillars in Jerusalem, they accepted his mission and agreed that Paul would go to the uncircumcised, while Cephas would go to the circumcised (2:9). However, Paul insisted that others violated the "truth of the gospel" (2:5, 14) when they insisted on circumcision (2:1–5) and refused table fellowship (2:11–14), for they were suggesting that gentiles must become Jews in order to be fully members of the people of God. Indeed, Paul's condemnation of Cephas concerned the latter's separation from gentiles at meals, a violation of the principle that there is no longer Jew or Greek. In the midrash on the Abraham story (3:6–29; cf. Gen 15:6), he claims that gentiles belong to the seed of Abraham and thus they have been incorporated into Israel. Believers are thus one in Christ because all people, like the Jews, are descendants of Abraham.

Paul consistently divides unredeemed humanity into two groups. He expresses his indebtedness to the Greeks and barbarians" (Rom 1:14), using the common terminology designating those who were shaped by Greek culture and those who stood outside of it and did not speak Greek (cf. Acts 28:2, 4; 1 Cor 14:11; Col 3:11).[7] More frequently he divides humanity into Jews and Greeks (Rom 1:16; 3:9; 10:12; 1 Cor 1:22; 10:32), which is evidently the equivalent of "Jews and gentiles" (Rom 9:24; 1 Cor 1:23–24).[8] Together, these groups encompass all humanity, all of whom are under the power of sin (Rom 3:9) and whom God calls into fellowship (cf. Rom 9:24). As Gal 3:28 indicates, these divisions belong to the "present evil age" (1:4) and reflect a people in need of redemption.

Did Paul assume that ethnic identities were erased in Christ? Many interpreters today maintain that Gal 3:28 calls for affirming differences.[9] We gain an insight when we observe Paul's own experience. In Galatians he recalls that his conduct "in Judaism" (1:13) was a thing of the past, using the

---

7. Cf. Plato, *Theaet.* 175a; Philo, *Abr.* 267. See other texts in BDAG, 166; Balz, βάρβαρος, EDNT 1:197–98. The Romans are here included among the Greeks.

8. Cosgrove, "Paul and Ethnicity," 273. See also Uzukwu, *Unity of Male and Female in Christ*, 138–39.

9. Cosgrove, "Paul and Ethnicity," 279. See Tucker, *Remain in Your Calling*, 115–35; Witherington, *Grace in Galatia*, 281–82; Brunk, *Galatians*, 179; Oakes, *Galatians*, 128–29.

term (*ioudaismos*) that appears nowhere else in his writings. When he describes his second trip to Jerusalem, he recalls that he presented the gospel that he preached to the gentiles (2:2), taking along Titus, a Greek (2:3). The pillars in Jerusalem agree that Peter will go to the circumcised and Paul to the gentiles (2:9). In the incident at Antioch, Paul confronts Cephas, who had withdrawn from table fellowship with gentiles, along with the other Jews (2:13). Paul says, "If you being a Jew live in a gentile way and not in a Jewish way, how do you compel the gentiles to be circumcised. He adds, "We ourselves are Jews by birth and not gentile sinners" (2:15). Here Paul employs the terms Jew and gentile for believers "who by nature" are Jews. Jewishness is both an ethnic designation ("by nature Jews") and a way of life.[10] Paul continues to distinguish between Jewish and gentile believers, and he insists throughout the epistle that gentiles not become Jews. However, while he condemns the distinctions that Cephas and the other Jewish Christ-believers have made, he asks that Jews compromise a badge of identity by eating with the gentiles. "For Paul, commitment to Christ is of higher priority than the maintenance of Jewish practices."[11]

The claim that there is no longer "Jew or Greek" (3:28) appears at the end of the midrash on Gen 15:6. Indeed, Gal 3:28 is the elaboration of the conclusion in 3:26, according to which "all are children of God through faithfulness to Christ Jesus." This declaration forms an *inclusio* with 3:7–9, which first announces that all are saved by faithfulness (*pistis*) and are the children of Abraham. The conclusion that, as a result of Abraham's faithfulness, those who are faithful are his children presupposes the ancient Mediterranean notion that an individual is made of his or her ancestors, so that status, character, and identity are conferred by one's ancestors.[12] Paul continues the image of patrilineal descent, recalling the promise to Abraham's seed (3:16; cf. Gen 13:15), concluding that the "seed" is not plural but singular. Whereas in Jewish tradition, the "seed of Abraham" referred to the physical descendants of the patriarch and those who were incorporated through circumcision, Paul argues that it refers to one person, that is, to Christ, the corporate person in whom "everyone who has faith in Jesus Christ" (3:26) and "as many as" have been baptized have put on Christ (3:27) become Abraham's children. "All" (3:26) and "as many as" (3:27) lead to the conclusion that "there is no longer Jew or Greek." Thus the gentile readers of Galatians are Abraham's seed and heirs of the promise (3:29).

10. See Barclay, *Pauline Churches and Diaspora Jews*, 12.

11. Barclay, *Pauline Churches*, 21.

12. Johnson Hodge, *If Sons, Then Heirs*, 19–42.

In the allegory about Hagar and Sarah, Paul insists that all who believe in Christ are the children of the free woman (4:23–21). He concludes the letter describing the gentile community as "the Israel of God (6:16)." As he argues consistently, those who believe in Christ are the children of Abraham (cf. 2:15–16; 3:6, 8, 26–29; Rom 4:10–12). They are encouraged to look to biblical history as the story of "our fathers" (cf. 1 Cor 10:1).[13] Paul envisions a community composed of Jews and Greeks that is united by faithfulness toward Christ. Although there is "no longer Jew or Greek," he assumes that differences still exist; both uncircumcised gentiles and circumcised Jews are children of Abraham because they are both "one in Christ." The focus of the argument, therefore, is not on the preservation of identities, but on the unity in Christ of all who are faithful. While Paul says nothing about the abolition of ethnic identities, he treats ethnicity as *adiaphora*.

Paul's major concern in Galatians is that gentiles are children of Abraham without becoming Jews. He does not object to the continuation of the Jewish practice of circumcision, but he insists that gentiles not be circumcised. As he indicates in 5:6, circumcision (and presumably the food laws) has become *adiaphora*, for what actually matters is faith in Christ. Jews and gentiles are "one in Christ" (3:29); therefore, their primary identity is their allegiance to Christ. Paul exemplifies the situation of Jewish Christ-believers in his claim that he "died to the law" in order to live to God (cf. Gal 2:19). This new community is not, as later church fathers suggested, "a third race." Nor has Paul established a new religion, for those who are "one in Christ" are also the "seed of Abraham." Gentiles, therefore, have become "honorary Jews."[14] Paul's reference to Titus, a Greek Christ-believer (2:3) suggests that ethnicity still exists but that the primary identity of Jews and Greeks is based on their faith in Christ.

Paul addresses this issue briefly in 1 Cor 7:17–24 in a digression within his response to the Corinthians' inquiry about whether to marry. Having reiterated that believers maintain the marital status that they had prior to their conversion, Paul applies this principle to ethnicity and slavery. The questions, "Was anyone at the time of his call already circumcised?" and "Was anyone at the time of his call uncircumcised?" assume that the Corinthian church is composed of both Jews and gentiles. Both the circumcised and the uncircumcised should remain as they were when God called them. The reason for this answer is that "circumcision is nothing and uncircumcision is nothing." The task for both is to "keep the commandments" (7:19).

13. Barclay, *Pauline Churches*, 13.

14. Engberg-Pedersen, *Paul on Identity*, 97.

J. Brian Tucker maintains that this is a call to maintain ethnic identity. "The kind of identity that Paul seeks to create is one that sees previous social identities as maintaining their fundamental significance, rather than as something to set aside as irrelevant."[15] However, Paul's reason for remaining in their current situation corresponds to similar statements in Gal 5:6 and 6:15: In the new creation, those identities have been relativized. Ethnic identity, like marriage, belongs to the age that is passing away (cf. 7:29–32). While Paul assumes that Jewish Christ-believers will continue their practices, his primary concern is not the maintenance of social identities but the recognition of the provisional nature of ethnic identity. Ethnic identity remains because believers live between the times. Similarly, Paul's question, "Were you a slave when called?" (7:21) and the advice to remain in that situation presupposes the irrelevance of the current social identity (on slavery, see below).

He speaks in 1 Cor 9:19–23 of fashioning different identities for himself as he describes himself a servant of all for the sake of the gospel. He became "as a Jew to Jews," as if he were not already a Jew, and "as one under law," as if he were not under the law. To those "outside the law," he became "outside the law." Paul suggests that he places himself outside the traditional categories of ethnicity as he is a servant of all.

He speaks in the present tense in 2 Corinthians, describing himself as a Hebrew, an Israelite, and a descendant of Abraham (11:22). In Phil 3:5–6, Paul boasts of his Jewish identity, calling himself a "Hebrew of Hebrews" and recalling that he was circumcised on the eighth day, from the tribe of Benjamin, and a Pharisee, but now regards that identity as "loss" and "garbage" by comparison with the new identity in Christ. The logic of the contrast implies that the greater the value of his Jewish identity, the greater still the value of his identity in Christ. In that case, Phil 3:2–11 assumes the real value of Jewish identity. Nevertheless, Paul's choice of words reflects a very deprecating term to use of one's own ethnicity.[16]

The issue of ethnicity is a central focus of Romans, as scholars in the last generation have observed. In the first four chapters, Paul demonstrates his ethnic consciousness by declaring that the gospel is the power of God to salvation "for everyone who believes, both Jew and Greek" (1:16), for "Jews and Greeks are both under the power of sin" (3:9). By emphasizing "all" (*pantes*), Paul declares that the righteousness of God is "for all who believe" (1:16; 3:22; 4:11), indicating that both Christ-believing Jews and gentiles share a common identity based on faithfulness to Christ. As in his argument

15. Tucker, *"Remain in Your Calling,"* 76.
16. Cosgrove, *"Paul and Ethnicity,"* 281.

in Galatians, Paul maintains that the gentile believers are the children of Abraham (cf. 4:18).

He expresses his anguish for his "own people, [his] kindred according to the flesh" (Rom 9:3) who have not obeyed the message of Christ, introducing the extended discussion about the destiny of Israel in chapters 9–11. Those Jews who have not believed in Christ are merely kinsmen "according to the flesh" (9:3, 8; cf. 9:5). Because these children of the flesh are not children of God (9:8), Paul's task is to make his "flesh" (*sarx*, NRSV "people") jealous in hopes that they will ultimately become Christ-believers, reversing the situation described in 9:1–5. He describes himself in the present tense in Romans as an Israelite and a descendant of Abraham from the tribe of Benjamin (11:1). Using the image of the olive tree as an image for the people of God, he describes the gentile believers as the branches grafted onto the olive tree (11:16–24), which is Israel. By contrast Jews who have not believed in Christ have been broken off from the same tree. As a warning to the gentiles who have been grafted in, Paul indicates that God can graft the branches that have been cut off back into the olive tree (11:23–24). The genuine olive tree in the present, according to Paul, is composed of gentile believers and the remnant of Jewish Christ-believers. This situation is not, however, permanent, for Paul reaches the climactic conclusion in 11:26, declaring that "all Israel"—those for whom he grieves in the present—will be saved in the future (11:26). His desire for a united community composed of Jews and gentiles will ultimately be a reality. The olive tree will have "all Israel," who will become Christ-believers, including those who are now merely Israel "according to the flesh" (9:3), and the gentile Christ-believers. Paul does not anticipate separate identities but a single olive tree composed of Christ-believing Jews and gentile believers. Together, they now belong to the true Israel.

Paul anticipates this conclusion in 2:25–29 in his condemnation of those who do not keep the law, indicating that physical circumcision is not the sign of Jewish identity. Circumcision benefits only when one keeps the law (2:25). Paul asks, "If the uncircumcised keep the just requirements of the law, will not their uncircumcision be reckoned as circumcision?" (2:26). As Paul indicates later, those who are under the power of the Spirit, including gentiles, keep the just requirements of the law (8:4). Thus gentiles are Jews "*where it really matters*."[17] Paul has constructed a new form of Judaism, "one that consists of *all* (and only those) who—through Christ faith—*fulfill* "the law of Moses."[18]

---

17. Engberg-Pedersen, *Paul on Identity*, 97 (emphasis Engberg-Pedersen).

18. Engberg-Pedersen, *Paul on Identity*, 97.

The description of the strong and the weak in Rom 14:1—15:13 prob-ably has ethnic overtones, reflecting the realities of a church composed of Jews and gentiles. While Paul does not mention ethnic distinctions until 15:8–9, the differences of opinions probably suggest ethnic and cultural dif-ferences. Indeed, the argument of the entire epistle culminates in the call for accepting those who have differences of opinions inasmuch as the righ-teousness of God "for all who believe" (1:16; 3:22; 4:11, 16) is the founda-tion for the community composed of Jews and gentiles who inevitably have differences of opinion. The "weak in faith" eat only vegetables and observe specific days (14:5) while the "strong" (cf. 15:1) eat everything (14:2). The "weak" are evidently maintaining Jewish food laws. While no Jewish law re-quires the abstinence from meat, in instances where the Jews did not know the source of the meat, they refrained from eating it.[19]

The different practices may reflect the practices of different house churches. Paul acknowledges this diversity of opinion and insists that both groups welcome one another into their respective house churches (15:7; cf. 14:1). While Paul agrees with the strong (15:1), he does not force the weak to surrender their position for the sake of unity. The "weak in faith" may maintain their practices, but they should not stand in judgment on the strong (14:4). Nor should the strong condescend to the weak (14:3). The major burden lies with the strong, for Paul insists that they not put a stumbling block before the "weak in faith" (14:13) but that they bear the weaknesses of the weak and not please themselves (15:1–3). To glorify God with one voice is not to erase all differences but to acknowledge the others whose opinions are different.

Paul accepts the diversity of ethnic groups. In Romans, the basis for accepting others is that "Christ received them" (14:3; cf. 14:9). Furthermore, inasmuch as both groups stand before the God who is judge of all (14:10–12), neither group should stand in judgment on the other. However, while Paul apparently acknowledges the legitimacy of Jewish and gentile believers, he does not suggest the "(post)modern idea that every ethnicity should be protected because it is precious to its bearers."[20] Indeed, while he acknowl-edges the rights of those who remain law-observant, he characterizes them as "weak in faith" (14:1–2). Thus the significance of their observance of the law is greatly reduced.[21]

19. In numerous cases Jews refrained from eating meat because they did not know its source (Dan 1:8, 12–16; 10:3; Jdt 8:6; 10:5; 12:1–2).

20. Cosgrove, "Paul and Ethnicity," 287.

21. Barclay, *Jews in the Mediterranean Diaspora*, 386.

We see no evidence in his letters that Paul was concerned to honor and protect specific ethnic identities of gentiles, whom he typically lumps together under that generic name or under "Greek" as a term for non-Jews. Moreover, the idea that ethnicities, as cultural heritages, deserve social protection is a modern idea off the intellectual map of ancient Mediterraneans, including Paul.[22]

Paul indicates that commitment to Christ can simultaneously encompass various cultural particularities.[23] Thus although Paul claims a righteousness apart from the law, he never forbids its practice by Jews or Jewish Christians, and in Rom 14 he goes to some lengths to defend their rights to observe food and sabbath customs. He does not outlaw circumcision (for Jews); he regards it as an *adiaphoron* that counts for nothing compared with "faith working through love" (Gal 5:6; 6:15; cf. 1 Cor 7:19).[24] However, Daniel Boyarin insists that even this apparent "tolerance" of difference is ultimately intolerant of the Jewish conviction that circumcision cannot be a matter of indifference:

> What will appear from the Christian perspective as tolerance, namely Paul's willingness—indeed insistence—that within the Christian community all cultural practice is equally to be tolerated, from the rabbinic Jewish perspective, is simply an eradication of the entire cultural value system which insists that our cultural practice is our task and calling in the world and must not be abandoned or reduced to a matter of taste, but is the very core of their identity.[25]

Boyarin correctly observes that tolerance of cultural difference is actually intolerant of those for whom the maintenance of their cultural traditions cannot be a matter of taste but is the essence of their core identity.[26]

> As Rom 14–15 indicates, Paul's protection of the rights of law-observant Christians to keep sabbath and food laws in fact subtly undermines their social and cultural integrity, since they are forced to acknowledge the equal validity of non-observance while being allowed (with some condescension) to observe. Thus even if Paul does not "eradicate" cultural differences, his

22. Cosgrove, "Did Paul Value Ethnicity?," 289.

23. Cosgrove, "Did Paul Value Ethnicity?," 278.

24. Cosgrove, "Did Paul Value Ethnicity?," 278.

25. Boyarin, *Radical Jew*, 32; cf. 9–10.

26. Barclay, "'Neither Jew Nor Greek,'" 212.

relativization of their significance somehow threatens the very seriousness with which they are taken by their practitioners.[27]

As Paul argues in Galatians, there is "no longer Jew or gentile" because gentiles have been incorporated into Israel. He preaches a "de-restricted, open Judaism,"[28] attempting to create multiethnic communities under the umbrella of the seed of Abraham. Paul does not obliterate cultural particularities but relativizes them.[29] According to Buell and Hodge, "Paul asks gentiles or Greeks to reject their gods, religious practices, and stories of origin and to adopt instead the God of Israel, Christ, the narrative of Israel, and its founding ancestor."[30] He demands that gentiles abandon practices that are prohibited in the Torah (cf. 1 Thess 4:5), and he requires that Jews recognize the legitimacy of gentile converts as participants in the "Israel of God" (Gal 6:6). They may maintain their Jewish observances, but in Christ these practices become *adiaphora*.

PAUL AND SLAVERY

Although slavery is not the primary issue in Gal 3:28, in the context of his argument for the inclusion of gentiles in the people of God, Paul declares that there is no longer "slave or free." According to Hans Dieter Betz, the statement in 3:28 can be interpreted in two ways: "As a declaration of the abolishment of the social institution of slavery or as a declaration of the irrelevancy of that institution, which would include the possibility of its retention."[31] The overwhelming evidence in the early churches suggests that only the second option was viable. Indeed, in many instances freed slaves were no better off.[32]

Paul cannot divorce himself from the ancient economy, for slavery remains a reality in society. Slaves were probably included in the household

27. Barclay, "'Neither Jew Nor Greek,'" 212.

28. Theissen, *Social Reality of the Early Christians*, 219.

29. Barclay, "'Neither Jew Nor Greek,'" 211.

30. Buell and Johnson Hodge, "Rhetoric of Race and Ethnicity in Paul," 249.

31. Betz, *Galatians*, 193.

32. Wright, *Paul and the Faithfulness of God*, 1:12. See also de Vos, "Once a Slave, Always a Slave?," 104: "Despite what many scholars appear to have assumed, manumission—in and of itself—would not have made any significant difference to the actual relationship between Philemon and Onesimus. Since the Graeco-Roman world was a strongly collectivist, authoritarian and patriarchal society that understood people in terms of fixed and unchanging stereotypes, the prevalent attitude would have been one of 'once a slave, always a slave'. Manumission had no significant effect on that."

baptisms, as the household codes suggest (cf. Eph 5:21–6:9; Col 3:18–4:1). In some instances, slaves probably became Christ-believers without their masters (cf. 1 Pet 2:18–25) while in other instances the masters became Christ-believers without the slaves (e.g., Philemon). Undoubtedly, this domestic situation created a dilemma for the churches.

The presence of slaves among Paul's churches is indicated in his instructions to slaves in 1 Cor 7:17–24, a passage that appears in the larger context of Paul's advice on marriage. In response to a letter from the Corinthians, Paul states the governing idea for the chapter: "It is good for a man not to touch a woman" (7:1), which he clarifies repeatedly in his advice for believers to remain as they are (1 Cor 7:7–8, 17–20, 25–27). He advises the unmarried to remain as he is (7:8), but he advises married believers to remain married (7:10). Paul follows a pattern in which the advice is regularly followed by a caveat:

> It is good for a man not to touch a woman
>> But because of fornication each man should have a wife and each woman her own husband (7:1–2).
>
> To the unmarried and widows . . . it is good to remain as I am (7:8).
>> But if they do not have self-control (7:9; cf. 7:2), let them marry.
>
> To the married, . . . not to separate (7:10)
>> But if she separates, let her remain unmarried or be reconciled (7:11).
>
> To the rest I say if a man or woman has an unbelieving spouse, do not separate (7:13),
>> But if the unbelieving spouse separates, the brother or sister is not bound (7:15).
>
> Let each of you lead the life that the Lord has assigned (7:17).
>> Example: Circumcised? Do not remove the marks of circumcision (7:18).
>> Reason: Circumcision does not mean anything (7:19).
>
> Were you a slave when called? (7:21)
> Don't let it be a care to you.
>> But if you can gain your freedom, make use. . . . (7:21)
>
> Virgins, married, unmarried: remain as you are (7:25–28).
>> But if you marry, you do not sin (7:28).

Paul's advice to slaves in 1 Cor 7:21 is one of the most perplexing issues of interpretation in the NT, as the translations indicate. Interpreters debate the meaning of *chrēsai* ("make use"),[33] and the standard translations reach different conclusions—whether Paul is advising slaves to "make use" of their present situation (NRSV) or to "make use" of the opportunity to be free (NIV). The pattern of instructions followed by "if" clauses suggests the answer. The imperatives suggest a specific course of action (remain where you are). The "if" clauses suggest the caveat, a different course of action that is possible (i.e., "but if the unbelieving spouse separates, the brother or sister is not bound," 7:15; "if you marry, you do not sin," 7:28). When Paul sets up one premise (being a slave), he urges one action (do not be concerned). However, when he sets up a subsequent, different premise (if you can become free), he urges a different action (be concerned and take it).[34]

Even if Paul suggests that slaves may avail themselves of the opportunity for freedom, the point is that slavery is largely irrelevant. When he asks, "Were you a slave when you were called?" he adds, "Do not be concerned about it" (7:21), suggesting that slavery does not matter. Just as circumcision and uncircumcision are nothing, slavery is not an ultimate matter. Indeed, Paul gives the basis for his advice to slaves in 7:22, as *gar* suggests. The one who is called as a slave is "a freedperson (*apeleutheros*) of the Lord," and the free person who is called is a "slave of the Lord," for all have been bought with a price (1 Cor 6:20).

Paul directs slaves (and others) not to try to change their status but only because that status will change soon enough—as the new age comes in its fullness and the old age passes away.[35] As Paul's advice to virgins suggests (7:25–28), believers should not be concerned about their status because of the "present distress." He elaborates on this expression in 7:29–31. Given the proximity of the parousia, Paul concludes that it is not wise for believers to be concerned about their status. Since the form of this world will soon pass away (7:31), believers should not be concerned about the affairs of this age.[36] According to Schrage, "The freedom granted by Christ and the service to Christ belong together and relativize the inner-worldly differentiation and

33. BDAG, 1087.

34. Harrill, "Paul and Slavery," 587. "This kind of grammatical construction—the depiction of one situation followed by a direction, then the depiction of a second situation followed by a new direction with the phrase "rather use" (*mallon chrēsai*)—finds parallel in a number of Greek authors." See Deming, "Diatribal Pattern in 1 Cor 7:21–22," 130–37.

35. Hinkle Shore, "Freedom of Three Christians," 395. See also Still, "Pauline Theology and Ancient Slavery," 29.

36. Still, "Pauline Theology and Ancient Slavery," 29.

realities of slavery and freedom. If the slave is a freedman of the lord and the free person is a slave of Christ, then the freedom and bondage are the only matters that transcend all standards and human classifications" (2.142). Thus Paul relativizes slavery. He identifies himself as a *doulos* (Rom 1:1; 2 Cor 4:5) of Christ and assumes that all believers are *douloi* of Christ (Rom 6:16–17; cf. Col. 4:12). Indeed, he encourages believers to be slaves of one another (Gal 5:13).

Paul's message to Philemon also addresses the challenge of placing the claim that "there is no longer slave or free" into practice. Although the letter involves slavery, it is oblique about the actual circumstances that prompted the letter and the actual nature of Paul's request. Indeed, only in verse 16 does Paul mention slavery. According to tradition, Onesimus is a runaway slave although the text never describes him in those terms. More recently, interpreters have concluded that Onesimus has come to Paul to act as *amicus domini* in a dispute with Philemon.[37] The parallel with Pliny's letter to Sabinianus suggests that the letter to Philemon reflects a similar situation. Pliny writes on behalf of Sabinianus's freedman, who has come to Pliny expressing sorrow for his actions and asking him for his intervention. Pliny then writes, asking for mercy for the unnamed freedman.

Although the occasion of Philemon is uncertain, Paul explicitly declares that Onesimus has become a Christ-believer through Paul's efforts while the apostle was in prison. Paul has become his father, and Onesimus is his child (10). Indeed, Paul speaks in intimate terms of Onesimus, calling him his own heart (*splachna*, 12).[38] The reality of Onesimus's conversion forces Paul to face the consequences of this change in status and to take painful measures to protect the former slave when he is sent back to his master.[39] That is, this slave belongs to a family relationship that has become possible only through the saving work of Christ. Elsewhere, Paul similarly describes Timothy as his child (Phil 2:22), and he describes himself as a father to his churches (1 Cor 4:14–15; 1 Thess 2:12–13). He admonishes (1 Cor 4:14), punishes (1 Cor 4:21), and encourages (1 Thess 2:12–13) them while modeling the conduct that he expects of them (1 Cor 4:16). Inasmuch

37. For alternative views of the occasion of Philemon, see Fitzmyer, *Letter to Philemon*, 17–22.

38. The term, literally referring to the bowels, was commonly used in antiquity for the seat and source of love. Cf. BDAG, 938. Paul frequently employs the term for the affection that is present in the community. Cf. 2 Cor 6:12, "you are constrained in your affections" (*splachna*); 2 Cor 7:15, Titus's "heart goes out to you"; Phil 1:8, "I long for you with the affection (*splachna*) of Christ"; Phil 2:1, "If there is . . . any compassion (*splachna*) and sympathy." Every Christian should be clothed with it (Col 3:12), for it is the sign of brotherly love (C. Spicq, *splachna*, TLNT 3:274).

39. Lategan, "Reconsidering the Origin," 282.

as *doulos* appears only once in this brief letter, more is at stake than a domestic dispute between master and slave.

While Onesimus has recently become Paul's child in the faith, Philemon had entered the family at some time earlier—perhaps while Paul was in Ephesus (v. 19). With Paul is Timothy "the brother" (1) as he writes to Philemon, "the beloved," and Apphia, "the sister" (v. 1). Paul establishes a family relationship that includes Onesimus, Philemon, and Apphia, as well as Paul himself.

The thanksgiving (vv. 4–7) indicates the intimate relationship in Christ as Paul prepares the way for his request to Philemon. As in the other letters, Paul expresses thanks for Philemon's love and faithfulness (v. 5) to the Lord and all the saints, referring to two of the familiar triad of faith, hope, and love (cf. 1 Cor 13:13; 1 Thess 1:3). This duality is commonplace in Paul's letters as inseparable concepts (Gal 5:6; Eph 1:15; 3:17; 6:23; Col 1:4; cf. 1 Thess 3:6; 5:8), signifying the most fundamental aspects of Christian conduct.[40] Paul describes this relationship in Gal 5:6 as "faith working through love." As the most frequently mentioned moral concept, love is primarily the bond among the siblings in the community of faith, as the reference to Philemon's love "for all the saints" indicates.

While Paul expresses gratitude for Philemon's love and faith for the saints, he prays that it will be active in the future, as he suggests in the implied petition "in order that the fellowship of your faith (*koinōnia tēs pisteōs sou*) may be active in the full knowledge of everything good" (v. 6).[41] The *koinōnia* of faith is the partnership of the people of God (cf. Phil 1:5) that is based on their *koinōnia* with Jesus Christ (1 Cor 1:9; 10:16; Phil 3:10) and shared participation in the Spirit (Phil 2:1). Anticipating the request that follows, Paul prays that this fellowship will become active. He also gives thanks that Philemon has refreshed the hearts (*splachna*) of the saints (v. 7). Thus Paul's thanksgiving portrays the intimate family relationship that Philemon has demonstrated. The house church is held together by the bonds of kinship.

This family relationship is the basis for the request that Paul makes. Having expressed thanks for Philemon's love (v. 5) and prayed that his partnership (*koinōnia*, v. 6) may be active, Paul appeals to Philemon on account of the latter's love (v. 9) and his partnership (v. 17). Paul is sending Onesimus back to Philemon (v. 12), describing him in the intimate terms that one uses for a family member (my *splachna*). Paul's wish is that Onesimus might

40. See Thompson, *Apostle of Persuasion*, 112–13.

41. Cf. Phil 1:3–11. Paul's thanksgiving (1:3–8) is the basis for his petition that (*hina*) the community will "love more and more in full knowledge."

remain with Paul "in order that Onesimus might serve [him] on Philemon's behalf" (13) just as Timothy serves him "as a child to his father" (cf. Phil 2:22). Paul does not indicate the status of Onesimus if Paul has him for himself (v. 13) "for a little while" (v. 15) to serve him in the gospel. He mentions only his intimate familial relationship to him.

While Onesimus was absent from Philemon "for a little while," Philemon has "him forever" (v. 15) with a new status: "no longer as a slave, but more than a slave, a beloved brother" (16). Here Paul mentions the *doulos* for the first time. In legal terms, Onesimus remains a slave, but Paul wants Philemon to recognize him as more than that "in the flesh and in the Lord."[42] "In the flesh" probably refers to the legal reality of slavery while "in the Lord" refers to the new relationship in Christ. The situation has irrevocably changed—through his conversion the former slave has become a son to Paul (v. 10). Just as Philemon and Apphia are siblings to Paul, so also is Onesimus. "Here Paul is able to imagine at least one household embodying the new age in the midst of the old. Each of the letter's three principal characters appears to be bound by roles belonging to the old age,"[43] yet upon closer inspection, they embody the new age. While he does not seek to alter the fact that legally and structurally they remained master and slave, he wants to bring about a fundamental change in the nature of their relationship as master and slave.[44] A new symbolic universe came into being in which the roles of Paul, Philemon, and Onesimus fundamentally changed: "Master and slave have been replaced by brother, son and father as part of a redefined understanding of the household of God."[45]

Only in verse 17 does Paul make a request: "If you have me as a partner (*koinōnos*), welcome (*proslabou*) him as you would welcome me." That is, Paul now indicates that the *koinōnia tēs pisteōs* becomes active in Philemon's response to Paul's request. The root word *proslambanō* is the language of hospitality between equals.[46] Paul expects Philemon to treat Onesimus as an honored guest. As a host receiving guests meant protecting their guests and their honor at all cost, being attentive to their needs, and offering them the very best that was available.[47] Such language suggests a fundamental change in the relationship between Philemon and Onesimus because hospitality was offered only between social equals. "In other words, Paul expects

---

42. Fitzmyer, *Philemon*, 114.

43. Hinkle Shore, "Freedom of Three Christians," 395.

44. De Vos, "Once a Slave," 102.

45. Lategan, "Reconsidering the Origin," 282.

46. De Vos, "Once a Slave," 103.

47. De Vos, "Once a Slave," 103.

Philemon to treat Onesimus as his social equal—indeed, as an honored guest—from this point on. As a host, receiving guests meant not insulting them, protecting them and their honor at all cost, being attentive to their needs, and offering them the very best that was available.[48]

Paul probably does not insist that Philemon liberate Onesimus, although his suggestion that Philemon will do even more may be a suggestion of ultimate liberation.[49] While he does not seek to alter the fact that legally they remained master and slave, the relationship between slave and master has fundamentally changed. Paul, Philemon, Apphia, and Onesimus are siblings in Christ. Paul has thus transformed the common understanding of slavery. Even if Philemon has Onesimus forever, their relationship has changed, for there "is no longer slave or free."

Slavery is a reality in the disputed letters. While Paul acknowledges the reality of slavery, he mitigates its effects by giving instructions to masters. Paul assumes the existence of households composed of extended families, including masters and slaves. His advice to slaves is commonplace in antiquity. However, he gives reciprocal responsibilities to masters (*kurioi*), instructing them to "treat [their] slaves kindly and fairly," knowing that they have a *kurios* in heaven (Eph 6:9; Col 4:1).

PAUL AND GENDER

While elsewhere Paul declares that the church is a community without distinctions between slave and free and Jew and gentile (1 Cor 12:13; Col 3:11), only in Galatians does he affirm that there is "no longer male and female" (3:28). As scholars have observed, Paul echoes Gen 1:28, altering the "neither . . . nor" to "male and female." That is, the community lives in the new creation, where the division of male and female has been erased. This affirmation comes in a context where the issue involves Jews and gentiles who are now one in Christ. Paul's affirmation in such a context indicates that he is citing a slogan, perhaps a baptismal confession.

The full membership of women is evident in Paul's churches. Unlike the associations of Paul's time, Paul's churches included women members. As the baptism of entire households indicates (Acts 16:15; 18:8; cf. 1 Cor 16:16), the churches mirror the ancient household, which included householders, wives, slaves, and children. When he writes to the *adelphoi*, he assumes the presence of a demographic that was unprecedented in antiquity.[50]

48. De Vos, "Once a Slave," 103.

49. De Vos, "Once A Slave," 104.

50. Thompson, *Church according to Paul*, 238.

Paul undoubtedly includes women when he calls for reciprocal responsibilities. Women are included when he insists that "each" builds on to the building under construction (1 Cor 3:10) and when he describes the church as a body in which God has given "each" (Rom 12:3) a measure of faith and a manifestation of the Spirit for the common good (1 Cor 12:7, 11). Both men and women exercise the ministries mentioned in Rom 12:3–8 and 1 Cor 12:4–11. When "each one has a hymn, a lesson, a revelation, a tongue, or an interpretation" in the assembly (1 Cor 14:26), women are not excluded.[51]

Occasionally Paul mentions specific women who are active in the life of the church. Euodia and Syntyche, for example, have "struggled beside" (*synēthlēsan*) Paul in the gospel (Phil 4:3). The image suggests that they were active with Paul in the proclamation of the gospel in the midst of great opposition. As a *diakonos* of the church in Cenchrea and a "benefactor (*prostatis*) of many" (Rom 16:1–2), Phoebe has a recognized function within the church. Paul mentions numerous other women in the greetings in Romans 16, indicating their active participation in ministries.

In Rom 16 Paul mentions specific women who are active in the life of the church. Prisca (Priscilla in Acts) is always named along with Aquila (Rom 16:3–5a; 1 Cor 16:19; 2 Tim 4:19; cf. Acts 18:2, 18, 26). Together they are coworkers with Paul, who "risked their neck" on Paul's behalf. Paul mentions another pair, Andronicus and Junia, who are "prominent among the apostles" (Rom 16:7); they may be a husband-and-wife team. Paul mentions several women who "labored" in the Lord. Mary (16:6), Tryphaena and Tryphosa (16:12), and Persis (16:12) worked hard in the Lord. Paul commonly uses the verb *kopiaō* for evangelistic work (cf. 1 Cor 4:12; 15:10; 16:16; Gal 4:11; Phil 2:16; 1 Thess 5:12).[52]

At Corinth both men and women pray and prophesy (1 Cor 11:2–16). However, Paul still assumes a clear difference in status between the sexes, as the dress code indicates. While the circumstances behind Paul's instructions are uncertain,[53] he clearly maintains that men should dress as men (with uncovered head) and women should dress as women (with covered head) because of the order of creation (11:3–9).[54] He announces the fundamental

51. Thompson, *Church according to Paul*, 238.

52. Thompson, *Church according to Paul*, 239.

53. See Schrage, *Der erste Brief an die Korinther*, 2:491. One does not know whether Paul has been informed about this issue from the Corinthians' letter to him (cf. 1 Cor 7:1) or from the report of Chloe's people (cf. 1 Cor 7:1). Also uncertain is the custom to which Paul refers with regard to head coverings. Evidence does not suggest that Greek or Roman women customarily covered their head during religious rites. More likely is the suggestion by Schrage (2:493–94) that Paul is appealing to a Jewish custom.

54. A consensus has emerged that the women in Corinth were expressing their

principle in 11:3, describing the order of creation and preparing for the argument about head coverings with the metaphorical use of *kephalē* (head) before giving instructions about the literal head coverings in 11:4–16.

Because *kephalē* in 11:3 is not a common metaphor in the Old Testament, interpreters have debated the significance of the image. Some suggest that *kephalē* does not mean ruler but source.[55] However, the order of creation in 11:3 echoes Philo's description of God's creation of the world and his frequent use of *kephalē* to speak of preeminence.[56] *Kephalē* can mean both source and sovereignty in a hierarchical relationship grounded in creation.[57] One may compare the subordination indicated in 1 Cor 15:28, where Paul anticipates the time when the son "will be subjected to the one who has put all things in subjection to him."

He apparently runs into difficulties explaining the reasons for the instructions inasmuch as he first speaks of the man's precedence, giving an egalitarian answer, indicating that men and women depend on each other (11:11–12). The point is not the annulment of sexual (or cultural or social) differences but the unity of practice of both men and women as believers before God.[58]

While women both pray and prophesy in the Corinthian church (1 Cor 11:2–16), Paul does not erase the distinction between men and women. At the conclusion of the instructions on public worship (11:2—14:40), he also places restrictions on acceptable speech in the assembly (14:33b–36), declaring, "Let the women be silent in the churches, for it is not permitted for them to speak, but to be in subjection, as the law says." Because of the apparent contradiction with the prophesying and praying by women

---

emancipation, perhaps with reference to the claim that there is "no longer male and female" (Schrage, *Der erste Brief an die Korinther*, 2:245). However, Paul does not indicate that he is addressing a particular abuse. His argument probably suggests only that the Corinthians have asked questions about proper attire.

55. See Scroggs, "Paul and the Eschatological Woman," 283–303, esp. 297; see also Murphy-O'Connor, "1 Corinthians 11:2–16 Once Again," 265–74, esp. 269–70.

56. When Philo describes the nature of the universe, he speaks of heaven as the *kephalē* (*Post.* 53.5–6) and earth as the "foot" (*Somn.* 1.145). The head is the governing part of the body (*Opif.* 11) and the seat of reason (*Leg.* 1. 70.6; 171.6). Because of the preeminence of the head to the body, the head may rightly be called "king" (*Leg.* 3.15). Philo also uses *kephalē* for the preeminence among people. Esau is the *kephalē* of all members of his clan (*Congr.* 66.1). He describes Ptolemy Philadelphus, saying, "As the head is the highest of the body, so is he head of the kings" (*Mos.* 2.230). For additional texts, see Thompson, "Creation, Shame, and Nature," 248–49.

57. Thompson, "Creation, Shame, and Nature," 249.

58. Lategan, "Reconsidering the Origin," 102.

(11:4–5), numerous scholars regard the passage as an interpolation.[59] However, textual evidence for an interpolation is nonexistent. Moreover, we have no evidence that a scribe ever corrected the argument of Paul, as the interpolation theory suggests.[60] Thus if the passage is not an interpolation, one must determine how it coheres with 11:2–16. In a context of glossolalia and prophecy where others were told to be silent for the sake of order (14:28), the women were also told to be silent. While women prayed and prophesied in the assembly, the women addressed in 14:33b–36 were not engaged in prophetic speech; thus they are told to be silent.

While interpreters debate the extent and nature of the restrictions on women, a dialectic is present in Paul's instructions. Women are full members of the congregations, and they pray and prophesy alongside the men, but in the present the differences still exist, as the dress code indicates. In the present the women conform to cultural expectations about the attire of the women.

CONCLUSION

Paul describes a new creation in which "there is no longer Jew or Greek, slave or free, male and female," but his communities still live in a world where those distinctions exist in practice. However, they are all relativized in Christ. J. Louis Martyn urges a "bifocal" reading of Gal 3:28 that simultaneously sees the world as it is in Christ yet still remains in the old age. Consequently, Paul never fully places this ideal in practice. Just as Paul remains a Jew, Jews remain Jews, even in Christ, and gentiles remain gentiles. Paul permits Jews to maintain traditional Jewish practices, but he does not demand that they do so. Slavery is not abolished in Pauline churches, but it is relativized. Men and women are one in Christ, but gender differences remain in the church. Martyn attributes to Paul an apocalyptic "bifocal vision" that is rooted in his apocalyptic understanding. As Paul indicates in 1 Cor 7:29–32, believers live "as though they were not" (*hos mē*). Paul "noticed as not noticing that some of his colleagues were women and not men." We might say, in Martyn's concept, Paul cares about ethnicity without caring.[61]

59. The reasons given for concluding that the passage is an interpolation are the following: (1) the apparent contradiction with 11:2–6, (2) the textual instability of the passage (some manuscripts place it at the end of the chapter), (3) terms that are not used elsewhere in the Pauline corpus, (4) the apparent interruption of the flow of argument on prophecy and glossolalia. Schrage, *Der erste Brief an die Korinther*, 3:482–85.

60. See Jervis, "1 Corinthians 14.34–35," 53.

61. Martyn, "Galatians 3:28," 44.

5

Citizens of Heaven

Paul and the State

Like Jesus before him, Paul says surprisingly little about Roman power or politics, although he established communities in three Roman colonies (Antioch of Pisidia, Corinth, Philippi) and was frequently confronted by Roman magistrates elsewhere. His letters do not address public affairs but speak of the welfare and moral transformation of the communities he establishes. In response to his proclamation of "Christ crucified," those who receive this message become members of a network of communities whose only loyalty is to Jesus Christ. These communities, which transcended the boundaries of class, ethnic origin, and gender,[1] were unprecedented in the ancient world, forming a subculture within the larger society. A major task of community formation, although rarely mentioned, was the relationship between this community and the society dominated by the Roman presence.

Although Paul instructed communities explicitly on their conduct toward the Roman state only once in the undisputed letters (Rom 13:1–7; cf. 1 Tim 2:1; Titus 3:1), as the herald of the one crucified by the Romans, he was consistently confronted by Roman authorities and a populace that was loyal to Rome. On at least one occasion he received the Roman punishment of beating with rods (2 Cor 11:25; cf. also 2 Cor 6:5; 12:10). Both the "battle with the wild beasts in Ephesus" (1 Cor 15:32) and the danger of death in the province of Asia (2 Cor 1:8–9) indicate life-threatening conflicts (cf. also

1. Wright, *Paul and the Faithfulness of God*, 383.

86

Rom 16:4).[2] The accusation that these people are "turning the world upside down" (Acts 17:6) probably reflects accurately the reaction of communities wherever he preached. When he preached in Thessalonica, he was "shamefully mistreated," preaching "in spite of great opposition" (1 Thess 2:1–12). Local hostility to Paul in these cities often turned into hostility from Roman authorities and their representatives. In 2 Cor 11:32, Paul reports a plan to arrest him in Damascus. The Nabatean king Aretas, a Roman vassal, had the city watched in order to arrest Paul. The apostle escaped arrest by having himself let down in a basket through a window in the wall (2 Cor 11:32–33). Paul did not always escape arrest, however, for he was "in prison many times" (2 Cor 11:23)[3] and wrote letters from prison before he was ultimately executed by the Romans.

Since Paul was repeatedly in conflict with Roman authorities, the communities that he left behind had to determine their level of participation in civic life. On the one hand, the fact that Erastus was the *oikonomos* in Corinth (Rom 16:23) suggests that at least some believers continued to hold public office. Believers also were present in Caesar's household (Phil 4:22). While the precise roles of the *oikonomos* of Corinth or the members of Caesar's household are unknown, their presence among Roman authorities indicates that some believers were active in city or imperial affairs. On the other hand, Paul's communities would inevitably get the attention of the Roman authorities, for whom the Pax Romana required the religious cohesion of the empire. From the point of view of Roman officials, communities gathering in unusual combinations, binding themselves to a cause, were perceived as a threat to this cohesion.[4] Their withdrawal from the sacrificial offerings to the gods of the household, city, and empire and their exclusive allegiance to the one God was a move without precedent, and it would have been distressing to the local populace.[5] Their exclusivist claims were "so impious in the eyes of ancient pagan observers and critics that they were accused of atheism."[6]

Foreign cults had already been banned in the city of Rome, for groups of people meeting together with their own structure and way of life, unrelated to the official structures of the state, were considered dangerous.[7] The Romans sought to restrict and channel the numerous religious movements

2. Schnelle, *First Hundred Years of Christianity*, 264.

3. See Wengst, *Pax Romana and the Peace of Jesus Christ*, 73.

4. Wright, *Paul and the Faithfulness of God*, 1278.

5. Hurtado, *Destroyer of the Gods*, 53–54.

6. Hurtado, *Destroyer of the Gods*, 56.

7. Wright, *Paul and the Faithfulness of God*, 383, 1278.

within the common bond of the Pax Romana.[8] In addition, the lifestyle of the Christians, which in many respects differed from the norms and customs of their environment, provoked the hostility of the populace (cf. 1 Pet 4:4).[9] Thus when the community of the disciples confessed the crucified Messiah Jesus after Easter, they took on a political burden as well.[10]

THE POLITICAL SIGNIFICANCE OF PHILIPPIANS

Paul's letter to the Philippians offers a window into the tense relationship between believers and the state. He writes from prison to this Roman colony (1:7, 12–13), where the Roman citizens were registered in the list of the citizens of *tribus Voltinia*,[11] when the apostle was probably anticipating execution at the hands of the Romans (1:21–26). His conflict with Roman power is evident in his reference to the praetorian guard (1:13). His imprisonment undoubtedly raised questions about the community's own status in this Roman colony. His exhortation not to be intimidated by the adversaries (1:28) and statement that they are partners in tribulation (4:14) suggest that they share in Paul's struggles (1:30). His readers were also anxious (cf. 4:6) about their potential conflict with Roman magistrates.

Paul responds to the vulnerable community with the call for unity and solidarity among them. Indeed, the *propositio* of the letter is the encouragement, "live out your citizenship (*politeuesthe*) in a way that is worthy of the gospel of Christ (1:27),"[12] which anticipates the later affirmation that "our citizenship (*politeuma*) is in heaven" (3:20). While Paul commonly uses the verb *peripatein* (literally "to walk," cf. Rom 6:4; 13:13; Gal 5:16; Eph 4:1; 1 Thess 4:1) for moral conduct, he deliberately chooses a word that has political significance.[13] The word choice indicates the conflict with impe-

---

8. Schnelle, *First Hundred Years of Christianity*, 265.

9. Wright, *Paul and the Faithfulness of God*, 1302.

10. Wengst, *Pax Romana and the Peace of Jesus Christ*, 72.

11. Pilhofer, "Philippi zur Zeit des Paulus: Eine Ortsbegehung," 13.

12. The NRSV renders the phrase "live your life in a manner worthy of the gospel." Paul uses the term *politeuesthe* nowhere else in the letters in describing the moral life. His most common verb for ethical conduct is *peripatein* (lit. "to walk around" (cf. Rom 6:4; 8:4; 13:13; 1 Cor 3:3, 7, 17; Gal 5:16; Phil 3:17; 1 Thess 4:1, 12). *Politeuesthai*, which is drawn from political life , means literally "conduct yourselves as citizens." It is used for someone who lives according to the norms of the polis. Cf. BDAG 846.

13. Vollenweider, "Politische Theologie im Philipperbrief?," 459.

rial Rome. Christ-believers are citizens of another, superior realm.[14] Paul's statement thus reflects a conflict of loyalties for Christ-believers in Philippi.

The citizenship that is worthy of the gospel is maintained only with the exercise of communal solidarity, as Paul indicates in 1:27b—2:5. Believers stand in "one spirit, one soul" (1:27). This challenge, like the encouragement to be "of the same mind" (*to auto phronein*) in 2:2 (cf. 4:2), echoes the ancient language of friendship, a frequent theme among the philosophers.[15] It also recalls the ancient discussions of *homonoia* (agreement, harmony), which distinguished the ideal polis.[16] Paul has thus applied ancient political rhetoric to describe the church as the ideal polis.

The theme of friendship in antiquity implies the presence of enemies. It was necessary for Athens to unite against the threat of Sparta. The Greeks had to unite against the barbarians.[17] Paul formulates the citizenship that is worthy of the gospel in agonistic terms. The Philippians are "striving side by side" (*synathlountes*) in the Gospel.[18] As Paul indicates in 1:28, the community faces adversaries, and suffering is their destiny (cf. 1 Thess 3:1–5).

This solidarity can be attained, according to Paul, if believers reject the values of their culture, "in humility (*tapeinophrosynē*) counting others better than" themselves (2:3).[19] Believers are able to "have the same mind" (*to auto phronein*, 4:2) when they "have among themselves the mind (*phroneite*, 2:5) of Christ."[20] The centerpiece of the letter is the poetic narrative in 2:6–11, describing the one who modeled the selfless conduct commended in 2:1–5. In describing one who "did not count equality with God a thing to be grasped" (2:6) but "emptied himself" by exchanging the "form of God" for the "form of a slave," Paul offers a counternarrative to the common depiction of Hellenistic rulers. Paul's description has echoes of Roman emperors, who were regarded as "equal to God" but grasped for power. Nearly every description of emperors of the first century depicts them as "grasping their power through

---

14. Popkes, "Zum Thema 'Anti-imperiale Deutung neutestamentlicher Schriften,'" 862.

15. On the philosophical discussions of friendship, see ch. 6.

16. Vollenweider, "Politische Theologie im Philipperbrief?," 460.

17. Vollenweider, "Politische Theologie im Philipperbrief?," 462.

18. *Synathlein* is an image drawn from military activity. Cf. BDAG 964. Paul envisions soldiers standing side by side as a single unit.

19. Outside of Paul, *tapeinophrosynē* is used only in Josephus (*B.J.* 4.494) and Epictetus (*Diatr.* 3.24.56; 4.6.8), exclusively in a negative sense. The term is unknown prior to Paul. See Becker, *Paul on Humility*, 24.

20. Contrary to the standard translations, the best rendering is not a call to have the same mind *in you* that was in Christ (a call for imitation), but "have the same *among you* that you have in Christ."

self-assertion, greed, rivalry, violence, and murder."[21] The self-emptying of Christ is the antithesis of the self-exalting Hellenistic ruler.[22]

The conflict with Rome is further indicated in the claim that "he humbled himself, becoming obedient to death, even death on a cross" (2:8). That he "humbled himself" recalls the earlier encouragement to the readers to adopt humility as a way of life (2:3). The added phrase, "even death on a cross," indicates the absolute nadir of the descent and the epitome of shame and is a reminder of the Roman method of execution. As Roman writers indicate, it is the most shameful form of death, particularly offensive to Roman ears.[23] According to Cicero (Rab. Perd. 5.16), the word cross should be far removed from the "thoughts, eyes, and ears" of Roman citizens."[24]

Conflict between the new community and Rome is nowhere more present than in the confession that all beings will acknowledge that "Jesus Christ is Lord" (2:11). A man crucified by the Romans receives the highest status through the direct intervention of God.[25] The designation of Jesus as the Lord to whom "every knee will bow" would have been especially troublesome to the Roman audience, for whom only Caesar is lord.[26] As one condemned by the Roman government (Phil 1:12–26), Paul knows that one who dies condemned by Rome was offensive to Roman ears, especially in Philippi. While the confession of the universal reign of Christ is offensive to the Romans, it is the basis of the solidarity of the community that recognizes that Jesus Christ is Lord.

Paul continues this claim for the universal sovereignty of the exalted Christ in 3:20–21, declaring that "our citizenship (politeuma) is in heaven, and it is from there that we are expecting a Savior, Jesus Christ." This terminology echoes the poetic narrative of 2:6–11. The heavenly politeuma stands in contrast to the Roman politeuma. The community awaits the one who has been made universal Lord. Contrary to Roman propaganda, the Caesar is neither lord nor savior. While loyal citizens of this Roman colony would gladly welcome a visit from the Caesar and acclaim him "savior and lord," Christ-believers look forward to the one who will return as universal sovereign. Just as Christ was transformed from his humble status to glory,

21. Tellbe, *Paul between Synagogue and State*, 256.

22. Vollenweider, "Der 'Raub' der Gottgleichheit," 283.

23. Popkes, "Zum Thema 'Anti-imperiale' Deutung neutestamentlicher Schriften," 861.

24. Thompson and Longenecker, *Philippians and Philemon*, 72.

25. Schnelle, *First Hundred Years of Christianity*, 264.

26. A Greek inscription from the time of Nero contains the formulation "Nero the kyrios of the world." Cf. NW I/2:239–56. Cited in Schnelle, *First Hundred Years of Christianity*, 265.

believers will also be transformed. Undoubtedly, this conviction created a conflict of loyalties among Christ-believers and would have been considered seditious.[27]

COUNTER-IMPERIAL TERMINOLOGY?

Pauline terminology in all of the letters inevitably raised questions about the community's relation to the Roman state, as Adolf Deissmann observed more than a century ago, describing the "polemical parallelism between the cult of the emperor and the cult of Christ."[28] Besides the obvious examples of *theos, theou huios*, and *kyrios*, he noted the use of king (*basileus*), coming (*parousia*),[29] and *epiphaneia*[30] as special imperial terminology.[31] In recent years, scholars have supplemented and developed Deissmann's insight with the claim that Paul's language is parallel to imperial claims in many respects.[32] The term *gospel (euangelion)*, according to N. T. Wright, "cannot but have been heard as a summons to allegiance to 'another king.'"[33] The terms *Christos, Lord*, and *Son of God* would also have been regarded as a challenge to the empire, for these were royal titles suggesting that the believers honored another king than Caesar. According to Wright, the announcement of the revelation of the justice (*dikaiosynē*) of God (Rom 1:17; 3:21) was a challenge to the imperial claim that the Caesar had brought justice to the empire. The climactic claim of the renewal of creation in Rom 8 was subversive for a community whose emperor claimed to rule the whole world.[34] God's justice demands loyalty (*pistis*), just as Caesar's claim also

27. Popkes, "Zum Thema 'Anti-imperiale Deutung neutestamentlicher Schriften,'" 862.

28. Adolf Deissmann, *Light from the Ancient East*, 337–78.

29. See 1 Thess 2:19; 3:13; 4:15; 5:23. NRSV renders it as "coming." In the Hellenistic period, it was used for either a divine visit or the formal visit of a sovereign and his joyous visit to the city that has prepared for him. Spicq, *Parousia*, TLNT, 3:53–54. See Harrison, "Paul and the Imperial Gospel," 83, for texts illustrating the widespread use of *parousia* and *epiphaneia* for the visit of the emperor or other magistrates to the cities: "It would seem, then, that Paul has seized upon a familiar imperial motif to allay Thessalonian fears regarding the dead in Christ."

30. See 1 Tim 6:14; 2 Tim 1:16; 4:1; Titus 2:12. *Epiphaneia* was used for an emperor who is visiting or making a joyous entry into a city, granting favors to his subjects. Spicq, TLNT 2:67.

31. Deissmann, *Light from the Ancient East*, 333–73.

32. See Wright, "Letter to the Romans," 404.

33. Wright, "Paul's Gospel and Caesar's Empire," 165.

34. Wright, "Paul and Caesar," 188.

required loyalty.[35] According to Richard Horsley, the term *ekklēsia* to designate the community of believers as an alternative society was "set sharply over against the established *ekklēsia* in Corinth."[36] Paul's instruction to the community to conduct its own affairs separate from the dominant society (Cor 6:1–11) subverted the very basis for the unity of the cities in the Roman Empire.[37] When Paul warns the Thessalonians, "When they say 'there is peace and security,' then suddenly destruction will come upon them" (1 Thess 5:3), he employs a phrase that was associated with the Pax Romana.[38] "Peace and security" was a slogan that expressed the political stability and the beneficence of Roman rule (Tacitus, *Hist.* 2.12; 4.74; Josephus, *Ant.* 14.160; 15.348).[39] Paul places the Roman ideology of peace, security, and prosperity in opposition to his view of the imminent end.[40] Thus on the one hand, he creates the connection with the vocabulary of Rome "but at the same time makes it clear that his message surpasses the realities of the Roman Empire by far."[41]

The rhetoric of the alternative universal movement, with its own king and norms for citizenship inevitably resulted in conflict with the Pax Romana. Consequently, less than a decade after Paul's letter to the Romans, the Christians had become sufficiently problematic that Nero blamed the fire of Rome on them. According to Tacitus, Nero blamed the fire on them in order to put an end to the rumor that he had caused the burning. The fact that they were treated as scapegoats indicates that they were already widely considered enemies of the Roman Empire.[42] Tacitus describes them as "loathed for their crimes" and known for their "hatred of the human race." Fifty years after Paul, Pliny regarded the Christians as a dangerous nuisance.[43]

Paul's use of terminology that resonates with the Roman audience raises the question of how deliberately he shaped his language to confront the claims of Roman authorities by offering an alternative to Roman rule. One cannot doubt that ancient listeners would have heard in the Christian

---

35. Wright, "Paul and Caesar," 188.

36. Horsley, "Rhetoric and Empire—and 1 Corinthians," 91.

37. Horsley, "Rhetoric and Empire," 91.

38. Schnelle, *First Hundred Years*, 266.

39. Malherbe, *Letters to the Thessalonians*, 303.

40. Schnelle, *First Hundred Years*, 266.

41. Schnelle, *First Hundred Years*, 266; Wengst, *Pax Romana and the Peace of Jesus Christ*, 77–78.

42. Wengst, *Pax Romana and the Peace of Jesus Christ*, 72.

43. Wright, *Paul and the Faithfulness of God*, 383.

claims a challenge to Roman power.[44] Interpreters in the last decade have argued that Paul was deliberately confronting Roman power by using its familiar language. Horsley argues that Paul's message was one of social and political protest in which the arrogance and brutality of empire was the main target.[45]

While his terminology resonates with the Roman populace, it also is derived from the Septuagint.[46] Paul lives within the narrative world of the Septuagint, where the terms *kyrios, christos, euangelion, ekklēsia,* and *dikaiosynē* are deeply rooted. While the terms would have challenged imperial power and made conflict inevitable, they are not evidence of a comprehensive and intentional "anti-imperial" theology of Paul.[47] His churches form alternative ways of life, but they do not define themselves as a world in opposition.

Although Paul's claims inevitably created conflict with Rome, there are no direct statements that are explicitly anti-Roman or critical of Rome in the letters. As a general principle, the use of common language does not entail an antithetical relationship between the entities using the same terms.[48] Even if he did use words such as *parousia* and *epiphaneia* that were familiar to the Roman audience, his purpose was likely to describe the return of Christ in terms that were intelligible to the Roman audience.[49] Paul can speak of the community's leaders as *diakonoi* and *leitourgoi* of God (1 Cor 3:5; Rom 15:16) but can also label the political authorities *diakonoi* and *leitourgoi* (Rom 13:4, 6). If Paul is a *diakonos,* there is no indication that Caesar is not.[50]

THE RULERS OF THIS AGE

Paul speaks explicitly of the believers' relationship to governmental authorities only in Rom 13:1–7. However, interpreters have suggested that the reference to "the rulers of this world who crucified the Lord Jesus" (1 Cor 2:8) is

44. See Barclay, "Why the Roman Empire Was Insignificant to Paul," 377.

45. See Horsley, "Paul and Empire—1 Corinthians," 94–95.

46. See Bird, *Anomalous Jew,* 216.

47. Schnelle, *First Hundred Years,* 267.

48. Barclay, "Why the Roman Empire Was Insignificant to Paul," 377. See also Bryan, *Render to Caesar,* 91: "Terminological parallels say nothing about the use of the word; the context determines the meaning."

49. Strecker, "Taktiken der Aneignung," 124. Strecker (123) observes that the focus of 1 Thess 4:13–17 is the fate of the living and the dead at the return of Christ rather than on anti-Roman polemic.

50. Barclay, "Why the Roman Empire Was Insignificant to Paul," 376.

a reference to Roman rulers.[51] This passage appears within the larger context of Paul's response to the partisanship in Corinth (1:10–17; 3:1–5) in which the partisans of Paul, Apollos, and Cephas engage in the kind of partisan politics that was common in the ancient cities. In challenging the Corinthians' emphasis on human wisdom, Paul presents the message of the cross, which is foolishness according to human standards but is a demonstration of the wisdom of God (1:24), which is wiser than human wisdom (1:25).

This is a wisdom among the mature, "not of this age or the rulers of this age" (2:6). Paul assumes the rabbinic distinction between "this age" and "the age to come" (cf. 10:11; Gal 1:4), distinguishing between the "wisdom of this age" and the divine wisdom, which belongs to the coming age that has now been revealed (cf. 2:10). Only those with the epistemology of the new age recognize the divine wisdom. Inasmuch as the world did not know wisdom (1:21), the "rulers of this world that is passing away" (2:6) "did not know" the divine wisdom. Consequently, they crucified the Lord of glory.

Scholars debate the identity of the "rulers (*archontes*) of this age." Some maintain that the reference is to cosmic powers while others maintain that it refers to political officials. In some instances the term is used for supramundane powers that exercise lordship inimical to God (cf. Matt 9:34; 12:24; Mark 3:22; Luke 11:15; John 12:31; 14:30; 16:11; Eph 2:2).[52] In the Gospels, the term is also used for Jewish rulers (Luke 14:1; 23:13; 24:20; John 3:1; 7:26, 48; 12:42) and the rulers of the gentiles (Matt 20:25). In Acts the term is used for the Jewish leaders who were responsible for the death of Jesus (Acts 3:17) and for political leaders in various cities (14:5; 16:19; 23:5). The "rulers of this age that is passing away" are those who arrested and executed Jesus (cf. 1 Thess 2:15). They represent the cosmic rulers who will ultimately be destroyed by the exalted Lord (cf. 1 Cor 15:24). Unlike the believing community, which has a new epistemology derived from divine revelation (1 Cor 2:10), the "rulers of this age" did not know the divine wisdom. They belong to the world that is passing away (cf. 1 Cor 7:29–30). Thus those who are engaged in partisan politics within the church cannot receive the divine wisdom because their epistemology belongs to this age.

51. See the discussion in Schrage, *Der erste Brief an die Korinther*, 1:252–53. See also Merk, *archōn*, EDNT 1:168.

52. Merk, *archōn*, EDNT 1:167.

ROMANS 13 WITHIN THE CONTEXT OF THE LETTER

Paul's explicit instructions about the believers' relationship to the state appear in Rom 13:1–7 within the context of his appeal to the community not "to be conformed to this age" (Rom 12:1). This appeal introduces the extended ethical exhortation in 12:1—15:13. Having announced that God has intervened to reveal divine righteousness (1:17; 3:21), inaugurating the new age, he maintains that believers now live in the new age as the result of their faithfulness (1:16–17; 5:1). According to chapters 5–8, those who are baptized have entered the new age (Rom 6:1–11) and now walk in "newness of life" (6:4), putting to death the desires of the old existence (6:12–21) through the power of the Spirit (8:1–17), awaiting the ultimate redemption of their bodies (8:23–25). Paul describes Christian existence as the interim between the "now" of the new age (Rom 3:21; 8:1) and the "not yet" of the final consummation (Rom 5:1–11; 8:31–39).

Having described the existence in the interim between the inauguration of the new age and the consummation in chapters 5–8,[53] Paul describes this behavior in greater detail in 12:1—15:13, instructing believers not to be "conformed to this age" (12:2). As the inclusion with the declaration that "salvation is nearer that when you believed" (13:11) and "the day is at hand" (13:12) indicates, the moral life takes on urgency because "the night is far spent." Consequently, the readers should awaken from their sleep, putting away "the works of darkness" (13:13) and "putting on" the Lord Jesus (13:14). This *inclusio* places Paul's discussion within an eschatological framework as he encourages the believers to live appropriately "between the times." Paul was firmly convinced that with the death and resurrection of Jesus the new eschatological age has dawned, but it will be completely established only with Jesus's second coming. He expects the readers to live up to the expectations of the new age.[54]

This ethical advice stands in sharp contrast to the bleak portrayal of humankind in 1:18—3:20. To live in the new age is to abandon slavery to the flesh (cf. 6:12–21) and the pursuit of arrogance and self-interest (12:3) and to live within the community of the new age (12:3–8). Old boundaries of ethnicity have been taken away, and now they live together in the body of

---

53. Chapters 9–11 also anticipate the ultimate consummation when "all Israel will be saved." The ethical advice in 12:1—15:13 continues the exhortation that readers not "be wise among themselves" (11:25; cf. 12:3). By living in a multiethnic community (12:1—15:13), believers are not "conformed to this age" (12:2).

54. Constantineanu, "Bible and the Public Arena," 152.

Christ (12:3–8) in which all members exercise their gifts for the sake of the whole community.

As in Paul's ethical instructions in all the letters, the love for others within the community is the paramount ethical norm. Indeed, 12:9—13:8–11 is framed by references to love within the community; the conduct of the strong and the weak is also determined by love (14:15) within the community. Troels Engberg-Pedersen has argued persuasively that the command for unhypocritical love (12:9a) forms a bridge between the image of the body in 12:3–8 and the description of "the essential character of in-group behavior" that Paul has described from the beginning of the chapter.[55] In 12:9b–13 Paul gives illustrations of love within the community, remaining focused on in-group behavior. Believers "love one another with mutual affection" and "outdo one another in showing honor" (12:10), "rejoice with those who rejoice," "weep with those who weep" (12:15), contribute to the needs of the saints (12:13), and live in harmony with one another (12:16).

Paul's instructions on the believers' relation to the government in 13:1–7 does not stand alone but is the continuation of instructions on relations with outsiders in 12:14, 17–21. He instructs believers, "Bless those who persecute you" (12:14) and do not "return evil for evil" (12:17), but do the good to all and be at peace with all (12:17–18) if it is possible, "so far as it depends on" them (12:18). He insists that believers not render vengeance but leave room for the wrath of God (12:19). He challenges them to do good for the enemies (12:20) and to overcome evil with good (12:21).

As an example of doing good to all people (12:17–18), Paul instructs the readers, "Let every soul be submissive to governing authorities" (*pasa psychē exousiais hyperexousais*, 13:1), which introduces a unit (13:1–7) that is different in style from the ethical instructions in the context. One may observe the structure of the argument:

Let every soul be subject to the governing authorities (*hyperechousais*)

Reason (*gar*): There is no authority except from God

And those authorities that exist have been instituted by God.

Result (*hōste*): whoever resists authority resists what God has appointed.

Reason (*gar*): Rulers are not a terror to good conduct but to bad.

Do the good, and you will receive its approval

Reason (*gar*): For it is God's servant for your good

Reason (*gar*): For he does not bear the sword in vain.

55. Engberg-Pedersen, "Paul's Stoicizing Politics in Rom 12–13," 165.

Therefore one must be subject, not only because of wrath, but also because of conscience.

For the same reason, you also pay taxes,

Reason (*gar*): For the authorities are God's servants (*diakonoi*).

Unlike the other instructions in the context, this unit is supported by an extended argument, as *gar* (v. 1), *hōste* (v. 2), and *gar* (vv. 3 and 4) indicate. The content of the imperative in 13:1 is repeated in 13:5. Verses 6, 7 repeat the imperative in terms of paying taxes and paying debts.

Because the form of the passage, with its three imperatives (13:1, 6, 7; cf. 13:5) accompanied by a reason (13:2–4, 6) differs from the surrounding exhortation, Ernst Käsemann describes it as "an alien body in Paul's exhortation,"[56] although he sees no reason to doubt its authenticity. Others, however, have suggested that the passage is an interpolation into the exhortations.[57] While Paul may be adapting a common topos, the instructions fit into the argument of Rom 12:1—15:13, especially the instructions about behavior toward outsiders in 12:14–21. Thus the imperative "be submissive to the governing authorities" elaborates on the advice to bless the persecutors (12:14), to render no evil for evil (12:17), to do what is noble "in the sight of all" (12:17), and to be at peace with all (12:18). Consequently, James Dunn takes 13:1–7 as the center of the chiastic structure evident in chapters 12–15.[58] Similarly, David Horrell and N. T. Wright regard 13:1–7 and 12:14—13:7 respectively as the centers of a similar structure in 12–13.[59]

These instructions present a challenge to interpreters who insist that Paul is offering an anti-imperial message. Some argue that 13:1–7 is a "hidden transcript" that is so subtle in its subversive intent that only the insiders would recognize its subversive intent.[60] Others describe the passage as irony.[61] However, Paul's numerous imprisonments, his invitation for his

---

56. Käsemann, *Commentary on Romans*, 352.

57. See Kallas, "Romans XIII.1–7: An Interpolation," 365–74.

58. Dunn, *Romans*, 705.

59. Horrell, "Peaceful, Tolerant Community and the Legitimate Role of the State," 86–87: "Thus, chapters 12–13 seem to have a roughly chiastic structure (ABCB'A'), opening and closing with the theme of transformation (12:1–2; 13:13–14), inside which is the theme of love, first along with a series of practical admonitions that embody it (12:9–21), and second as the commandment which summarises the whole law (13:8–10). If these approximately balancing sections form the AB/B'A', then the section in the middle is evidently Rom 13:1–7, linked by key words both to what precedes and follows it." See also Wright, "Letter to the Romans," 9.703.

60. See Lim, "Double-voiced Reading of Romans 13:1–7 in the Light of the Imperial Cult," 1–10. Robinson, "Hidden Transcripts?," 55–72.

61. See Carter, "Irony of Romans 13," 209. "The original audience of the letter shared with Paul a common experience of oppression at the hands of the authorities and were

listeners to "turn to God from idols" (1 Thess 1:9)—including the Roman gods—and his claim that Jesus is Lord suggest that Paul saw no need to conceal his criticism of Roman religion.[62] Furthermore, the place of the passage in the larger context of 12:14–21 indicates that the instructions fit well with Paul's instruction to "overcome evil with good" (12:21) and to "be at peace with all people" (12:18).

The presence of a topos that appears nowhere else in the undisputed letters suggests that it is a response to the changing political situation in Rome. As the edict of Claudius (Suetonius, *Claudius* 25.4) suggests, Roman authorities are now aware of this group, distinguishing it from the Jews. Paul's exhortation for believers to acknowledge the government authorities may be understood against the background of the increasing tension between the church as it is developing as an independent movement and the Roman authorities.[63] The emphasis on the payment of taxes could be a response to the current situation, for protests in Rome against the increasing taxes under Nero had erupted,[64] and Paul may have been trying to urge Roman Christians not to participate in the protests and not to have an attitude of protest.[65]

"Every person" (*pasa psychē*) refers to everyone in the community of faith. *Hypotassō*, to subordinate oneself to an ordered structure,[66] is used elsewhere for the subordination of wives to husbands (Col 3:18; 1 Cor 14:34) and for the relationship of believers to one another (cf. 1 Cor 16:16;

---

aware of the abuses that took place in the opening years of Nero's reign. The consequent implausibility of Paul's language would have alerted his readers to the presence of irony. They would have been able to set aside the surface meaning of the discourse and to recognize that Paul was using the established rhetorical technique of censuring with counterfeit praise. While the passage can be read as a straightforward injunction to submit to the authorities, an ironic reading of the text results in a subversion of the very authorities it appears to commend."

62. Bird, *Anomalous Jew*, 226. For a thorough critique of the methodology of those who argue for the hidden transcript, see Heilig, *Hidden Criticism?*

63. Schnelle, *First Hundred Years*, 267. See also Wright, "Paul and Caesar," 190. "The fact that Paul needs to stress the need for civil obedience tells fairly strongly, if paradoxically to my case. It implies that, without some restraining counsel, some might have heard his teaching to imply that the church was to become . . . under obligation to rebel violently against human rulers."

64. See Dunn, "Quietism," 60. In *Annals* 13, Tacitus reports that the year 58 was marked by persistent public complaints regarding indirect taxes. This report suggests the strong likelihood that in the years prior to 58 the collection of taxes was a sensitive matter.

65. Schnelle, *First Hundred Years*, 267. According to Tacitus, *Ann.* 13.50–51, in AD 58 continued protests against the oppressive taxation occurred.

66. BDAG, 1042.

Eph 5:21). Paul indicates that the opposite of subordination here is "to resist (*antitassō*)."[67] That is, two possibilities exist for believers in their relationship to government officials: either to submit or to resist. It would not have occurred to Paul that Christians would be participants in the state. He is working within the situation as it stands.[68] All Christians could do was to live within the structures that existed, accommodate to them, as everyone had to, and seek to benefit from whatever rules or rights the governing authorities granted.

As the apostle's terminology shows, he has in view very different local and regional authorities. He is not so much thinking of institutions, but of organs and functions, ranging from the tax collector to the police, magistrates, and Roman officials. It deals with the circle of power with whom everyone came into contact.[69] Paul is (not) giving a general theology of the state but is giving the commonsense advice that all those who were not in power followed. In view of the recent conflict between the Jews and the Romans, Paul may be advising believers to maintain a low profile and continue to care for each other. Thus the relationship to the authorities is one example of the believers' encounter with outsiders.

Paul supports the imperative with reasons in 13:1b–4 (cf. *gar*, v. 1; *gar*, v. 3). According to the first reason, "there is no authority except from God, and those government authorities have been instituted by God" (13:1b). As the root words *hypotassō/tassō* indicate, believers submit (*hypotassō*) to the established order that God has arranged (*tassō*). That God institutes governments is a familiar theme in the Old Testament. No king can rule unless he is called by God. No power exists in the pagan world without God's consent (cf. Cyrus, Isa 41:1–5, 25–29; 45:1–4). God "changes times and seasons, deposes kings and sets up kings" (Dan 2:21; cf. 4:17). According to Prov 8:15–16, God says, "By me kings reign, and rulers decree what is just." Josephus shows a similar understanding when he states that "no ruler attains his office save by the will of God" (*B.J.* 2.140).

David Flusser has demonstrated a similar view in the Dead Sea Scrolls. This community, which understood itself to be living in the last days, looked forward to its war against the "sons of darkness" and its conquest of Israel and then the world.[70] In the meantime, they had to determine how they should live in the interim. While they hate the "sons of darkness," they submit to the authorities at the same time, awaiting the day of God's vengeance,

67. BDAG, 90.

68. Dunn, "Quietism."

69. Käsemann, *Romans*, 354.

70. Flusser, "Jewish Origins of the Early Church's Attitude toward the State," 300.

recognizing that God will ultimately defeat the powers of darkness.[71] The belief that God has preordained the course of events results in a passive approach among the Qumran sectarians. Thus Paul is following Jewish tradition and expectations. This is the position of any Jewish community when it is under foreign rule.

Jews in the diaspora probably took comfort in the claim that rulers govern only because God has given them the authority, for they assumed that rulers were responsible before God and subject to God's final judgment. This conviction reassured Jewish communities that those who oppressed Jewish subjects would come under the judgment of God sooner or later—as Nebuchadnezzar discovered in the Daniel story (4:13–17, 23–25; 5:20–21).[72] The point of Wisdom's assertion that kings receive their dominion from God was to warn them that the Most High would punish those who did not rule rightly or walk in the purpose of God. Similarly, in 4 Macc 12:11 the tyrant is rebuked for abusing his responsibility given to him as king from God.[73] One may compare Jesus's words to Pilate, "You would have no power over me unless it had been given to you from above" (19:11).

Although Paul instructs believers to be submissive to the authorities, the affirmation that "there is no authority except from God" (13:1) would not have been acceptable to imperial officials. While imperial authority is affirmed, it is subordinated to God. As N. T. Wright has indicated, "In a world where rulers have been accustomed to claim divine honours, the statement that they hold their office as a vocation from the one God (13:1) constitutes a major demotion."[74]

The logical consequence of this claim (cf. *hōste*) is that resistance against government authorities is a resistance against God (13:3), resulting in God's judgment on those who resist. Having instructed believers to bless those who persecute and to do the good to outsiders (12:17, 21; cf. 12:2), he again insists that believers "do what is good" (13:3), knowing that the official is a servant (*diakonos*) for what is good (13:4). After encouraging them not to take vengeance (*ekdikountes*) but to "leave room for the wrath of God (12:19), he asserts that the role of the magistrate is to "execute wrath" (*ekdikos eis orgēn*, Rom 13:4). The instruction to do what is good (13:3) and not evil (13:4) clarifies the nature of submission to the established order as Paul appeals to the conventional understanding of the good.[75] Paul is

71. Flusser, "Jewish Origins of the Early Church's Attitude toward the State," 300.

72. Dunn, "Quietism," 64.

73. Dunn, "Quietism," 64.

74. Wright, *Paul and the Faithfulness of God*, 1303.

75. See Engberg-Pedersen, "Paul's Stoicizing Politics," 169: "At the time and place

not giving a theology of the state but is offering an example of the call to "take thought of what is noble in the sight of all" (12:17), of being "at peace with all" (12:18), and of overcoming evil with good (12:21). His advice is consistent with traditional Jewish teaching about how to live appropriately under alien rule.[76]

The nature of the resistance is evidently the withholding of taxes (13:6). The repetition of the call for submission (13:5) leads to the two imperatives in 13:6–7: pay taxes (13:6) and "pay your debts to all" (13:7). Paul's reason for paying taxes—[the authorities] "are servants (*leitourgoi*) for this very thing"—recalls the early reason for submission to the authorities: the authority is a servant (*diakonos*) to execute wrath on the wrongdoer (13:4). The second imperative, "Pay to all what is due them" (13:7), expands on the need to recognize authorities as well as other outsiders. Paul includes the payment of different types of taxes—taxes (*phoron*) and revenue (*to telos*) accompanied by respect (*phobos*) and honor (*timē*). That is, believers recognize the need for order in society, and they contribute to it. He presents an active and positive involvement of the Christian in the world, advocating practices that are conducive to a meaningful and peaceful life in the larger society. In his exhortations, "Paul gives primacy to practices of reconciliation as the appropriate Christian attitude to, and relationship with, the wider world, including the authorities."[77]

The instruction to "owe no one anything" (13:8a) suggests the believers' continuing relationship with outsiders and the need to pay others what is due to them. To fulfill one's obligations to others in the society is central to the goal of living "at peace with all people." The phrase, "owe no one anything, except (*ei mē*) to love one another" (13:8), marks a transition from relationships with outsiders (i.e., "no one") to a resumption of the relationship to the in-group ("one another") that was the subject of 12:3–14, 15–16. Troels Engberg-Pedersen has observed that Paul has not extended the love command to outsiders in this instance but has instructed the believers to "bless" those who persecute them (12:14), be at peace with all (12:18), be subject to the authorities (13:1, 5), do the good, and pay taxes (13:6–7).[78] "Love one another" (13:8) defines the in-group responsibilities of the community. It recapitulates the earlier command to "love one another with mutual affection" (12:10). One may observe the frequency of the command

---

of the writing of these two texts there was a conventional view of the good, divinely installed ruler to which one might appeal without further ado—and then use the appeal for one's own purposes."

76. Wright, *Paul and the Faithfulness of God*, 1303.

77. Constantineanu, "Bible and the Public Arena," 152.

78. Engberg-Pedersen, "Paul's Stoicizing Politics," 166.

to "love one another" in the Pauline correspondence (Gal 5:13–14; 1 Thess 3:12; cf. Eph 4:2) and the pervasiveness of the command to love in all the Pauline correspondence, which, with rare exceptions, is aimed at the believing community rather than outsiders. Moreover, *allēlōn* ("one another") appears with numerous verbs to designate the care that believers take for each other (cf. Rom 12:10, "love one another . . . outdo one another in showing honor"; 12:16, "live in harmony with one another"). Thus the submission to the governing authorities is an expression of the community's obligation to do the good to outsiders. By bringing in again *agapē* from chapter 12, Paul is reiterating the relationship between the community's obligation to the in-group and its obligation to outsiders.

The statement that the one who loves the other has "fulfilled the law" (13:8) recalls the similar observation in Galatians, according to which Paul maintains that "the whole law is fulfilled in one word, "love your neighbor as yourself" (5:14). In both Galatians and Romans, the neighbor is the fellow believer.

As the concluding comments of Rom 13 indicate, Paul's instructions for the believers' relationship to the governmental authorities is framed by an eschatological consciousness. Believers live in the new age (cf. 12:1–2), but the moment has arrived "to awaken from sleep" (13:11), for "salvation is nearer than when we became believers" (13:11). Indeed, "the day is near" (13:12). The imminence of the end places the ethical life in perspective (13:13–14). The underlying issue is the relation between this world and the new age.[79] Having instructed believers not to be conformed to this age inasmuch as they have entered the new age, Paul does not call believers out of this world as if they no longer had any responsibility to the present creation.[80] According to Frank Matera:

> Paul was keenly aware that believers are already, in some sense, citizens of heaven (3:20). Likewise, he firmly believed that "the present form of this world is passing away" (1 Cor 7:31). But he was not ready to dispense believers from the created order. . . . Although he knew that believers were already participating in the new age through the gift of the Spirit, he recognized the necessary role that governing authorities play in maintaining an ordered society.[81]

Inasmuch as the world is passing away (1 Cor 2:6), according to Paul, a confrontation with Rome is scarcely necessary. Paul consistently reminds

79. Matera, *Romans*, 302.
80. Matera, *Romans*, 302.
81. Matera, *Romans*, 302.

his readers that "the time is short" (1 Cor 7:29; cf. Rom 13:11–14; 1 Thess 5:1–11). His advice to the Corinthians to regard marriage, possessions, and all human activities "as though they were not" (1 Cor 7:29–31) probably applies to all institutions. Indeed, his advice that "those who deal with the world as though they had no dealings with it" (1 Cor 7:31) indicates the provisional nature of all institutions. At the present Christ is enthroned at the right hand of God and will reign until he puts all enemies—every ruler and every authority and every power—under his feet (1 Cor 15:24–25). While these claims are antithetical to Roman ideology, the imminent victory of Christ precludes a revolutionary challenge to Rome.[82]

CONCLUSION

Few passages have had as much impact on Western society as Rom 13:1–7. It has been used to justify blind obedience to autocratic regimes and is the favorite passage for those who are in power. Luther appealed to it to support the princes against the peasant revolt, and the German Christians appealed to it to support the evils of the Third Reich. In more recent times it has been used by Christians to justify inhumane governmental practices, including the mistreatment of immigrants. The passage has been the focus of attention in debates over civil disobedience and the participation of the church in politics.

The challenge for Christian interpreters is that this text was written in a specific historical context that is different from our own. It was addressed to people who lived in an autocratic society in which the only options were to submit or rebel. It does not address the numerous situations that believers now face with respect to the state: the response to unjust laws or the circumstances in which Christians may practice civil disobedience. Nevertheless, Paul's statements about believers and the state offer insights for Christians in the current situation.

Paul's major concern in all the letters was to guide his communities toward their transformation into the image of Christ, a process that began with their turning away from the "many gods and many lords" (1 Cor 8:6) in the cities of the Mediterranean. In this pluralistic society, a religion that demanded conversion to the one Lord inevitably created conflict with families and neighbors, and ultimately with the local magistrates. Consequently, Paul consistently refers to the sufferings that accompany his ministry and the conflicts between his communities and their neighbors. A worldwide movement composed of alternative *ekklēsiai* was an obvious threat to the

---

82. Taubes, *Political Theology of Paul*, 53–54.

cohesion of the empire. Believers who confess that Jesus Christ is Lord will continue to be in tension with the state.

Because of his focus on the moral formation of his communities, Paul rarely speaks of the relationship of believers to the political situation. The Roman Empire, like other institutions, belongs to the world that is passing away (cf. 1 Cor 7:31). Consequently, Jacob Taubes correctly observes that the *hōs mē* ("as if not"), which he applies to marriage, joy and sorrow, and business relations in 1 Cor 7:29–31, also applies to the believers' relationship to the state and politics.[83] Living before the impending eschaton serves to relativize those institutions that are temporary. Thus Paul neither engages in active resistance to the Roman state nor encourages his communities to do so. Because Paul anticipates a time when the exalted Lord will destroy "every ruler and every authority and power" (1 Cor 15:24), believers live within the state, demonstrating a concern for the public good but devote their ultimate loyalty to the risen Lord.

Because "our citizenship is in heaven" (Phil 3:20), our ultimate loyalty to the Christian faith places political allegiance in perspective. While Christians seek the good of all humankind, acting as good citizens in their respective countries, their loyalty to the political party and the state is limited by their fidelity to the lordship of Christ. The interests of the state in maintaining order and doing the good may frequently be compatible with the goals of the Christian community, but they are sometimes incompatible. Christians recognize that Jesus Christ is the Lord of all nations, and they recognize their responsibility to demonstrate compassion beyond the borders of their own country.

---

83. Taubes, *Political Theology of Paul*, 53.

6

Is Paul among the Philosophers?

Although Paul receives little notice in the non-Christian literature in the first century, he is an unprecedented figure in antiquity, as his continuing influence indicates. He traveled throughout the Mediterranean world "from Jerusalem to Illyricum" (Rom 15:19) with his message and even planned to take his message to Spain (Rom 15:24). He established communities in the cities where he preached and maintained contact with them through his letters and emissaries. His letters included friendly exhortations for proper conduct (1 Thessalonians, Philippians) and extended theological arguments clarifying his gospel (e.g., Galatians, Romans).

How would Paul have been perceived by ancient observers? He was, as Michael Bird has suggested, "an anomalous Jew"[1] inasmuch as he is without parallel in the Jewish tradition. Consequently, interpreters have looked to Greek and Roman parallels to the work of Paul. A vast literature in the last century has maintained that Paul was acquainted with ancient philosophy and that observers would have identified him as a philosopher. Indeed, Christian writers in antiquity recognized the similarity between Paul and the moral philosophers. An anonymous Christian in the third century, recognizing the similarities between Paul and Seneca, even composed a correspondence that was supposed to have taken place between the two.

---

1. Bird, *Anomalous Jew*. The designation was earlier used by Barclay, *Jews in the Mediterranean Diaspora*, 381–93.

Several contemporary philosophers, most of whom are non-Christians, have taken an interest in Paul in the last generation. Alain Badiou, Jacob Taubes, Giorgio Agamben, and Stanislas Breton, working at an interface of religion, politics, and philosophy in the secular world, have found in Paul a significant conversation partner.[2] Paul advocates a universalism that is important for contemporary political life. He proclaims the universality of truth, the conviction that what is true is true for everyone, and that the truth should be known by everyone. These philosophers consider Paul a radical subversive figure who challenges the existing order. Alain Badiou, for example, is drawn to the way that Paul's whole thought and practice is oriented to and founded upon a singular event that transforms Paul himself and becomes the basis for a reshaped humanity.[3] Paul both declares and enacts its truth in the practical reshaping of life in faithfulness to the event.[4] Paul is the militant who, like Lenin, established subversive cells of followers. "What is clear is Paul's paradigmatic fidelity to a new and impossible event, a creation from nothing, an essentially unconditioned grace which follows no rational order, no cosmic structure and no moral rule."[5]

THE MISSION AND PRACTICE OF PAUL AND THE PHILOSOPHERS

Philosophers in the first century formed communities in which the teacher and students maintained regular contact with each other. The four great schools of philosophy continued to gather students and teach according to the traditions of their founders: the Academy of Plato, the Lyceum of Aristotle, the Garden of Epicurus, and the Porch of Zeno.[6] The major philosophical concern in the first century was not the acquisition of a theoretical system but the shaping of good character within the household and within the individual person.[7] The philosopher functioned as a therapist guiding the soul to its essential self.[8]

In comparing Paul's ministry with that of the philosophers, interpreters have observed that he shared their sense of mission and the intense focus

2. See the discussion in Barclay, "Paul and the Philosophers," 171–84.

3. Badiou, *Saint Paul.*

4. Barclay, "Paul and the Philosophers," 173.

5. Barclay, "Paul and the Philosophers," 178.

6. Johnson, *Constructing Paul,* 180.

7. Johnson, *Constructing Paul,* 180.

8. Divjanović, *Paulus als Philosoph.*

on the shaping of moral character.[9] E. A. Judge maintained that observers would have compared Paul's communities with a philosophical school.[10] Stanley Stowers argued that Paul taught in private homes as the philosophers had.[11] Stowers also advanced the suggestion, first proposed by Rudolf Bultmann in 1910, that Paul's use of the diatribe is indebted to the philosophers. Loveday Alexander in 1995 asked to what extent Paul's activity as a preacher was similar to the teaching activity of Hellenistic philosophers. She compares "going to church" with "going to school" as well as the authority of Paul with a founding figure of a philosophical school. She demonstrated the commonalities as well as the differences and concludes: "The model of the school is an important tool for the imaginative understanding of Paul's world and the options open to him for penetrating it, as well as for understanding the reactions of that world to Paul."[12] Kristin Divjanović maintains that Paul would have been perceived as a philosopher.[13]

A Conversion Experience and Divine Calling

Like numerous philosophers, Paul attributed his work to a conversion experience and divine calling (cf. 1 Cor 9:1; 2 Cor 4:4–6; Gal 1:15–21). The theme of the philosopher's conversion is common in the philosophical literature. In turning to philosophy, the philosopher turned to himself, coming to his senses. According to Epictetus, "There was a time when I made mistakes, but now no longer, thanks be to God" (*Diatr.* 4.4.7). Plato and Xenophon attribute Socrates's wisdom to a divine call at the oracle of Delphi.[14] The Stoic Zeno also made the radical change in his life to pursue philosophy after an encounter with the oracle (Diogenes Laertius, *Lives* 7.2). Diogenes fled to the oracle after he had debased the coinage in Sinope and then came to Athens, where he encountered Antisthenes. "From that time forward he was his pupil, and, exile as he was, set out upon a simple life" (Diogenes Laertius, *Lives* 6.20). Others, including Plato, Phaedo (Diogenes Laertius, *Lives* 2.105), Aristippus of Cyrene (Plutarch, *Curios.* 516C), and Alcibiades (Plato, *Symp.* 218D), made the sudden turn to philosophy upon encountering Socrates (cf. Diogenes Laertius, *Lives* 3.4–6). In most instances, a man of low social status or unsavory background makes the radical change to

9. Johnson, *Constructing Paul*, 184.

10. Judge, "Early Christians as a Scholastic Community," 4–15.

11. Stowers, "Social Status, Public Speaking and Private Teaching," 65–66.

12. Alexander, "Paul and the Hellenistic Schools," 82.

13. Divjanović, *Paulus als Philosoph*, 19.

14. Divjanović, *Paulus als Philosoph*, 33, 186.

philosophy after hearing the oracle or encountering an esteemed teacher such as Socrates.[15] The many conversion narratives have one thing in common: the description of a decisive event that results in the turn to philosophy.[16] The turn to philosophy was accompanied by a radical new lifestyle.

Paul also claims that his mission rests on a divine call. Although Acts gives the most dramatic portrayal of Paul's conversion and call (chs. 9, 22, 26), the apostle also attributes his authority and mission to a divine call in his letters. He made a radical change from a devoted Pharisee (cf. Gal 1:13–14; cf. Phil 3:2–6) to a messenger of Jesus Christ. The risen Lord appeared to him (1 Cor 9:1; 15:6), and the light "shone in [his] heart to give the light of the knowledge of the glory of God in the face of Jesus Christ" (2 Cor 4:6). Consequently, Paul consistently mentions his calling (Rom 1:1; Gal 1:15; cf. 2 Cor 1:1) as the basis for his mission. However, Paul envisions his role and identity in prophetic terms, comparing himself to Jeremiah (Gal 1:15; cf. Jer. 1:5) and the servant of Deutero-Isaiah (cf. Isa 49:1). He speaks with authority to his communities, claiming that he speaks for God (cf. 1 Cor 1:18–25; 2:6–17; Gal 1:12). Thus he speaks with the power of God (1 Cor 2:1–5; 1 Thess 1:5–6). His mission to the gentiles brings the "light to the nations" to bring salvation "to the end of the earth" (Isa 49:6).

Models for Imitation

Philosophers insisted that their pupils seek models of virtue to imitate. Seneca writes to his pupil Lucilius, "Find some man of high character, and keep him ever before your eyes, living as if he were watching you and ordering all your actions as if he beheld them" (*Ep.* 11.8–10). Examples could be mythical figures,[17] family members, historical figures (*Ep.* 6.5), or philosophers from the past such as Socrates (Plato, *Apol.* 21D) or Zeno. According to Seneca,

> Cleanthes could not have been the express image of Zeno's life if he had only heard his lectures; he shared in his life, saw into his hidden purposes, and watched to see whether he lived by his own rules. Plato, Aristotle, and the whole throng of sages who, each in his own way, derived more benefit from his character than from the words of Socrates. It was not the classroom of

15. Divjanović, *Paulus als Philosoph*, 54–57.
16. Divjanović, *Paulus als Philosoph*, 89.
17. Heracles was a common model for imitation (*Div.* 183).

Epicurus, but living under the same roof, that made great men
of Metrodorus, Hermarchus, and Polyaenus. (*Ep.* 6.6)[18]

Philosophers also presented themselves as models for imitation among
their students. Inasmuch as the philosophers focused not only on theory
but on a way of life, their life and teaching were inseparable. According to
Xenophon, Socrates presented himself as an example.

> Don't you see that to this day never would I acknowledge that
> any man had lived a better or pleasanter life than I? For they live
> best, I think, who strive to become as good as possible. And the
> pleasantest life is theirs who are conscious that they are grow-
> ing in goodness. And to this day that has been my experience;
> and mixing with others and closely comparing myself to them,
> I have held without ceasing to this opinion of myself. And not
> I only, but my friends cease not to feel thus towards me, not
> because of their love for me . . . but because they think that they
> too would rise to be the highest in goodness by being with me.
> (*Mem.* 4.8.6)

Seneca's self-descriptions and personal examples attest to the success
or failure of his own efforts to attain the good, the philosophical ideal. Seneca indicates his own personal struggles and weaknesses in his endeavor.
The example of his own life verifies his teaching (*Ep.* 71.7). Since the moral
advice is given in the context of friendship, it possesses the authority and the
persuasiveness of affection.[19]

Philosophers and Paraenetic Letters

The philosophers' concern with moral formation is evident in the paraenetic
letters that they wrote to guide their pupils. The idea of guiding a protégé's
character development by means of letters goes back to Epicurus. The letters
of Seneca to Lucilius, however, are the only extant extended correspondence
of this type from antiquity. For example, Seneca describes his own moral
progress as an example for Lucilius in *Epistle* 6 (LCL).[20]

> Seneca to his own Lucilius, greeting. I feel, my dear Lucilius,
> that I am being not only reformed, but transformed. I do not
> yet, however, assure myself, or indulge the hope, that there are

18. See Fiore, *Function of Personal Example in the Socratic and Pastoral Epistles*, 183.

19. Fiore, *Function of Personal Example in the Socratic and Pastoral Epistles*, 89.

20. See also Cancik, *Untersuchungen zu Senecas Epistulae morales*, 75. See Seneca,
Ep. 6.1–5; 7:1; 8:1–3; 26:4–5; 63:14; 68:8–9; 71:30; 71:36; 76:1; 76:5; 87:3–4; 102.1–2.

no elements left in me which need to be changed. Of course there are many that should be made more compact, or made thinner, or be brought into greater prominence. And indeed this very fact is proof that my spirit is altered into something better—that it can see its own faults of which it was previously ignorant. In certain cases sick men are congratulated because they themselves have perceived that they are sick.

I therefore wish to impart to you this sudden change in myself; I should then begin to place a surer trust in our friend- ship—the true friendship, which hope and fear and self-interest cannot sever, the friendship in which and for the sake of which men meet death. I can show you many who have lacked, not a friend, but friendship; this, however, cannot possibly happen when souls are drawn together by identical inclinations into an alliance of honorable desire. And why can it happen? Because in such cases men know that they have all things in common, especially their troubles.

Several of Seneca's letters consist of a theoretical argument in the in- dicative mood followed by prescriptive paraenesis in the form of the im- perative.[21] Epistles 74 and 76, for example, are paraenetic letters in which Seneca offers a theoretical foundation that is the basis for the imperative.[22] In *Epistle* 74, for example, Seneca begins with the premise that "the chief means of attaining a happy life [consists] in the belief that the only good lies in that which is honorable" (74.1). After a series of examples, Seneca concludes with the challenge for Lucilius to follow the good life of honor (74.10, 16). One finds a similar progression in the other letters of Seneca.

Like Seneca's letters, Paul's letters are also aimed at the moral forma- tion of his communities. Paul frequently offers a theoretical and theologi- cal foundation for his paraenesis. Paul's letters were, however, written to communities and intended to shape the collective identity and ethos of the group. Nothing in ancient letter writing corresponds to the authoritative voice of Paul, who speaks not only for himself but also for God. In the letters in which he needs to assert his authority, he identifies himself as an apostle sent by God.[23] In some instances he writes in response to crises while in other instances he writes to continue building the foundation that he laid when he was in the community (e.g., 1 Thessalonians).

---

21. Cancik, *Untersuchungen zu Senecas Epistulae morales*, 16.

22. Cancik, *Untersuchungen zu Senecas Epistulae morales*, 28.

23. Thompson, *Apostle of Persuasion*, 22.

Philosophers, Sophists, and Paul

According to Paul's contemporaries, his letters were "weighty and strong, but his speech was of no account" (2 Cor 10:10). As a public speaker, Paul was inevitably compared to the orators of his time, whose work drew the sharp critique of the philosophers. Indeed, the controversy between philosophy and rhetoric goes back to classical Athens and the beginning of the sophistic movement.[24] Socrates distinguishes between the genuine philosophy that aims at truth and moral improvement and the sophistry that is meant only to flatter and to please (cf. *Gorgias* 462b3–465e6). Consequently, in Plato's discussions, the true philosopher searches for truth while the "sophist" aims at persuasion to that which is neither true nor beneficial.[25]

The dispute between sophists and philosophers inevitably involved Paul, whose audiences compared him with the public speakers of his day (2 Cor 10:1). Consequently, Paul had to distinguish himself from the sophists, echoing the familiar criticisms made by the philosophers about the deceptive practices of the sophists. In 1 Thess 2:1–12, for example, Paul reminds the Thessalonians of his earliest ministry with them in a highly defensive tone that is presented in the antithetical terms ("not . . . but") sometimes used by the philosophers.[26] Interpreters have debated whether Paul is responding to criticisms from fellow believers or distinguishing himself from itinerant rhetoricians. Since the letter never suggests elsewhere that Paul is under suspicion from the Thessalonians, he is most likely distinguishing himself from the sophists. He spoke with *parrhēsia*, the virtue of the ideal philosopher (2:2).[27] His insistence that he did not speak with deceit (*planē*), impure motives (*akatharsia*), or trickery (*dolos*) recalls the common charges against the sophists. Similarly, Dio Chrysostom characterizes the ideal Cynic in negative and antithetic formulations designed to distinguish him from them. He speaks of the ideal philosopher who "with purity (*katharos*) without guile (*adolos*) speaks with a philosopher's boldness (*parrēsiazomenon*)."[28] Paul's statement that he speaks "not as pleasing people" (*anthropois areskontes*), engaging in flattery (*kolakeia*), or preaching "with a prctcxt for greed" (*pleonexia*) also echoes the common criticisms of the sophists. Dio says that the

---

24. Krentz, "Logos or Sophia," 285.

25. Krentz, "Logos or Sophia," 286.

26. See Malherbe, "'Gentle as a Nurse,'" 216–17.

27. NRSV: "We had courage in our God to declare to you the gospel of God" (*eparrhēsiasametha en tō theō*). *Parrhēsia*, "boldness, candor, freedom of speech, was the practice of speaking the truth in all circumstances, even to superiors. See Spicq, *parrhēsia*, TLNT 3:56. It is commonly contrasted to flattery.

28. Dio Chrysostom, *Or.* 32.11. Cited in Malherbe, "'Gentle as a Nurse,'" 214.

true philosopher will not preach for the sake of glory (*meta doxēs charin*), nor for personal gain (*meh' ep' argurio*),[29] nor as a flatterer.[30]

Paul also describes his coming to Corinth in anti-sophistic terms (1 Cor 2:1–5), indicating that he did not come to the Corinthians with "persuasive words of wisdom" (1 Cor 2:4).[31] His denial that he is not persuading people in Gal 1:10 indicates his familiarity of the charges that philosophers made against the rhetoricians. The claim that "the world did not know wisdom" is a disavowal of philosophy, for Paul's message has come by revelation rather than worldly wisdom. Paul distinguishes the wisdom that came by revelation from the "wisdom of this age" (1 Cor 2:6, 18).

Paul's debate with the opponents in 2 Corinthians also reflects the debate between philosophers and sophists,[32] which was still present in Corinth. In his defense, Paul claims, "We are not peddlers (*kapēleuontes*) like so many" (2:17), using a term that is used nowhere else in the New Testament. *Kapēleuein* can mean either "to hawk for profit" (i.e., to instruct for payment) or to falsify philosophical teachings or both.[33] Socrates describes the sophist as "a sort of merchant or dealer (*kapēlos*) in provisions on which a soul is nourished. For such is the view I take of him" (*Protag.* 313C). When his interlocutor asks what nourishes the soul, Socrates replies:

> With doctrines, presumably, I replied. And we must take care, my good friend, that the sophist, in commending his wares, does not deceive us, as both merchant and dealer do in the case of our bodily food. For among the provisions, you know, in which these men deal, not only are they themselves ignorant what is good or bad for the body, since in selling they commend

29. Cf. Dio Chrysostom, *Or.* 35:1, "I have come before you not to display my talents as a declaimer, nor because I want money, nor because I expect praise."

30. Malherbe, "'Gentle as a Nurse,'" 215. Dio Chrysostom has a long treatise on flattery (*Or.* 3.1–25). On flattery as the vice of sophists, see also Plato, *Gorg.* 466A–467A. While Paul makes only a succinct reference to flattery, a near contemporary, Dio Chrysostom, in his encomium in the third oration on kingship delivered before the emperor Trajan soon after his accession, contains a long condemnation of the role of flattery (*Or.* 3.1–25). There he contrasts "truth" (*alētheia*) and "frankness" (*parrhēsia*) with "flattery" (*thōpeia*) and "deceit" or "guile" (*apatē*) (3.12–13). In an early oration on kingship, he concludes the end of his encomium with the comment that this discourse (*logos*) will be delivered in all simplicity (*haplōs*) without any flattery (*kolakeia*). See Winter, "Entries and Ethics of Orators and Paul (1 Thessalonians 2:1–2)," 66.

31. Winter, "Is Paul among the Sophists?" 30.

32. Schmeller, *Der zweite Brief an die Korinther (2Kor 7,5–13,13)*, 2:164–69.

33. Schmeller, *Der zweite Brief an die Korinther*, 2:165. Forms of *kapēleuein/kapēlos* are used for shopkeepers, retailers, peddlers, and by extension any trafficker or merchant. *Kapēloi* had a reputation for falsifying what they sold. See Spicq, *kapēlos*, TLNT 255–57, for the reputation of *kapēloi* as unscrupulous merchants.

them all, but the people who buy from them are so too, unless one happens to be a trainer or doctor. And in the same way, those who take their doctrines the round of our cities, hawking them about to any odd purchaser who desires them, commend everything that they sell, and there may be some of these too, my good sir, who are ignorant which of their wares is good or bad for the soul. (*Protag.* 313D–E)

According to Plato's critique, the sophist "is a paid hunter after the young and the wealthy" and "a kind of merchant in articles of knowledge for the soul" (*Soph.* 231d). According to Plato's Socrates, rhetoric is "the occupation of a shrewd and enterprising spirit, . . . and in sum and substance I call it 'flattery'" (*Gorg.* 463d; cf. 467a). According to Lucian, "The philosophers sell their teaching like tavern keepers (*kapēloi*), and most of them (*hoi polloi*) mix their wine with water and misrepresent it (*dolōsantes*)."[34] According to Philo, "wisdom must not be that of the systems hatched by word-catchers and sophists who sell their tenets and arguments like any bit of merchandise in the market, men who forever pit philosophy against philosophy" (*Mos.* 2.212). Similarly, Paul claims that he does not "practice cunning or falsify (*dolountes*) God's word while "the many" (*hoi polloi*, 2:17), like the sophists, hawk the word of God for personal gain.

In 10:10 and 11:6 the opponents also resemble the sophists. When Paul concedes that his "bodily presence is weak and his speech of no account" (10:10), he recognizes the comparison to the sophists, who considered themselves superior to the philosophers by their more impressive appearance and rhetorical power. In 11:6 Paul partially accepts this judgment, conceding that he is an amateur in speech but not in knowledge. The antithesis of rhetorical power and knowledge is reminiscent of the conflict between rhetoricians and philosophers.[35]

PAUL'S ENGAGEMENT WITH PHILOSOPHY

While Paul shared the philosophers' focus on moral formation, one may debate the extent to which he was immersed in Greek philosophy. For a long time scholars have observed the phrases in Paul that echo philosophical

---

34. Lucian, *Hermot.* 59. Cf. Philo (*Moses* 2.12), "Philosophy—not that practiced by the wordmongers and sophists who sell their principles and reasonings like any goods at the market"; cf. *Spec.*4.51; *Mut. Nom.* 4.51.

35. Schmeller, *2. Korintherbrief*, 2:166.

expressions, especially those of Stoicism. He never alludes to the Stoic meta-physics, but he shares with them a focus on ethical progress.[36]

Life According to Nature

In Rom 1:18—2:29, Paul illustrates the dismal state of humankind, the ob-jects of God's wrath. They are "without excuse" (1:20; 2:1) because, in reject-ing the knowledge of God available to them (1:18–29, 32; 2:1–11), they fell under the power of sin (3:9). Paul's natural theology, according to which "the unseen things are seen in the things that are made," recalls Epictetus's claim that Zeus is present in the world and can be seen and understood (*Diatr.* 1.6.24).[37] Failure to acknowledge God results in enslavement to the passions (1:24–26). Paul illustrates submission to the passions, describing the women who exchanged the natural use (*physiken chrēsin*) for conduct that is "beyond nature" (*para physin*) in familiar Stoic language. He summa-rizes their offenses, indicating that those who acted contrary to nature did things that were not fitting (*kathēkonta*, 1:28), again using common Stoic terminology for the life that is not according to nature.[38]

Paul's argument resembles that of Epictetus, who says, "We must do what nature demands" and "observe what is in accordance with nature (*to kata physin*, *Diatr.* 1.26.1–2). Epictetus applied this principle to sexual relationships.

> And the male and the female [*to d' arren kai to thēlu*) and the passion (*hē prothumia*) of each for intercourse with the other, and the faculty which makes use of the organs which have been constructed for this purpose, do these things not reveal their artificer either? (*Diatr.* 1.6.9).

Epictetus's praise for the heterosexual relationship indicates why he con-demned the homosexual one.[39] Homosexual practice is not "in accordance with nature" (*kata physin*).

---

36. See Engberg-Pedersen, *Paul and the Stoics.*

37. Huttunen, "Stoic Law in Paul?" That the "unseen things" are "seen" also reso-nates with Platonic thought.

38. Stowers, "Paul and Self-Mastery," 535. The Stoics distinguished between acts that may on the whole be proper and good (*kathēkonta*, *officia* in Cicero; cf. *Fin.* 3.58–61) and acts that are through and through good (the *katorthōmata*, Cicero's perfectum officium, *Fin.* 3.61). See Arius Didymus, *Epitome* 5b2; 5b3; 5b9; 6q; 7b; 8a; 9.11a. See Engberg-Pedersen, "Stoicism in Philippians," 273.

39. Huttunen, "Stoic Law in Paul?" 50.

Paul also appeals to nature in his arguments about head coverings in Corinth (1 Cor 11:2–16). He instructs the Corinthians to maintain a clear distinction between the attire of men and women in worship, first appealing to the creation (11:3–12) to establish that women should pray and prophesy with heads covered while men should not cover their heads. Then he adds to the argument with two rhetorical questions, appealing to the Corinthians' judgment (11:13): "Is it fitting *(prepon)* for a woman to pray to God with the head uncovered?" *Prepein*, which is used nowhere else in the undisputed letters,[40] was common in Stoic argumentation.[41] Paul adds, "Does not nature *(physis)* teach you that it is a dishonor for a man to have long hair?" (11:14). His question is reminiscent of Epictetus, who also argued from nature: "Has not nature *(physis)* used even these [the hairs on the chin] in the most suitable way possible? Has she not by these means distinguished between the male and the female?" *(Diatr.* 1.16.9–14). Thus Paul moves from the argument based on the law (1 Cor 11:2–12) to an argument based on nature (1 Cor 11:13–14).

This argument is reminiscent of philosophical discussions that had taken place in Greece since archaic times.[42] Greeks sought an objective morality in the "unwritten law" given to humans by Zeus and applicable to all peoples. The view that these "laws" represented a divine standard was commonly accepted in philosophical circles. Against the Sophists, who argued that all ethical norms were relative, the philosophers attempted to connect the law to the natural order.[43]

> The goal of all these virtues is to live consistently with nature. Each virtue through its individual properties enables man to achieve this. For from nature he has initial impulses for the discovery of what is appropriate, for the balancing of his impulses, for acts of endurance, and for acts of apportioning. Each of the virtues, by acting in concert and by its own particular properties, enables man to live consistently with nature. (Arius Didymus, *Epitome of Stoic Ethics* 5b3)

The association of nature with the law of God was also made by Paul's near contemporary Philo. For Philo the demands of nature are rooted in

---

40. *Prepein* appears in Eph. 5:3; 1 Tim 2:10; Titus 2:1.

41. See Epictetus, *Diatr.* 1.22.1. *Prepein* is placed alongside *dikaion* (just). Panaetius gave *prepein* a central significance and called on humankind to conduct a way of life toward a goal that corresponds to one's nature as a rational being (cited in Schrage, *1. Kor* 2.520.) Cf. Arius Didymus, *Epitome* 5d.

42. See Brookins, "Natural Hair," 177–78,

43. Brookins, "Natural Hair," 177.

the laws of Torah.[44] According to *Opif.* 3, "The world is in harmony with the law, and the law with the world, regulating his doings by the purpose and will of nature." Indeed, many individual laws are presented as the laws of nature. Philo is vitriolic in his denunciation of men who transgress the boundaries set by nature. In *Spec.* 3.37–50, Philo describes pederasty as a "shame" even to mention 3.37, 49). Passive partners transform the male nature to the female, "counterfeiting the law of nature," 255. He consistently describes sexual aberrations as a violation of the natural law. According to *Abr.* 135, the inhabitants of Sodom "threw off their necks the law of nature." In his discussion of sexual laws (*Spec.* 3), he consistently interprets the law of Moses to demonstrate that the dictates of nature provide the norm for human existence.

Overcoming the Passions

When Paul describes the tortured person who says "I do not do what I want, but I do the very thing I hate" (Rom 7:15) and "I can will what is right, but I cannot do it" (Rom 7:18), he is apparently familiar with the philosophical discussion of Medea, who killed her own children, saying, "I am being overcome by evils. I know that what I am about to do is evil but passion is stronger than my reasoned reflection and this is the cause of the worst evils for humans" (*Medea* 1077–80). Twice she hesitated as she reflected that another course of action would be better (1040–48; 1056–58). But she finally determined that her desire for revenge is stronger than her reasoned reflections.

These words became the classic text for philosophical discussions of *akrasia*, lack of self-mastery.[45] Socrates acknowledged that the view of the masses is that people do not do the good because of the power of pleasure or pain but insisted that acting against what was right was impossible. The Stoics and Platonists maintained that the weakness of the will was derived from ignorance or false beliefs. Paul's near-contemporary Seneca wrote a *Medea* of his own based on Euripides's work. Epictetus also reflected on the story of Medea, citing the popular view of reason and emotion (*Diatr.* 1.28.6–8). The interlocutor asks, "Cannot a man, then, think that something is profitable to him, and yet not choose it?" Epictetus answers, "He cannot." The interlocutor replies, citing Medea, What about [Medea] who said:

> Now, now, I learn what horrors I intend;
> But passion overmasters sober thought?

44. Najman, "Law of Nature and the Authority of the Mosaic Law," 55–73.
45. Stowers, *Rereading of Romans: Justice, Jews and Gentiles*, 260.

Epictetus answers, "It is because she regards the very indulgence of her passion and the vengeance against her husband as more profitable than saving her children." When the interlocutor replies, "Yes, but she was deceived," Epictetus replies, "Show her clearly that she is deceived, and she will not do it; but until you show it, what else has she to follow but that which appears to be true?"

Analogies to Rom 7:15, 19 appear widely in the philosophical literature. The words of Medea were circulated in discussions about the role of the passions and knowledge of good and evil in moral psychology.[46]

Worship and Ethics

Paul's ethical instructions in Rom 12:1–3 also echo Stoic language. After his extended argument for the ultimate salvation of both Jews and Greeks (1:13—11:36), Paul encourages his readers, "I appeal to you by the mercies of God to present your bodies a living sacrifice wholly acceptable to God, which is your spiritual worship (*logikēn latreian*)" (12:1). *Logikē latreia* is a well-known philosophical concept to describe the relationship between human beings as *logikoi* and God as logos.[47] Epictetus states that as *logikos* human beings do well to worship God with hymns and songs. "If I were a nightingale, I should be singing as a nightingale; if a swan, a swan. But as it is, I am a rational being (*logikos eimi*); therefore, I must be singing hymns of praise to God (*Diatr.* 1.16.20–21; 1.16.15–19; 3.26, 39–30). The proper worship was to imitate God, the logos. Seneca says, "The honor that is paid to the gods lies, not in the victims for sacrifice, though they be fat and glitter with gold, but in the upright and holy desire of the worshipers. According to Seneca, the proper worship consists not in cultic ceremonies but rather in a "will that is reverent and upright" (*Ep.* 115.5; cf. *Ep.* 95).

Of utmost importance was the worshiper's way of thinking. Paul urges his readers to be transformed by the renewing of their minds so that they will discern the will of God, reversing the corrupt minds described in chapter 1. Thus the transformed mind (*nous*) is the prerequisite for the *logikē latreia*.[48] Seneca states, "One who has learned and understood what he should do and avoid is not a wise man until his mind (*animus*) is metamorphosed (*transfiguratus est*) into the shape of that which he has learned (*Ep.* 94.47–48; cf. *Ep.* 6.1–3).

---

46. Stowers, *Rereading Romans*, 264.
47. Thorsteinsson, "Paul and Roman Stoicism," 23.
48. Thorsteinsson, "Paul and Roman Stoicism," 25.

Paul further echoes Stoic thought, encouraging his readers not "to think of themselves more highly than they ought to think, but *phronein eis to phronein*—to think" (*phronein*) so as to mind a proper moderation (*eis to sōphronein*). Here Paul employs a play on words on the root *phron-*, probably recognizing that *phronēsis* was one of the four cardinal virtues (*phronēsis*). As a rule, the Stoics adhered to the four cardinal virtues—*phrōnesis, sōphrosynē, dikaiosynē, andreia*. Paul's audience would scarcely have missed the reference to the cardinal virtue of *phronēsis*. Paul shares with his contemporaries the view that proper behavior is the result of a correct perception.[49]

The image of the church as a body, which Paul first introduces in 1 Corinthians (10:16–17; 12:12–27) and employs again in Romans (12:3–8), is further developed in Colossians and Ephesians. Although interpreters have sought to identify the background of the image in the concept of corporate personality in the Jewish tradition, they have found no reference to Israel as a body. The image was, however, commonplace in Greek political speeches on concord. The image is employed by Seneca, Dio Chrysostom, Epictetus, and others.[50] The image is used in the famous speech of Menennius Agrippa's attempt to quell the revolt by the plebeians. In the story, the other parts of the body rebel against the belly, a situation that Agrippa compares to the revolt of the people against the state. He uses the fable to say that "the common good" demands mutual assistance. Consequently, all parts of the body are indispensable, and no one should disparage the apparently useless belly. "No one of their parts either has the same function or performs the same services as the others" (Dionysius of Halicarnassus, *Ant. Rom.* 6.86.1). He also speaks of the need for the diversity that is necessary for unity. Within a commonwealth there is a variety of people, and each is necessary for the proper functioning of the body.

Others employ the imagery. A frequently chosen part was the head, usually displayed as the ruling or superior part of the body.[51] Eyes were frequently used, as were hands and feet. The image of diseases and injuries in the body were common in speeches on concord. Diseases had the potential to spread throughout the body (Dio Chrysostom 2.34.20). Sometimes the injuries to the body were compared to flaws in the body politic.

Agrippa makes the following points in his comparison of the body to the commonwealth: 1) the body has many parts, each of which is indispensable; 2) the parts of the body work for the common good; the body parts

---

49. Thorsteinsson, "Paul and Roman Stoicism," 26.

50. See Lee, *Paul, the Stoics, and the Body of Christ*, 31–40.

51. Lee, *Paul, the Stoics, and the Body of Christ*, 40.

Friendship

work together in unity; 3) some use the distinction between soul and body to describe the role of the head in governing the body.

Echoes of Stoic ethics can be found in other Pauline letters. In Phil 1:10, for example, Paul prays that God will help the community "determine what is best" (*dokimazein hymas ta diapheronta*). Similarly, Paul says to his law-keeping interlocutor, "You know the will of God and approve the better things (*ta diapheronta*, Rom 2:18)."[52] This phrase is indebted to Greek philosophy. Its converse is *adiaphora*, the things that are indifferent (cf. Epictetus, *Diatr.* 2.5.7; 1.20.12).

Interpreters have recognized that Philippians contains numerous echoes of philosophical discussions. For example, the phrases derived from ancient concepts of friendship play an important role although Paul never uses the terms *philia* or *philos*.[53] Paul's encouragement that the Philippians strive side by side "with one soul" (Phil 1:27) is reminiscent of Aristotle's description of friendship (Aristotle, *Eth. nic.* 1168b [9.8.2]), which was subsequently used by others (cf. Diogenes Laertius, *Lives* 5.20). In addition to using this typical phrase, Paul employs variants that reflect similar conceptions. Timothy is "of equal soul" (*isopsychos*, 2:20), and Paul encourages the Philippians to be "fellow souls" (*sympsychoi*, 2:2).

The terms *koinōnia* and *phronein* are central to the language of friendship in antiquity.[54] Closely related to the concept of the "one soul" is the affirmation that friends "think the same thing" (*to auto phronein*). Because friends share the one soul, they think the same thing.[55] Paul employs this phrase, which became commonplace in antiquity, to encourage the community, especially Euodia and Syntyche "to think the same thing" (2:2; 4:2). He employs the phrase elsewhere (Rom 12:16; 15:5; 2 Cor 13:11). In Phil 4:10–20, Paul begins this section by conveying his joy at the Philippians' expression of concern for him (*to hyper emou phronein*, 4:10). Such concern

52. BDAG, 239, "The things that really matter." Cf. Oberlinner, *diapherō*, EDNT 1.315. See also Engberg-Pedersen, "Stoicism in Philippians." The negative *adiaphora* is of special significance in Aristotelian logic and ethics. The Cynics and Stoics call *adiaphoron* the middle sphere between virtue and vice and the related good and evil. See Diogenes Laertius 6.105, "Whatever is intermediate between virtue and vice they, in agreement with Ariston of Chios, account as indifferent (*adiaphora*)." Cf. Diogenes Laertius 7.160; Arius Didymus, *Epitome of Stoic Ethics* 6c, 6f, 7a, 11f.

53. Interpreters have demonstrated affinities between Philippians and the ancient letters of friendship. See Fitzgerald, "Philippians in the Light of Ancient Discussions of Friendship," 142. For a challenge to the designation of Philippians as a letter of friendship, see Still, "More Than Friends?," 53–66.

54. See Briones, "Paul and Aristotle on Friendship," 64.

55. Fitzgerald, "Philippians in the Light of Ancient Discussions of Friendship," 145.

expresses the common concern of friends for one another.[56] One may compare his plea to the Corinthians to "say the same thing" (1 Cor 1:10).

Koinōnia also played a significant role in ancient concepts of friendship. Aristotle says that "friendship is *koinōnia*" (*Eth. nic.* 1171b33). "All affection (*philia*) consists in partnership" (*koinōnia*, *Eth. nic.* 1161b [8.12.1]). The Stoics described it as sharing (*koinōnia*) and an agreement (*homonoia*) in living (*SVF* 3.24.22; 3.27.3). Paul mentions it for the first time in the thanksgiving in 1:5, expressing his gratitude for the Philippians' *koinōnia* in the gospel. It continues throughout the letter; Paul uses *koinōnia* and its cognates a total of six times (1:5, 7; 2:2; 3:10; 4:14–15).

Paul's statement that he has learned to be content (*autarkēs*, 4:11) echoes a familiar theme in philosophy. Self-sufficiency was the ideal of the Cynics and Stoics.[57] According to the *Epitome of Arius Didymus*, virtue has many names, including self-sufficiency (*autarkēs*), for it "suffices for the person who has it; free from want, because it removes any want; and enough, because it is adequate for our usage and extends every need in life" (11h). For Diogenes the Cynic, *autarkeia* meant, on the physical plane, contentment with the bare necessities of life, and on the spiritual level, complete detachment from the world and worldly values. Teles wrote a tractate, *peri autarkeia*.

Autarkeia reflects one dimension of friendship in antiquity. The relationship between *philia* and *autarkeia* had been discussed for centuries by philosophers, including Aristotle, the Stoics, the Neopythagoreans, who attempted to mitigate the conclusion that friends are superfluous for the self-sufficient individual (Diogenes Laertius, *Lives* 2.98). *Autarkeia* has become widely used by people of many persuasions, in most instances without the intellectual or psychological baggage of Stoicism.[58]

Vices and Virtues

Scholars have observed that the form of the ethical list is rare in the Old Testament but a common feature in both the Greco-Roman ethical instruction and Paul. The most prominent list in antiquity was the catalog of cardinal virtues attributed to Plato, which shaped the consciousness of a major portion of Greek ethical thought. In several dialogues (*Phaed.* 69c; *Resp.* 427E; *Leg.* 631c; 963a), Plato lists wisdom (*sophia* or *phronēsis*), courage (*andreia*), self-control (*sōphrosynē*), and justice (*dikaiosynē*) as the four cardinal

56. Fitzgerald, "Paul and Friendship," 332.
57. Malherbe, "Paul's Self-Sufficiency (Philippians 4:11)," 819.
58. Malherbe, "Paul's Self-Sufficiency (Philippians 4:11)," 820.

virtues (*aretai*).[59] For ancient writers each of the cardinal virtues was a form of knowledge, as the common introduction of each of the virtues as *episteme* indicates.[60] The four cardinal virtues later played an important role among the Stoics, who also divided them into subcategories.[61] Aristotle abandoned the fourfold form, adding other virtues to the list.[62] Greeks also named four cardinal vices (*kakiai*): folly (*aphrosynē*), intemperance (*akolasia*), injustice (*adikia*), and cowardice (*deilia*).[63] The cardinal vices were sometimes placed alongside the cardinal virtues (Stobaeus, *Ecl.* 2.59). Just as each of the cardinal virtues was a form of knowledge, the vices were regarded as a form of ignorance (*agnoia*).

The primary concern of the Greek ethical tradition, as reflected in the cardinal virtues and vices, was the well-being of the individual.[64] Philosophy provided the knowledge and skills by which one could attain *eudaimonia*. This goal could be reached only when the individual overcame those irrational forces that prevented one from acquiring the cardinal virtues, the path to human flourishing.[65]

While Paul also frequently gives lists of vices and virtues, his lists rarely overlap with those in the philosophical tradition. Paul employs the term *aretē* only once (Phil 4:8) and never mentions any of the Greek cardinal virtues in the undisputed letters.[66] Nor does he mention aristocratic and humanistic ideals such as *kalokagathia, eleutheriotes, megalophrosynē, megalopsychia, and megaloprepeia*. Thus while the form of the Pauline lists is reminiscent of Hellenistic lists, the former do not contain the central categories of the latter. In some instances, Paul balances vice and virtue lists (e.g., Gal 5:19–25; Phil 2:1–4) while in other lists he mentions only vices (Rom 1:18–32; 1 Cor 5:9–10; 6:9–11; 2 Cor 12:20–21). Sexual offenses (or offenders) appear in all the vice lists in the Pauline literature but do not

59. See the discussion in Philippo Ranieri, "Virtue," *Brill's New Pauly*, 15.458–59.

60. Cf. Stobaeus, *Ecl.* 2.59.4; *SVF* 3.262.

61. See Weber, *Das Gesetz im hellenistischen Judentum*. Stoic texts in Diogenes Laertius 7.92.126 and in *SVF* 1.199–204; 3.255–94; 1.406 = Diogenes Laertius, *Lives* 7.92; *SVF* 1.200= Plutarch, *Stoic rep.* 7, *SVF* 3.262, 264–66. See also Pohlenz, *Die Stoa* for Chrysippus; Wibbing, *Die Tugend- und Lasterkataloge im Neuen Testament*, 16.

62. Weber, *Das Gesetz im hellenistischen Judentum*, 349.

63. Stobaeus, *Ecl.* 2.59, 40; *SVF* 3.63; See Fitzgerald, "Vice/Virtue Lists," *ABD* 6:857.

64. Wibbing, *Die Tugend- und Lasterkataloge im Neuen Testament*, 18.

65. This information is drawn from my book, *Moral Formation according to Paul*, 88–89.

66. Echoes of the cardinal virtues appear in Acts and Titus. According to the Acts account of Paul's speech before Felix, Paul discussed "justice, self-control, and the coming judgment." According to Titus 2:12, God's revelation teaches the believer to live "soberly and justly and godly in this present world."

appear in Hellenistic vice catalogues.[67] The triad *porneia, akatharsia,* and *aselgeia* appears together in two instances (2 Cor 12:21; Gal 5:19) while each word in the triad appears in different combinations. *Porneia* is the most frequently listed among the vices mentioned by Paul.[68] The other repeated items in the lists (e.g., enmity, strife, jealousy, anger, envy, dissensions, factions (Gal 5:20–21; cf. Rom 1:29–31) point to vices that destroy community. Hellenistic writers also mention these vices that undermine the cohesion of the polis.

The list of positive attributes in Paul's writings overlaps minimally with the Hellenistic ethical lists. One example of the connection between Pauline and Hellenistic lists is the exhortation, "Whatever is true (*alēthē*), whatever is honorable (*semna*), whatever is just (*dikaia*), whatever is pure (*hagna*), whatever is lovely (*prosphilē*), whatever is commendable (*euphēma*). Although Paul mentions only one of the cardinal virtues ("whatever is just"), the list would have resonated with a Hellenistic audience because it reflects the popular values of the Greek polis.[69] However, the list, coming at the end of Paul's call for a new *phronesis* determined by the mind of Christ (2:5), derives its significance from the larger context of Philippians.

Paul's lists, unlike the Hellenistic lists, focus on life within the community of faith. Some of the qualities are consistent with Hellenistic values while others are derived from the biblical tradition. For example, some of the qualities of the fruit of the Spirit (Gal 5:22), including kindness (*chrēstotes*), gentleness (*prautēs*), and self-control (*enkrateia*), were virtues in the Hellenistic world.[70] Paul appropriates these virtues but places them under the heading of *agape*, which is the moral value that Paul mentions most frequently. In both the disputed and undisputed letters, humility (*tapeinophrosynē*) is a necessary dimension of the Christian life (cf. Phil 2:3; Col 3:12) while it is scorned in the Greco-Roman culture (cf. 2 Cor 10:1). Indeed, Jesus exemplified this quality when he "humbled himself" (Phil 2:7–8). While it is fundamental in Paul's thought, it is not a classical ideal.[71]

67. Vögtle, *Die Tugend- und Lasterkataloge im Neuen Testament,* 26; Wibbing, *Die Tugend- und Lasterkataloge,* 99.

68. Thompson, *Moral Formation according to Paul,* 94.

69. Thompson, *Moral Formation according to Paul,* 107.

70. See texts in Thompson, *Moral Formation according to Paul,* 101.

71. Judge, "St. Paul and Socrates," 106–16. Reprinted in Judge, *First Christians in the Roman World,* 677.

CONCLUSION

Paul shared with the philosophers the sense of mission, the passion, the desire to proclaim truth, and the intense focus on forming moral character among his readers. As in the case of rhetoric, Paul's dismissal of philosophy and his status as an *idiōtes* (2 Cor 11:6) without formal training in philosophy does not mean that he was unaffected, even if indirectly, by so conspicuous a feature of Mediterranean culture.[72] His letters give no evidence, however, that he had formal training in philosophy,[73] unlike Philo and the author of 4 Maccabees. Like his predecessors in the diaspora, he employed only the philosophical language that was useful to him, placing it within a framework that was incompatible with any philosophical school.[74] E. A. Judge notes correctly,

> In a mixed society of that kind one simply picks up and uses the vocabulary and technical ideas and fashionable notions of the time, wherever they come from. If one is the kind of independent thinker that Paul is, one is simply building out freely from that, exploiting the material rather than subjecting oneself to it.[75]

72. Johnson, *Constructing Paul*, 180.

73. Johnson, *Constructing Paul*, 180.

74. See Johnson, *Constructing Paul*, 184: "For the doctrines of Stoicism, as for the other Greek philosophical schools, the best that can be said is that Paul picked and chose what was useful or, perhaps better, made use of what he had picked up here and there. In this sense, when it comes to philosophy, the characterization of Paul at the Areopagus in Athens by the Stoics and Epicureans . . . as *spermologos* is not entirely unfair." See also Malherbe, "Paul's Self-Sufficiency (Philippians 4:11)," 823: "As he does elsewhere, then, Paul uses the moral philosophical language of his day, but places it in a larger framework quite foreign to the philosophical tradition that he uses."

75. Judge, "St. Paul and Socrates," 675.

7

The Church and the World in the Johannine Literature

The Johannine literature, written at the end of the first century, addresses internal and external crises within the church. The three letters of John and especially the Gospel of John are characterized by a distinctive view of the Christ event, which is indicated in their own world of language, thought, and imagery, especially in their christological focus. They share the conviction that the Savior came in the flesh (John 1:14; 1 John 1:1–4; 4:2; 2 John 7), a sharp distinction between light and darkness (John 1:5; 8:12; 12:35, 46; 1 John 1:5; 2:8–9, 11), and an emphasis on love for members of the community (1 John 2:10; 3:10–11, 14, 21, 23; 4:20; 5:1; 2 John 1, 5; 3 John 1). Even Revelation, the only book in the Johannine tradition that bears the name of John, shares points of contact and symbolism with the other Johannine writings, although most interpreters exclude it from treatments of Johannine theology.[1]

The Gospel of John and the Johannine epistles apparently address different stages in the life of the community.[2] In the Gospel of John, believers face a crisis as they are being expelled from synagogues (9:22; 12:42; 16:2)

1. See Johnson, *Writings of the New Testament*, 462, 513–15.

2. For the argument that the sequence of the writings is 2 John, 3 John, 1 John, Gospel of John, see Schnelle, *First Hundred Years of Christianity*, 345.

because their confession that Jesus is the Son of God has alienated them from the larger Jewish community, leaving them as a minority group in a hostile climate. John indicates his purpose in telling his narrative: that the readers may believe that Jesus is the Christ, and that, believing, they may have life in his name (20:31), despite their rejection by the larger populace. Because of the textual variant in 20:31, interpreters debate whether John is written so that the believing community may "continue to believe" or is intended as a missionary document: that the world may "come to believe."[3] Undoubtedly, the Gospel addresses a minority community, offering examples of those who came to faith through the healing activities of Jesus as a reason for them to continue believing. However, Michael Gorman has suggested that an ambiguity is present in John's statement of purpose; the Gospel is written so that disciples will "continue to believe" in the midst of a crisis of faith, and those who believe will bear witness so that others may believe.[4]

The occasion for the Johannine letters is the internal dispute between the letters' recipients and the "many antichrists" (1 John 2:18) who deny that Jesus is the Christ (2:22; cf. 5:1) who came in the flesh (1 John 4:2; 2 John 7). While the Gospel of John focuses on the conflict with outsiders, the Johannine letters explicitly confront the divisions within the community—the disputes over the nature of Christ and the conflict over leadership within the community (3 John). Nevertheless, while the Gospel and the epistles of John address different stages in the crises facing the community, they share the common theme of Christ and culture. The author of 1 John encourages the readers, "Do not love the world or the things that are in the world because the love of the Father is not in them" (1 John 2:15). According to H. Richard Niebuhr's typology, 1 John is the major example of Christ against culture[5] while the Gospel of John is the first example of Christ the transformer of culture.[6]

Like Paul (see ch. 3), the Gospel of John does not speak of Christ and culture but of Christ and the world (*kosmos*). Indeed, this Gospel speaks of the relationship between Jesus and the *kosmos* more than any other writer. The word *kosmos* appears no less than seventy-eight times in the Gospel. It appears most often on the lips of Jesus (fifty-nine times) but is also used by the narrator (twelve times) and other speakers (seven times).[7] Thus the

---

3. Major witnesses ℵ and B have *pisteuēte*, "continue to believe," while other important witnesses (e.g., A C D) have *pisteusēte*, "come to believe."

4. Gorman, "John: the Nonsectarian, Missional Gospel," 38–39.

5. Niebuhr, *Christ and Culture*, 48.

6. Niebuhr, *Christ and Culture*, 196.

7. Klassen-Wiebe, "In the World but Not of the World," 10.

relationship between the church and the world is a primary issue in both the Gospel and the Johannine letters.

SPEAKING THE LANGUAGE OF THE WORLD

Although the Gospel of John was written for a believing community that is not "of this world" (17:6), its language and concepts were intelligible to the larger culture.[8] The *kosmos* is one of the principal concepts of Greek thought.[9] The Hebrew does not have a precise term for *kosmos* but normally employs the phrase "the heavens and the earth" (cf. Gen 14:19; Exod 20:11).[10] The term is, however, frequently employed in the LXX, particularly in the Book of Wisdom, which reflects the influence of Greek philosophy. Wisdom employs such expressions as "the creation of the world out of formless matter" (Wis 11:17), the presence of Wisdom when "God made the world" (9:9), the "whole world" (11:22; 17:19), and "the structure of the world" (7:17). *Kosmos* is also used for the society that inhabits the universe.

More than any other ancient writer, Philo of Alexandria brought the concept of the *kosmos* into Judaism.[11] Within the Platonic-Stoic background against which he wrote, Philo could not avoid raising issues about the *kosmos*, bringing philosophical reflection to bear on the Bible. In the LXX text of Gen 1, he found the basis for distinguishing the "universe, incorporeal, we know, and discerned by the intellect alone" (*Migr.* 103 LCL), which is the model of this world.[12]

The logos, which is mentioned only in the prologue (1:1, 14), was a term that echoed the works of Philo of Alexandria as well as the philosophical tradition. Greco-Roman traditions are familiar with expressions such as "in the beginning" (*en archē*).[13] The Gospel of John and 1 John speak of truth more than other NT writings. The search for truth was the primary concern in philosophical and religious literature.[14] Similarly, the language

8. Schnelle, *First Hundred Years of Christianity*, 345.

9. Marrow, "Kosmos in John," 90.

10. Marrow, "Kosmos in John," 93.

11. Marrow, "Kosmos in John," 94.

12. Marrow, "Kosmos in John," 94.

13. Anaxagoras of Clazomena (496–428 BC) writes, "In the beginning everything was chaotic; but reason (*nous*) divided and ordered it." Cited in Kierspel, *Jews and the World*, 88.

14. According to Plato, (*Gorg.* 526d), "By searching for truth I strive to make myself as perfect as possible in life and, when the time comes to die, in death." Cf. also Plutarch, *Is. Os.* 2: "To aspire to the truth is to incline toward divinity—especially the truth concerning the gods. This type of study and research is like an ascent toward the

of light and darkness as metaphors for truth and falsehood are well known in the philosophical literature; to be in the truth is to be in the light.[15] Niebuhr maintains that John has intentionally transformed the images of culture with his insistence that Jesus Christ embodies the highest values of Greek culture.[16] According to Udo Schnelle, "One cannot avoid the impression that the language of the prologue is intentionally open to all kinds of traditions and requires the knowledge of both Jewish and Hellenistic bodies of literature in order to be understood." Schnelle concludes,

> When Jesus Christ is identified in the prologue with the guiding concept of Greco-Roman culture and history and education, a distinctive claim is suggested: in the Logos, Jesus culminates the ancient history of religion and the intellectual quest; he is the origin and goal of all being. This claim was taken up by the apologists and developed further until it flowed finally into the christological debates of the third and fourth centuries.[17]

THE ONE WHO HAS COME INTO THE WORLD

The prologue sets the stage for the major themes in the Gospel of John, especially the relationship between Christ and the world. The fact that "he was in the world, and the world was made through him" (John 1:10a and b) indicates that the world, unlike God and the logos, had a beginning.[18] The creation includes the physical world (1:2; cf. 17:5) as well as humanity (cf. 1:10; cf. 6:33; 12:19).[19] The *kosmos*, therefore, is neither positive nor negative but simply neutral, the earthly realm of existence (e.g., 16:21; 17:5; 21:25).[20] When the disciples say "Show yourself to the world" (7:4) and when his opponents say "the world has gone after" Jesus (12:19), the term is used in a neutral sense. John speaks of the world in neutral terms also when he

---

holy things, a more religious task than any ritual or priestly function." Cited in Spicq, *alētheia*, TLNT 1:66.

15. In Parmenides, and especially in Plato, to be in the truth is to be in the light (*Resp.* 7.517 b–c; 518 c); "one must open the soul's eye and look up toward being, which gives light to all things" (*Resp.* 7.540a). See Bultmann, *Theology of the New Testament*, 2.17. Cf. Spicq, *phōs*, TLNT 3:473.

16. Niebuhr, *Christ and Culture*, 202.

17. Schnelle, *First Hundred Years of Christianity*, 360.

18. Raabe, "Dynamic Tension: God and World in John," 133.

19. Matera, *New Testament Theology*, 294.

20. Klassen-Wiebe, "In the World but Not of the World," 11.

mentions Jesus's hour "to depart out of this world" (13:1; 16:28) and the example of when "a child is born into the world" (16:21).

God's creation in John's Gospel is good. In contrast to the view of the later Gnostics, John regards the physical, material, and temporal realities in positive terms. "Natural birth, eating, drinking, wind, water, and bread and wine are for this evangelist not only symbols to be employed in dealing with the realities of the life of the spirit but are pregnant with spiritual meaning."[21] Niebuhr adds that the creation of the world by the Word and the incarnation of the Word in flesh indicate his positive view of the world,[22] even if this world is corrupted and in need of salvation.

As the one who was with God from the beginning, he was the outsider who "came into the world" (1:11), "was made flesh" (1:14), and "exegeted God" (1:17). One may observe the frequency of the verbs for Jesus's coming (*erchomai*), going away (*hypagein*), and being sent (*apostellein*, *pempein*) into the world (1:9), all of which presuppose his preexistence and John's positive concern for the world. Jesus was the light coming (*erchomenon*) into the world (1:9, 11; 3:19; 12:46) from heaven (3:31). He came from the father (5:43; 16:28). He did not come on his own (7:28) but knows from whence he came and where he is going (8:14). He did not come to judge the world but to save the world (12:47) and to witness to the truth (18:27). Jesus responds to Pilate's question, "Are you the king of the Jews," declaring "for this I came into the world, in order that I might witness to the truth" (18:37).

The Johannine Jesus repeatedly claims that he did not come on his own but was sent by God. John apparently uses the verbs *apostellein* and *pempein* interchangeably.[23] This theme is closely connected with the preexistence and incarnation of the Son. John uses *apostellein* frequently to describe Jesus's mission. God loved the world and sent his son to save the world (3:16–17). Jesus's works demonstrate that the Father sent him (5:36–37). At the tomb of Lazarus, Jesus prays that the people will know that God sent him (11:42). Eternal life is to know that the people know God and the one whom God sent (17:3). Similarly, John frequently uses the verb *pempein* to say that God sent his son. Jesus does the works of the one who sent him, does the will of the one who sent him (4:34; cf. 6:38; 9:4). Jesus honors the one who sent him (5:23) and calls for listeners to believe in the one who sent him (5:24). The one who sent him has witnessed about him (5:37). No one comes to Jesus

---

21. Niebuhr, *Christ and Culture*, 197.

22. Niebuhr, *Christ and Culture*, 197.

23. See Hahn, *Theologie des Neuen Testaments*, 1.605: "The key motif for understanding John is the sending motif. Here one sees the fundamental connection of theology and Christology. Both terms for sending, *apostellein*, which appears 19 times, and *pempein*, which occurs 28 times, are interchangeable."

unless drawn by the one who sent him (6:44). His teaching is not his own, but that of the one who sent him (7:16). Jesus does not speak on his own, but the one who sent him gave him a commandment (12:49; 14:24). The one who sent him is true (7:29–30). His judgments are those of the one who sent him (8:16). The one who sent him has not left him alone (8:29). The one who has seen him has seen the one who sent him (12:45). Those who receive him also receive the one who sent him (13:20).

Jesus is the prophet who has come into the world (6:14; cf. 11:27), the "lamb of God that takes away the sin of the world" (John 1:29; cf. 1 John 2:2). As the bread that has come down from heaven, he gives life to the world (6:33, 38, 41). He is the light of the world (8:12; 9:5) and the savior of the world (4:42; 12:42). Jesus is the outsider who enters the world "from above" to save the world (John 3:17; 5:34; 12:47), the bread from heaven who has come down from heaven (6:33, 38, 41). Those who believe in him drink "rivers of living water" (7:38) and live eternally (11:25–26). They will no longer live in darkness (12:46) but become "children of light" (12:36). He did not come to condemn the world "but in order that the world might be saved through him" (3:17; cf. 12:47). They will do even greater works than the Savior (14:12), while those who do not believe will die in their sins (8:21). These greater works involve the extending of the mission of Jesus.[24]

Just as Jesus has come into the world, he will return to the unity with the Father. The Johannine Jesus declares, "I go away to the one who sent me" (7:33). He knows where he has come from and where he is going (8:14); he came from God and he goes back to him (13:3), and where he goes the disciples cannot follow (8:22). Those who are in darkness do not know where he is going (12:35), nor do the disciples understand where he is going (14:5). Jesus indicates to the disciples that he goes to the Father (14:28). In the high priestly prayer, Jesus says, "And now I go to you" (17:13).

THE REJECTION BY THE WORLD

The prologue introduces John's dialectical view of the world that is maintained throughout the Gospel. Because the world came into being through the agency of the Word (1:10), John often presents a positive view of it. However, there would be no need for God to send his Son into the world unless the world were in need of salvation.[25] God sent Jesus into the world to bridge the gap, to supply what the world lacks since this need can be met

24. Ruiz, *Der Missionsgedanke des Johannesevangelium*, 175.

25. Matera, *New Testament Theology*, 295.

only by a source outside the world.[26] The world that Jesus enters is a world dominated by the evil ruler (12:31; 14:30; 16:11) and needs salvation.[27] The prince is the father of all evil, a murderer from the beginning; he is the father of lies (8:44) and has many children, who embody the lifestyle of their father.[28]

Jesus has come into the world to save it from the power of darkness. As the prologue indicates, he was the light shining in the darkness (1:5, 9), and those who believe in him become children of God (1:12). God loved the world so much that he sent his son so that they would not perish but have eternal life (3:15–16). Indeed, a frequent theme is that Jesus gives life (4:14, 36; 5:24, 40; 6:40; 10:28; 12:25; 17:2–3; 20:31). John uses many metaphors to describe what Jesus brings to the needy world. He is bread and water because he brings life to a world that hungers and thirsts and harbors death (6:33, 51). He brings light to the world that is in darkness (8:12; 9:5; 11:9) and truth to the world that exists in what is false.

As the prologue indicates, the world is a place of darkness, and the light "did not overcome it" (1:5). The Son was in the world, but the world did not know him (1:10), and he came "into his own, and his own did not receive him" (1:11). As the Johannine Jesus elaborates, "This is the judgment, that the light has come into the world, and people loved the darkness rather than the light because their deeds were evil" (3:19). The world hates the light because the light reveals the wickedness of its deeds.[29] Therefore, the world of darkness does not receive the one who brings light.

The rejection of the one who came into the world is a constant theme in John's Gospel. Because Jesus is the heavenly one, the world cannot receive him (3:11; 5:43; 14:17) or believe in him. As Jesus tells Nicodemus, "My witness you do not receive" (3:11). Jesus tells the Jews, "I have come in the name of the Father, and you do not receive me" (5:43). While many believed (2:11; 4:39; 7:31; 8:30; 10:42; 12:11), most of the hearers, including the rulers (12:42), did not believe (5:38, 47; 6:36, 64; 8:45; 10:25; 12:37). Indeed, the book of signs concludes with the rejection by the world. "Although he had performed so many signs in their presence, they did not believe in him" (12:37). When the advocate comes to replace Jesus, the world is not able to receive his message (14:17).

A distinctive feature of John's Gospel is the frequent use of the expression "the Jews" (*hoi ioudaioi*), to whom Jesus presents his claims. The term

26. Klassen-Wiebe, "In the World but Not of the World," 11.
27. Klassen-Wiebe, "In the World but Not of the World," 12.
28. Kok, "As the Father Has Sent Me, I Send You," 172.
29. Raabe, "Dynamic Tension," 136.

hoi ioudaioi occurs sixty-six times in the Gospel of John. In some instances it appears in a neutral sense. In other instances it refers to a subgroup among "the Jews," as in 3:1 ("ruler of the Jews"), 18:21 ("officers of the Jews"), and 19:21 ("chief priests of the Jews"). In one instance it denotes the geographic area of Judea (3:22). In other instances it is used in positive statements about the Jews. John acknowledges that "salvation comes from the Jews" (4:9, 22), insists that Abraham rejoiced to see Jesus's day (8:56), and claims that the Scriptures are about him (5:45–47). He also portrays Jewish sympathizers of Jesus (John 3:1; 8:30–31; 11:45; 12:11; 19:38a) and Jews who are amazed about Jesus's learning (7:15).[30] In some scenes they are a divided cohort seeking to decipher Jesus's unusual words or behavior (7:35–36; 8:31–59; 10:21–42; 11:45–53).[31]

However, the Jews remain Jesus's primary antagonists in John's Gospel, the embodiment of "his own" who did not receive him (cf. 1:10–11). Consequently, the hostility of "the Jews" is a frequent theme, especially in chapters 5–10.[32] When Jesus heals on the Sabbath, the Jews persecute him (5:16). When Jesus claims to be the bread that has come down from heaven, the Jews complain (6:41). The "Jews" are the cause of fear for those who believe in Jesus (7:13; 9:22; 20:19). In the most extended dialogue with the Jews, Jesus says, "But now you are trying to kill me, a man who has told you the truth that I heard from God" (8:40). He adds, "You are from your father, the devil, and you choose to perform your father's desires" (8:44). However, "the Jews" are not the originators of evil, for their disbelief originates from a superhuman power of evil, the devil. Some of the Jews, however, believe after witnessing the raising of Lazarus (11:45), while others report the event to the chief priests and Pharisees, who decide that Jesus must be killed (11:47–53). Thus while "the Jews" are ambiguous characters in John's narrative,"[33] they are the primary example of the world's rejection of Jesus.[34]

The world is darkness (1:5), and those who do not follow Jesus live in darkness (8:12). Those who do not believe walk in darkness (12:35). Those who believe in him do not remain in darkness (12:46). The coming of Jesus is the judgment of the world when the ruler of the world will be thrown out

30. See Kierspel, *Jews and the World in the Fourth Gospel*, 63.

31. Myers, "Just Opponents?," 164.

32. On the identity of the "*Ioudaioi*," see Bennema, "Identity and Composition of *hoi ioudaioi* in the Gospel of John," 242: "During the Second Temple period the referent of *Ioudaios* was extended from an ethno-geographic term for Judean Jews to a georeligious term for those who adhered to the Judaean religion (whether or not residing in Judaea)."

33. Myers, "Just Opponents?," 174–75.

34. Matera, *New Testament Theology*, 298.

(12:31); Jesus has overcome the world (16:33). However, the world is not able to receive the paraclete (14:17).

Because Jesus is not from this world, he speaks in ways that those who are "of the world" do not understand.[35] Jesus's hearers do not understand his statement that he will destroy the temple and rebuild it (2:19–21). When Nicodemus does not understand Jesus's statement that he must be born again (3:5), Jesus replies, "If I said earthly things and you do not know, how can you believe when I tell you heavenly things" (3:12). The Samaritan woman misunderstands his promise of living water (4:4:10–15). The opponents do not understand his statement about the bread of life (6:41–42). As he tells his opponents, "You are from below, and I am not of this world" (8:23). Similarly, Pilate does not understand Jesus's message about truth (18:38). Because Jesus speaks "heavenly things," the plot commonly focuses on the misunderstanding between Jesus and his interlocutors.

Jesus's claim results in the division between those who believe and those who do not. His disciples first believed in him when he manifested his glory (2:11). Those who believe will receive eternal life (3:16, 36). In the series of encounters between Jesus and others, many believed in his message. After Jesus spoke with the Samaritan woman, many of the Samaritans believed in him (4:39). Many in the crowd believed in him (7:31; 8:30; 10:42). As the prologue indicates, while the world neither knew nor received Jesus, the Johannine community "beheld his glory" (1:14) and "received grace upon grace" (1:16), as the first-person plural indicates. While John repeatedly speaks of the world that did not receive or believe that Jesus was the one sent by God, many believed. Many Samaritans believed him because of his word (4:41). At the climactic moment, Peter exclaims, "We have believed and we know that you are the holy one of God" (6:69). Jesus says, "If you do not believe that I am, you will die in your sins" (8:24). The man healed from his blindness speaks for the believing community, saying, "I believe" (9:38). Martha says, "I believe that you are the Christ" (11:27). Thus the message of Jesus divides humanity between those who believe and those who do not. The disciples believe, but they are surrounded by an unbelieving world.

While many believed him, the narrative is largely the report of those who do not believe in him, as the prologue indicates (1:10–11), for people prefer darkness to the light (3:19). Nicodemus does not believe (3:11). In the events that take place during feast days (5:1–10:42), this rejection is especially evident in the series of conversations between Jesus and the Jews. When he heals on the Sabbath, they reject his claim to be equal to the father,

---

35. Hahn, *Theologie*, 1.673.

and Jesus concludes, "Yet you refuse to come to me" (5:40). When he feeds the five thousand, he concludes, "You have seen me, and yet you do not believe" (6:36). When Jesus went to Jerusalem for the festival of booths, the Jews were attempting to kill him (7:1, 20, 25; cf. 8:40). On more than one instance the Jews took up stones to kill him (8:59; 10:31). John concludes the section, "Although he had performed so many signs in their presence, they did not believe in him" (10:36).

THE DISCIPLES AND THE WORLD: CHAPTERS 13–17

While the book of signs (1:19—12:50) presents Jesus's encounter with the world, including "the Jews," chapters 13–17 present Jesus's "last will and testament" to the disciples (chs. 13–16) and final prayer to God (ch. 17) in preparation for his departure. A major concern in this scene is the disciples' relation to the world after Jesus departs from it (13:1) to return to the Father.[36] The disciples—"his own" (13:1)—are those who have believed (cf. 2:11) when the world did not. Before Jesus gives instructions for their conduct after his departure from the world, he shares a meal in which only "his own who were in the world" are present at this last meal, which, like other meals in the ancient world, was an act of solidarity for family and friends.[37] By washing the feet of the disciples, Jesus turns social conventions upside down, engaging in an act normally performed by socially inferior persons.[38] The washing of the disciples' feet was not only an act of humble service but also an expression of the love that Jesus had for "his own" (13:1).[39] Having washed the disciples' feet, he instructs them to wash one another's feet (13:14), following his example (13:15). The reciprocal washing of feet was the sign of mutual love for each other and love within the community. Jesus's command extends beyond the actual washing of feet but is an example of a life of service and of the love that Jesus has for the disciples (cf. 13:1, 34; 15:9).[40] The expression "one another" (allēlōn),

36. This structure is affirmed by Gorman, "John," 147.

37. Van der Watt, "Ethics and Ethos in the Gospel according to John," 160.

38. Van der Watt, "Ethics and Ethos in the Gospel according to John," 160.

39. See van der Watt, "Radical Social Redefinition and Radical Love," 123: "The clearest example of such humble, selfless loving action can be seen in the story of Joseph and Aseneth. It is a love story in which Aseneth sends her slaves away and washes Joseph's feet herself as a token of her loving service to him" (Jos. As. 20). Other examples include Abigail, who offered to wash the feet of David's servants (1 Sam 25:41). Abraham washed the feet of his heavenly guests, according to T. Abr. A3).

40. Skinner, "Love One Another," 133.

which is commonly used for family relationships, indicates the solidarity of the community that is separated from the world. The interpersonal relationships are egalitarian; differences in status are suspended within the confines of the community.[41]

The transition from the reciprocity indicated by *allēlōn* in the washing of feet to the new commandment that they "love one another" (13:34) repeats the emphasis on reciprocity suggested by *allēlōn*, further indicating that the washing of feet is an expression of love as the necessary response to a hostile world. This love is patterned after the love of the Father and the Son. The Father loves the world (3:16), the Son (3:35; 10:17; 15:9; 17:23), and the disciples (17:23). Jesus loves the Father (14:31) and the disciples (13:1, 34; 15:9). This love is expressed in concrete deeds—not only in the washing of feet but also in giving one's life for others (10:17). The disciples respond to this divine love by loving Jesus in return (8:42; 14:15, 21). Thus the new commandment that they "love one another" is an extension of the love that flows from the Father and the Son.

Similarly, the Johannine epistles focus on the community's love for one another as they also live in a world that hates them (3:13). The one who hates his brother lives in darkness, while the one who loves his brother lives in the light (1 John 2:9–11; 3:11, 13–14; 4:11). The community has learned to love from the one who gave his life for them (3:16), so they give their lives for others in the family. Indeed, love takes on concrete form when believers take care of the physical needs of their siblings in the faith (3:17). The author invites the believers to love one another because love is from God (1 John 4:7).

The love command implicitly demarcates believers from the world. The metaphor of the vine and the branches also indicates the nature of the community and its separation from the world (15:1–8). The intimacy of the disciples is expressed in the repeated use of the verb *menein* (to abide). Jesus first speaks in the imperative, "Abide in me as I in you" (15:4), using the metaphor of the vine and the branches to indicate that only the branches that "abide" will bear fruit" (15:5). Jesus then indicates that the organic connection between the vine and the branches is a metaphor for the love that extends from the Father to the Son and then to the disciples (15:9), concluding with the encouragement for the disciples to "abide in [his] love" (15:10). This love is demonstrated in one's giving his life for his friends (15:13). As they love one another (15:12), Jesus's love abides in them. They are his friends (15:14) whom he has chosen from the world (15:16), but they remain in this relationship only as they love one another.

41. Van der Watt, "Radical Social Redefinition and Radical Love," 116.

This apparent withdrawal from the world places believers in a precarious position, for the world is hostile to them because Jesus has selected them from the world (15:19). Indeed, Jesus continues his encouragement for love within the community with the claims, "If the world hates you, know that it hated me first" (15:19) and "If they persecuted me, they will persecute you" (15:20). Indeed, John concludes that the world's hatred of the disciples is also the hatred of the Father, fulfilling the Scripture, "They hated me without cause" (15:25; cf. Ps 35:19; 69:5).

The Mission to the World

Interpreters have observed that the Johannine love command extends only to the disciples, designating the Johannine ethic as "sectarian." Wayne Meeks wrote that this Gospel

> defines and vindicates the existence of the community that evidently sees itself as unique, alien from its world, under attack, misunderstood, but living in unity with Christ and through him with God. It could hardly be regarded as a missionary tract. . . . It provided a symbolic universe which gave religious legitimacy, a theodicy, to the group's actual isolation from the larger society.[42]

In a later article, Meeks wrote that "the Fourth Gospel meets none of our expectations about the way ethics should be constructed," for the "only rule [of the Johannine Jesus] is 'love one another,' and that rule is both vague in its application and narrowly circumscribed, being limited solely to those who are firmly within the Johannine circle."[43]

Jesus's Mission to the World

Although interpreters have regarded John's emphasis on love within the community as evidence of its isolation from the culture, they fail to see the love command in its larger context of God's mission to save the world. As John 3:16 indicates, God loved the world and sent his Son to save the world, and only those who believe that God sent him will be saved (John 3:15, 16; 8:24; cf. 14:6). Passages recalling the coming of Jesus are frequently followed by a purpose clause.

"I came into the world for judgment, so that those who do not see may see, and those who do see may become blind" (9:39).

42. Meeks, "Man from Heaven in Johannine Sectarianism," 44–72 (here 70).
43. Meeks, "Ethics of the Fourth Evangelist," 318.

"I have come in order that they may have life" (10:10).

"I did not come to judge the world, but to save the world" (12:47).

"For this I came into the world, to testify to the truth" (18:37).

In addition, the numerous references to the sending of Jesus indicate the mission of Jesus. The frequent theme of John is that God sent Jesus into the world.[44] His teaching is not his own but that of the one who sent him (7:16; 14:24). He was sent to do the will of the one who sent him (4:14; 5:20; cf. 8:16, 29) so that people would believe in the one who sent him (5:24; 6:29). He will then return to the one who sent him (7:33). Here Jesus's missionary commission to the disciples is essentially the extension of Jesus's own sending by the Father.[45]

The numerous signs that Jesus performed (2:1—12:50) are examples of Jesus's mission to save the world. Even the request of the Greeks to see Jesus (12:20) reflects the significance of Jesus for the world. As the numerous dialogues in 1:19—12:50 indicate, Jesus brings life (1:4; 3:15–16; 4:14; 5:24, 26, 29, 40; 8:12; 10:28; 17:2–3; 20:31), light (8:12; 12:35–36), living water for the thirsty (4:11, 13–14; 7:38), and bread from heaven (4:32; 6:27) to those who are lost.

The constant theme throughout John is that the world did not know God (1:10; 8:27; cf. 3:10). Nor will the world know the paraclete who comes after Jesus's departure (14:17). Consequently, they will persecute believers because they do not know the Father and the Son (16:3). However, the disciples not only believe but they also know Jesus and the One who sent him. Jesus has made known to them everything that he has heard from the Father (15:15; 17:26; cf. 5:42). Because the disciples have been with Jesus, they know. The paraclete will guide them into all truth (16:13). Thus Jesus prays, "I have manifested your name to the people you gave me from the world. . . . They have known all things that you have given to me . . . they know that truly you have come from God" (17:7–8). The mission of Jesus is that the world might know the truth (8:23, 32) "so that [they] may know and understand that the Father is in me and I am in the Father" (10:38; cf. 14:20, 31).

The Mission of the Disciples

Jesus's mission is not only that the disciples believe but also that they may know him and the Father (13:35; 14:31; 17:23). The task of the disciples is to continue that mission, for they know what the world does not; in Jesus's

44. John employs *pempein* and *apostellein* interchangeably to describe the sending.

45. Schnelle, *Theology of the New Testament*, 740.

absence, they will bring the world to know God. Their love for one another (13:34–35) is not a withdrawal from the world but the means by which the world may know that they are the disciples of Jesus (13:34–35). They demonstrate their love in their willingness to lay down their lives for one another. Then they will bear witness. Their aim is not to withdraw from the world but to expand the circle of those who love one another. Their love for one another is thus not only a matter of internal cohesion but has a missionary intent. By their love for one another, "the world will know" that they are the disciples of Jesus (13:34). Their mission is to expand the circle of those who love one another by continuing the mission of Jesus.[46]

The incident of Jesus's encounter with the Samaritan woman in John 4:1–42 is paradigmatic of the mission of Jesus to save the world and the disciples' role in that mission. The Samaritan woman epitomizes for the readers the world of darkness. Besides being a Samaritan woman, regarded as unclean by the Jews, she was also one of notorious character, having had five husbands. Jesus's engagement with her in conversation was inconceivable in his own culture. His offer to her of living water (4:10) signifies the salvation that he offers to the world. As a result of this encounter, the woman becomes a witness and a missionary model of one who relates the story of the encounter to other Samaritans (4:29–30). Then many of the Samaritans believed because of the woman's testimony (4:39).

Before John reports of the Samaritans' belief, he indicates the involvement of the disciples as they bring food to Jesus (4:31), who responds with the usual Johannine symbolism, indicating that his food is to do the will of the one who sent him (4:34). This "food" is evidently the mission of Jesus to save the world. Jesus then describes his mission with the metaphor of the sowing and the harvest. Contrary to the literal understanding, Jesus refers to the eschatological harvest to eternal life in which he is engaged (4:36), indicating that the time for the harvest has come. The disciples enter into the mission of Jesus, joining in the harvest. Thus just as God has sent the Son (4:34), Jesus now sends the disciples to enter harvest of others. This harvest becomes evident when "many Samaritans believed" (4:39). This interlude in the story of the Samaritans anticipates the sending of the disciples into the world after Easter (20:21).[47]

---

46. Ruiz, *Der Missionsgedanke des Johannesevangelium*, 185.

47. Okure, *Johannine Approach to Mission*, 159; Ruiz, *Der Missionsgedanke des Johannesevangelium*.

The High Priestly Prayer and Mission

In the high priestly prayer (ch. 17), Jesus begins with the acknowledgement that "this is eternal life, that they know the only true God, the one sent by the Father (17:3)." He has prepared for his departure by making everything known to the disciples (17:7–8). The prayer focuses on the disciples' relationship to the world:

17:9: I am praying for them (the disciples). I am not praying for the world, but for those you have given me, for they are yours.

17:14: I have given them (the disciples) your word and the world has hated them, because they are not of the world.

17:16: [The disciples] are not of the world, even as I am not of the world.[48]

At the same time, Jesus insists that the disciples are in the world.

17:11: And I am no longer in the world, but they are still in the world, and I am coming to you.

17:13: I am coming to you now, but I say these things while I am in the world, so that they may have the full measure of my joy within themselves.

17:15: I do not ask that you take them out of the world but that you keep them from the evil one.[49]

The world appears to have two meanings in this prayer, just as it is throughout John's Gospel. On one hand, the world is the material creation that God loved and into which Jesus entered, while on the other hand it is the term for humanity's resistance to the truth in Jesus Christ. Both of these nuances are present in the high priestly prayer in the statements that Jesus and the disciples are "in the world" but not "of the world."[50]

Jesus begins the prayer (17:1–5) by reiterating the ultimate mission of God: "that they may know [God] and the one whom God sent" (17:3), thus suggesting that his work continues after his departure. In 17:6–19 he prays for the disciples whom God has given him, indicating that he has made known to them what he has received from God (17:6–8, 14). He does not pray for the world but for them. Jesus does not pray that God take them out of the world, but that he protect them from the evil one (17:15), "the ruler of this world" (12:31; 14:30; 16:11; cf. Matt 6:13), who is the agent of

48. See Skinner, "Love One Another," 37.
49. See Skinner, "Love One Another," 38.
50. Skinner, "Love One Another," 39.

ecclesial division.[51] Before he commissions the disciples to go into the world, he prays, "Sanctify them in truth." They, like Jesus (17:19), are sanctified, that is, not of this world. As sanctified ones—those who are set apart from the world—they are sent into the world. That is, Jesus prays that "those who are not of the world" have a mission to continue the work that God sent the Son to do in the world. The mission of Jesus is to save a broken world, and the disciples enter into that labor. Through the disciples, the world that does not know God will come to know God. As the high priestly prayer indicates, the task of the disciples is to continue the mission of Jesus to save the world.

The high priestly prayer is particularly rich in statements about the sending of the disciples and theological perspectives on the church's mission.[52] The primary missionary task is to witness (*martyrein*, NRSV "testify") on Jesus's behalf. John the Baptist first testified on Jesus's behalf (1:7, 15, 32, 34; 3:26; 5:33, 36). Jesus says to Nicodemus, "We speak of what we know and testify to what we have seen" (3:11). Jesus has no need to testify about himself (5:31), for both his works (5:36) and the Scriptures testify about him (5:39). The paraclete will testify on Jesus's behalf, and then the disciples will testify (15:26–27). *Martyria* is the language of the law court; witnesses declare the truth of what they have seen and heard (cf. 3:11; 4:39; 19:35). The disciples' testimony will lead others to believe (17:20). The one who saw the piercing of Jesus's side "testified so that you also may believe. His testimony is true, and he knows that he tells the truth" (19:35). Just as many believed because of the testimony (*martyrountes*) of the Samaritan woman (4:39–42), others will believe because of the testimony of the disciples.

In 17:20 Jesus even prays for those who will come to faith "through their word," a clear reference to the missionary activity of the Johannine school. The prayer is reminiscent of the earlier scenes where "many more believed because of his [Jesus's] word" (4:41; cf. 4:50). As the disciples abide in the word of Jesus, they share in his mission of extending life to others.[53] Jesus had said earlier in the narrative, "The words that I say to you I do not speak on my own; but the Father who dwells in me does his works" (14:10; cf. 14:24; 17:14). Thus the words of the disciples are the words of Jesus and the one who sent him.

The mission of the disciples is also evident when Jesus encounters the disciples after the resurrection and says, "Peace be with you; as the Father has sent me, so I send you" (20:21). This is John's equivalent of the

51. Gorman, *Abide and Go*, 116.

52. Schnelle, *Theology of the New Testament*, 740.

53. Gorman, *Abide and Go*, 122.

universal commissioning in Matt 28:18–20. The sending of the Son into the world makes possible and necessitates the sending of the disciples into the world.[54] The gift of the Spirit equips the disciples for their mission (20:22). Here Easter and Pentecost are combined; as in Acts (1:6–8), the Spirit empowers the community for a mission to the world.[55] It is not coincident that the risen Jesus charges his disciples with mission, for with the conclusion of the earthly work of the Son, his sending is transferred to the disciples. By the gift of the Spirit, they are authorized and equipped for their task of forgiving sins, that is, bringing people over from the realm of death into the realm of life.[56]

CONCLUSION

Contrary to Richard Niebuhr, the Gospel of John does not portray Christ as the transformer of culture but as the one who has come to save the world, which lives in darkness. The statement of purpose, "These things were written that you may believe that Jesus is the Christ, the Son of God, and that believing, you may have life in his name," summarizes the major themes of the book, which has presented a series of episodes demonstrating Jesus's mission to save a world of darkness. He writes a Gospel that the wider public can understand, employing the images that reflect the world's hunger and thirst for the flourishing life. "It not only completes the theological formation of the New Testament at the highest level but especially opens the way to Greco-Roman intellectual history through the concepts of the logos, truth, and freedom, and thus at the same time prepares the transition to the ancient church."[57] "According to Schnelle, "in the Logos, Jesus Christ culminates the ancient history of religion and the intellectual quest; he is the origin and the goal of all being."[58]

At the same time, Jesus speaks in "figures of speech" (*paroimiai*, 10:6; 16:25, 29) that even the disciples do not understand until after his departure, and he speaks "heavenly things" (3:12) that the world, including Nicodemus, does not receive, believe, or understand (3:10–12). According to John, salvation comes from the one who is "not of this world" but has come into the world to bring life. He assumes the resistance of the world, and he proclaims an offensive word: that "no one comes to the Father" except

54. Schnelle, *Theology of the New Testament*, 740.
55. Hahn, *Theologie*, 700.
56. Schnelle, *Theology of the New Testament*, 740.
57. Schnelle, *First Hundred Years of Christianity*, 360.
58. Schnelle, *First Hundred Years of Christianity*, 360.

through Jesus. Just as Jesus, who was not of this world, came into the world, he sends his disciples into the world to continue the work of Jesus. They go, equipped with the power of the Holy Spirit. Thus John proclaims both the hostility of the world to the Christian message and the mission of the church to the world.

8

The Other Voices

For believers who claimed to be God's chosen people, their relationship to society is a continuing issue, for conversion involves some level of separation from society and its institutions. However, as the authors of Hebrews, 1 Peter, and other writers indicate, separation is never complete. The witnesses speak the language of the dominant culture with varying facility and inevitably participate in its institutions as citizens, family members, and neighbors. Some believers are even married to unbelievers (cf. 1 Pet 3:1–6). All the writings describe how the communities maintain their separate identity and interact with the society.

THE EPISTLE TO THE HEBREWS

Like Paul, the author of Hebrews never mentions Greek writers, playwrights, or philosophers. However, his facility with Greek suggests his acquaintance with Greek culture. Eduard Norden describes Heb 1:1–4, along with the Lukan prologue, as "the best written period in the entire New Testament."[1] Similarly, Erich Grässer describes the author as "a great literary talent."[2]

---

1. Norden, *Die antike Kunstprosa vom VI. Jahrhundert v. Chr. bis in die Zeit der Renaissance*, 438.

2. Grässer, *An die Hebräer*, 1:46.

Hans von Soden called attention to the numerous examples of stylistic refinement.

> The author is a versatile and well-educated spirit. He has at his disposal a rich vocabulary (140 *hapax legomena*) that includes numerous words that appear nowhere else in the Bible, but are common in daily Greek usage (e.g., *nephos, nōthoi, gamos* for marriage, *elathon tines, klinein, prospheresthai tini* along with select compound words, verbs with *-zein*, substantives with *-sis*, composites such as *aimatekchysia, misthapodosia*). The linguistic diction is skillful, florid, . . . rich in fine syntactic phrases, beautiful periods; [the author] loves plays on words (5:8; 9:15–16, 10:38–39; 11:37; 13:14), striking images (6:7; 12:1–3), and sharply delineated antitheses.[3]

Although the author does not mention Greek philosophers, he demonstrates a basic familiarity with Greek philosophy and rhetoric throughout the homily, which consists primarily of a series of comparisons (*synkrises*) between the institutions of the Old Testament and the realities in the Christian faith. Indeed, the author employs "better" (*kreittōn*) thirteen times in the homily in addition to other comparisons.

The *synkrisis*, one of the most widely used modes of argumentation in Greek rhetorical theory, is a rhetorical device that takes persons, objects, or abstract concepts that are comparable in order to demonstrate either their equality or the superiority of one over the other.[4] It was included in the progymnasmata, the exercises in composition practiced in grammar schools.[5] Indeed, Theon shares with Hebrews the use of *kreitton* (114.16, 19; 115.2) to establish a comparison. In ancient literature the comparison of Greek and Roman heroes in the parallel biographies of Plutarch are the most famous examples. As Plutarch's *Parallel Lives* indicates, *synkrisis* can be the organizing principle of a speech.[6]

In Hebrews, transcendent heavenly realities are compared with earthly realities. The exalted Christ abides forever, while the angels are transitory

---

3. Von Soden, *Hand-Commentar zum Neuen Testament*, 6, my translation.

4. According to Theon, *synkrisis* is "language setting the better or the worse side by side." He adds, "Synkrises are not comparisons of things having a great difference between them. . . . Comparisons should be of likes and where we are in doubt which should be preferred because of no evident superiority of one to the other." Cited in Kennedy, *Progymnasmata,* 53. See also Kneepkens, "Comparatio," 2:293.

5. Kennedy, *History of Classical Rhetoric*, 78n.

6. Martin, "Philo's Use of Syncrisis," 281. See also Erbse, "Die Bedeutung der Synkrisis in den Parallelbiographen Plutarchs," 398–424. This paragraph originally appeared in *Perspectives in Religious Studies* 39 (2012) 366.

(1:5–13). At the exaltation, Christ became the high priest after the order of Melchizedek, which abides forever (7:3, 16, 24), in contrast to earthly priests who die and are continually replaced (7:23). Christ serves in a heavenly sanctuary as the high priest (8:1) while the priesthood of Aaron serves in an earthly sanctuary (9:1–5), a copy of the heavenly one (8:1–5). At the climax of the homily, the author declares that believers have not come to the earthly and tangible Mount Sinai (12:18) but to the heavenly city (12:22). At the end time God will shake the heavens and the earth, but only "that which cannot be shaken" remains (12:26–27).

The comparison between the heavenly eternal and the earthly transitory reflects the influence of Middle Platonism. Similar comparisons appear in the works of Philo and Plutarch. Plutarch says that "For that which really is and is perceptible and good is superior (*kreittōn*) to destruction and change" (*Is. Os.* 373).

The language also evokes Plato's theory of ideas (*Resp.* 7.514–17; *Leg.* 1.643c), according to which earthly matters are shadows of heavenly archetypes. Philo gave a Platonic interpretation to Exodus 25:40 (*QE* 2.52; *Leg.* 3.100–102; *Plant.* 26–27; *Mos.* 2.71–75), and the later church fathers also read the passage with Platonic lenses (Origen, *Hom. Exod.* 9.2; Eusebius, *PE* 12.19.1–9). With the Platonists, the author maintains the two levels of reality, according to which earthly matters are changeable while the heavenly world remains unchanged.

When the author describes Abraham as "going out," "as seeing the invisible one" (11:27), he evokes the language of Middle Platonism. The images of knowing and seeing invisible realities are commonplace in the literature of Middle Platonism. In describing God's role in creating the intelligible world as a pattern for the world of the senses, Philo describes the former as "a world discernible only by their mind" and the latter as "the world which our senses can perceive" (*Opif.* 19). Although the heavenly city is invisible for Philo, it is perceptible to the one who has the special capacity to see the invisible (*Post.* 15; *Deus.* 3; *Plant.* 17; *Praem.* 27). He speaks of the apprehensions of reality gained by the "soul's eye" (*Migr.* 39; cf. *Her.* 89). Similarly, Alcinous describes the deity as ineffable and graspable only by the intellect (*Epit.* 10.4).[7]

The heroes described in chapter 11 were "aliens" (11:9) who sojourned in a foreign land and "strangers (*xenoi*) and foreigners on the earth" (11:13). A familiar theme in Middle Platonism is the alien existence of those whose homeland is in the invisible world. According to Philo, the wise are appropriately called sojourners (*paroikountes*). The heavenly region, the place of

---

7. See Thompson, "What Has Hebrews to Do with Middle Platonism," 49.

their citizenship, is their native land; the earthly region is a foreign country in which they live as sojourners (*Conf.* 75–78; cf. *Q G* 4.74; *Somn.* 1.181). Those who migrate from their homes place their faith in God (*Her.* 99). According to *Congr.* 84–87, our task is to recognize our duty to hate the habits and customs of the lands in which we live, which are symbolized as Egypt and Canaan.[8] Jacob's temporary residence with Laban is symbolic of the soul's expectations of a city *(Somn.* 1.46).

The idea that one is a stranger on earth has deep roots in the philosophic tradition.[9] Plutarch's essay *De Exilo* describes the situation of literal exiles before concluding with reflections about exile as a metaphor for human existence. He cites the ancient words of Empedocles, "All of us . . . are sojourners here and strangers and exiles" (*Exil.* 607d). Because the soul has come from elsewhere, one may say that "the soul is an exile and a wanderer" (607e).

The echoes of philosophical language do not demonstrate that the author is a philosopher. Indeed, his fundamental message—that God "has spoken in these last days"—and the claim that the divine Son came into the world, suffered, and was exalted was incompatible with Middle Platonism. The author thus incorporates elements of Middle Platonism but rejects those parts that are incompatible with his Christian faith. He and the audience probably had an acquaintance with philosophy that was possessed by the educated people of the period.

Although the elegant Greek and the philosophical language suggest a level of acquaintance with Greek culture, the author consistently addresses a community that is alienated from its culture. In the early days after their conversion, they had experienced "a hard struggle with sufferings, sometimes being publicly exposed to abuse and persecution" (10:32–33). Some were imprisoned while all members of the community had suffered the confiscation of their property (10:34). No one had died (12:4), but some are still in prison (13:3). Consequently, a major theme is the endurance of suffering by the church (10:32; 12:5–11).

The author's task is to rebuild the symbolic world of a community that has been shaken by unfulfilled promises (cf. 11:33, 39). The vision of the ministry of Christ in the heavenly world and the community's own entrance to the throne of God in the present (cf. 4:14–16; 10:19–22) reassures the readers of the certainty of God's promises and offers motivation for the readers to endure (10:36–39). The author encourages the community by presenting Jesus as the pioneer in suffering. He is the pioneer

8. Thompson, *Beginnings of Christian Philosophy*, 60.

9. Feldmeier, *Die Christen als Fremde*, 27–38.

(*archēgos*) who has led the way for the community, reaching his present glory and honor only through the path of suffering (2:9–10). In the days of his flesh, he prayed "with loud cries and tears to the one who could save him from death" (5:7) and learned "obedience through what he suffered" (5:8). He "endured the cross, disregarding its shame" (12:2). Similarly, the heroes of faith in chapter 11 were outsiders in their own culture, having seen the future that others had not seen (11:13, 26–27). When Noah built the ark, he "condemned the world" (11:7). Abraham was a sojourner (11:9). Indeed, all the faithful people were "strangers on the earth" (11:13). Moses rejected the security of being Pharaoh's grandson, choosing rather "to share ill-treatment with the people of God than to enjoy the fleeting pleasures of sin" (11:24). The ancestors in the faith "were tortured, refusing to accept release" (11:35) while others suffered mocking and flogging and even chains and imprisonment.

> They were stoned to death, they were sawn in two, they were killed by the sword; they went about in skins of sheep and goats, destitute, persecuted, tormented—of whom the world was not worthy. They wandered in deserts and mountains, and in caves and holes in the ground. (11:37–38)

Ernst Käsemann, in his classic work on Hebrews, identifies the people with the title *Das wandernde Gottesvolk*; the English translation *The Wandering People of God* does not adequately capture the nuances of the title. Käsemann envisions a people on the move through difficult circumstances. The title evokes the scene comparing the believers to the wilderness generation who are on the path to the promised land (3:7—4:11). They follow the *archēgos* and forerunner (*prodromos*) to the heavenly world. The author gives a similar view of the heroes of faith as a model for a community that now endures marginalization (cf. 6:12). Its suffering is a time of discipline (12:5–11) that will ultimately yield the "peaceful fruit of righteousness to those who have been trained by it" (12:11). In the present they run the race, following the one who endured the shame that they now experience (12:1–2).

For the author, the world is a hostile place. In the peroration of the homily, he summarizes the believers' response to their culture, reminding the community that, just as the high priest discarded the bodies of the sacrificial animals "outside the camp" (13:11; cf. Exod 33:7–11; Lev 16:27), Jesus suffered "outside the gate" (13:12). The challenge for believers is to follow Jesus "outside the camp," bearing the abuse that their forerunner had suffered (13:13). The threefold use of the term "outside" (*exō*) and the compound "let us go out" (*exerchōmetha*) suggest that the term is the heart of this exhortation.[10] Thus they, like the patriarchs, are "strangers and pilgrims" in their own culture, accepting the shame of their outsider status.

Communal solidarity gives the strength to endure. Believers are siblings who journey together on the way, following the path of their forerunner (2:9–10; 12:1–2; cf. 6:20; 10:19–20). Jesus regards the community members as his siblings (2:12–13); he is like them in every respect (2:17), having experienced every temptation that they face (4:15). The ethic of Hebrews consists in caring and encouraging siblings in the community. The author recalls the earlier days when the community demonstrated love for each other and served the saints (6:10), and he desires that they demonstrate the same kind of zeal until the end (6:11). Their task is to "encourage one another each day" (3:12), to "stir one another up to love and good works" (10:24), and to see that no one is hardened by the deceitfulness of sin (3:13) or fails to attain the grace of God (12:16). He instructs them to maintain the same love, practicing hospitality toward one another (13:2) and visiting those who are in prison (13:3). He also insists on the communal solidarity in their sexual morality and their attitude toward possessions (13:1–6). After comparing the sacrifice of Christ to the Levitical sacrifices, the author concludes that the sacrifices that are pleasing to God are good deeds and fellowship (13:15–16).

Although the author demonstrates that he is at home in Greek culture, he encourages believers to accept their place outside the camp of its culture. He does not mention a mission to the culture or issues of interest to the society as a whole. The only reference to the surrounding culture is the memory of the occasion when they suffered the confiscation of their property and imprisonment. His central concern is the continuing viability of a community whose confession of Christ alienates them from the culture. Consequently, the ethical instructions involve the relationships within the community. Their challenge is to be an alternative community in their society.

ALIENS AND EXILES: 1 PETER

Like the epistle to the Hebrews, 1 Peter exhibits an acquaintance with Greek culture. Although the writer never mentions Greek writers or philosophers, he has a facility with the language that demonstrates his immersion in Greek literary culture, as E. G. Selwyn commented.

---

10. Backhaus, *Der Hebräerbrief*, 471.

> Its style is not only natural and unforced, indicating that it be-
> longs to one who not only wrote, but also thought, in Greek; but
> it exhibits a felicity of phrase, a suppleness of expression, and a
> wealth of vocabulary which betoken a mind nourished in the
> Greek spirit and tradition . . . and we may go further and say that
> it is the kind of correspondence which we find in the Greek tra-
> gedians and in Plato rather than that of writers such as Plutarch
> or Lucian. His mind is as much that of a poet as of a theologian.[11]

The polished Greek style of 1 Peter is a major reason that scholars have questioned the traditional attribution of the letter to Simon Peter, assuming that this facility with the language is unimaginable for a Galilean fisherman.[12]

The Exile Existence

Like the readers described in the second-century apology *Epistle to Diognetus*, who were "not distinguished from the rest of humanity by country, language, or custom" as they followed the local customs in "dress and food and other aspects of life" (*Ep. Diog.* 5:1 4), the recipients of 1 Peter also share the language and customs of the surrounding society. They live within the institutions of government (1 Pet 2:13–17), slavery (1 Pet 2:18–25), and marriage (1 Pet 3:1–6). Nevertheless, they are outsiders in their own land, as the opening address to the "elect exiles (*parepidēmoi*) of the diaspora (1:1)" indicates. The image of exile indicates their separation from the dominant culture and anticipates the major theme of this short letter.[13] While the author exhibits an acquaintance with Greek literary culture, probably no other New Testament author addresses the tensions between Christ and culture as thoroughly as 1 Peter.

Whereas the *Epistle to Diognetus* is written to explain the unusual behavior to suspicious outsiders, 1 Peter is written to encourage insiders as they face the challenges of living as exiles in their own land. Their exile existence is suggested in the opening blessing (1:3–12), which offers hope

---

11 Selwyn, *First Epistle of St. Peter,* 25. In this chapter, I will refer to the author as Peter although authorship is disputed. On the stylistic characteristics of 1 Peter, see Elliott, *1 Peter,* 41–79.

12. Schröger, *Gemeinde im 1. Petrusbrief,* 208.

13. *Parepidēmos* refers to one who stays for a while in a strange or foreign place, a "resident alien" (BDAG, 775). The term refers to those who were only passing through a city, not establishing themselves there. In the LXX, the Israelites present themselves as nomads, without hearth or home (Gen 23:4; Ps 39:13). See Spicq, *parepidēmos,* TLNT 3:42–43.

in the midst of the community's grief and testing (1:6–7). The nature of this testing becomes apparent in the consistent references to the community's exile existence and suffering. Believers suffer "for doing what is right" (3:14; cf. 2:19–20) and because they are Christians (4:16; cf. 4:1).

Peter encourages the readers to live in reverent fear during the time of their exile (*paroikia*). The word *paroikia* (1:17; cf. 2:11) reflects the social situation of "alien residence" in a foreign land. The image evokes the experience of the Israelites who, in several instances, resided in a land that was not their own. The *paroikoi* were exposed to the various forms of suspicion, hostility, and suffering that strangers in a foreign land commonly experience. Abraham was called to go from his country, his kindred, and his father's house (Gen 12:1). During a famine, Abraham went down to Egypt and resided as an alien (Gen 12:10). His grandchildren and the children of his grandchildren became "aliens in the land of Egypt" (Lev 19:34). Israelites later lived as exiles in Babylonian captivity. Even when they were secure in their own land, Yahweh commanded them to be different from the surrounding nations (Lev 18:1–4).[14] The author later addresses them as "aliens and exiles" (*paroikoi kai parepidēmoi*, 2:11), the key metaphor that 1 Peter employs to express the Christian relationship to culture.[15]

The image indicates their tenuous relationship with their culture (1 Pet 1:1; 2:11), implying a clear distance from the society's values and ideals.[16] The Christians live in a time of exile (*paroikia*) as if they are in a foreign country (1:17),[17] alienated from the "futile ways inherited from [their] ancestors (*patroparadotou*, 1:18),[18] which were dominated by ignorance

14. Elliott, *1 Peter*, 368.

15. Feldmeier, *Die Christen als Fremde*, 8. The combination of the two expressions *paroikoi kai parepidēmoi* occurs only in the Old Testament, namely in LXX Gen 23:4, Ps 38:13, and 1 Pet 2:11. In Gen 23:4 Abraham refers to himself as "a stranger and resident alien residing among you" in his negotiations with the Hittites. In reflecting on his own mortality, David says: "For I am your passing guest, an alien, like all my forebears" (Ps 39:12).

16. For example, the extremely rare *parepidēmos* is used by Polybius to refer to Greeks living in Rome, while Aristophanes of Byzantium (the grammarian, not to be confused with the poet) uses the term to describe the position of foreigners within a city. See Polybius, *Histories* 32.6.4 (the context involves how the Romans assisted the Greek resident aliens by opposing the tyrant Charops) and Aristophanes, *Nomina aetatum* (*fragmentum Parisinum*). Cited in Himes, "First Peter's Identity Theology and the Community of Faith," 119.

17. *Paroikia* is the state of being in a strange locality without citizenship (BDAG, 779).

18. According to Brox, "the author of 1 Peter is the first Christian, as far as we know, to use the word *patroparadotos* ('handed down from one's father/ancestors' [BDAG, 789])," which was normally used in a positive sense with a negative connotation for the lifestyle from which one has been liberated (*Der erste Petrusbrief*, 81).

(*agnoia*) and desires (*epithumiai*, 1:14; cf. 4:4). They remain foreigners in their own cities, alienated even from their families, because they have withdrawn from many of its activities.[19] The Christians in 1 Peter are not aliens and exiles because of their ethnicity or social class, inasmuch as Peter indicates that their neighbors are surprised that believers no longer join them in dissipation (4:3–4).[20]

Because the community has withdrawn from the society's activities, they are the objects of abuse from their neighbors, who "malign [them] as evildoers" (2:12; 3:16) and abuse them (3:16; 4:4). They suffer for the sake of righteousness (3:13); outsiders ask them to explain the "reason (*apologia*) for their hope" (3:15). They suffer for the name "Christian" (4:16), and they can only anticipate that a "fiery ordeal" of further testing will occur before the end (4:12–19). They may take comfort, however, in the fact that other believers (5:9) throughout the world experience the same suffering.

The author offers consolation to the readers' exile existence, indicating that Jesus was also rejected by his own society. He was the stone that the builders rejected (2:7–8). The author focuses on Jesus's suffering rather than on his death. He "suffered for" them (2:21), "suffered for sins" (3:18), and "suffered in the flesh" (4:1). When believers suffer, they follow in the footsteps of Jesus (2:21) and share in the sufferings of Christ (4:13). Thus the task of the community is to maintain their status as aliens and exiles in their own land, leaving behind their former practices.

A New Identity

Recognizing that exiles survive only as they live in communities, as Elliott has demonstrated, Peter describes a "home for the homeless," an identity that strengthens them when they suffer abuse. They are the "living stones" (2:5) who come to the "living stone" that was rejected by humankind, but chosen by God (2:4).[21] Together they are being built up into a spiritual house (2:5). The author provides an identity for them that separates them from their culture and incorporates them into Israel. They have, like Israel, been chosen by God (cf. Deut 7:7–11). They are not only exiles like Israel, but

19. Cf. the later charge against Christians by Minucius Felix, *Octavius* 12: "You do not go to our shows, you have no part in our processions, you are not present at our public banquets, you shrink in horror from our sacred games."

20. John H. Elliott advocated a thesis that the term *paroikoi* describes the social marginalization that Christians experienced before conversion. See his *A Home for the Homeless*, 48. However, the fact that the readers no longer join them in dissipation (4:3–4) indicates that they are marginalized as a result of their conversion.

21. Horn, "Christen in der Diaspora," 5.

"the elect exiles" of the diaspora (1:1) and an "elect race, a royal priesthood" (2:9), who have been called out of darkness into God's marvelous light (2:9),[22] a people who were once no people (2:10). The language of election and calling, drawn from Israel's Scriptures, indicates that this gentile community has been incorporated into the people of God.[23] They take on the collective identity of Israel as the people of God. Although the readers are gentile converts, they are instructed to live no longer like the gentiles (2:12; 4:3). The command to Israel, "you shall be holy" (Lev 19:2), is also the requirement for the church, for whom separation is not a misfortune but the vocation to which God has called the elect people. The exhortation to a new pattern of behavior (*anastrophē*, 1:15, 18; 2:12; 3:1, 16) is consistent with the incorporation into Israel's story. The behavior consists of abandonment of their former desires (1:14; 4:3), the malice, "guile, insincerity, envy, and slander" of their former lives (2:1), and the adoption of a new way of life of mutual love and support (1:22–23; 4:8), hospitality, and service to one another (4:9–10). This identity is the basis for their moral conduct.

The poetic blessing in 1:3–11 celebrates the fact that they are the privileged ones; they have been born again to a living hope and unfading inheritance (1:3–4, 23). Their current suffering is a test that will result in the salvation of their souls (1:9). Indeed, the sufferings of Christ are the culmination of the expectations of the prophets (1:10–12). As the author says, "They were not serving themselves, but you" (1:12); even angels desired to look at the days that the community now has seen (1:12). Their separation from the culture was nothing less than a ransom from their previous way of life (1:18).

They now live in a new family that shares their alien status. They belong to the "household of God" that will share in the fiery ordeal (4:17), which includes not only the local believers but also brothers and sisters throughout the world (5:9). Having been estranged from their physical families, they live in a new family that provides the loving care that they have lost. Peter urges the readers to have "genuine mutual love" and to "love one another deeply from the heart" (1:23; cf. 4:8). They practice hospitality to one another (4:8) and share their gifts (4:9–10). Together they are the living stones of a "spiritual house" (2:4). Thus they share their exile status as they share in the sufferings of Christ.

---

22. Cf. the prayer of Joseph in Joseph and Aseneth (8:9–10): "Lord, God of my father Israel, the powerful one of Jacob, who gave life to all [things], and called them from darkness to light, and from error to truth, and from death to life, you lord, bless this virgin and renew her by your spirit and form her anew by your hidden hand, and make her alive again by your life." Cited in Seland, *Strangers in the Light*, 66.

23. According to the classic election text, God chose Israel from all nations as an expression of divine love (Deut 7:7–8; 14:2).

Exiles and Society

While love and mutual support unite the believers and separate them from their environment, they nevertheless continue to interact with the existing society, living within the institutions of their own time. Their identity as the people of God (2:9–10) is now the foundation for the behavior that Peter encourages in the new section that begins in 2:11. "Aliens and exiles" (2:11) must now ask what practices of their culture they reject and which ones they continue. They do away with the "desires of the flesh" (2:11) that once characterized their existence (1:14; 2:1; 4:2) within their culture. Because they have separated themselves from many of the practices of their neighbors, they now live with the suspicions that they are "evildoers" (2:12; cf. 3:17; 4:15) who undermine the institutions of society. Consequently, the author introduces the instructions for life within society's institutions with the encouragement to demonstrate "good behavior among the gentiles" (2:12) to counteract their suspicions.[24] Their task is to do "good works" in order that others may "glorify God on the day of visitation" (2:12). Indeed, "doing good" (*agathopoiōn*) is a refrain throughout the letter. Believers are expected to be "do-gooders" with respect to government authorities (2:12), slavery (2:20), and the household (3:6). He concludes the insistence on doing good within these institutions by citing Ps 34:10–12, which appears to be written in a situation of marginalization.[25] The Psalmist encourages the listeners, "Those who desire life and desire to see good days, let them keep their tongues from evil and their lips from speaking deceit; let them turn away from evil and do good; let them seek peace and pursue it" (1 Pet 3:10–11). While suffering is a reality that they face, it is better to suffer for doing good than for doing evil (3:17; cf. 2:20; 4:19). By doing good they "will silence the ignorance of the foolish" (2:15).

In 2:13—3:7, the author offers specific examples of doing good, addressing Christian conduct within the institutions of the government (2:13–17), slavery (2:18–25), and marriage (3:1–7). In each instance he addresses believers who interact with unbelievers, and in each instance (2:13, 18, 3:1) he introduces the instructions with a form of *hypotassein* ("be submissive"), the conduct expected of everyone in the society. As Paul indicates in Romans 13:2, the opposite of submission is resistance (*antitassein*). The same term is used in the author's exhortation to those who are younger to submit (*hypotagete*) to the elders. As the etymology suggests, *hypo-tasso*, means "to

---

24. The author distinguishes the readers from the gentiles, although all evidence suggests that the readers are gentile converts. He has thus given them an identity as participants in Israel (cf. 1 Thess 4:4).

25. See Williams, *Good Works in 1 Peter*, 248.

place oneself under an ordered structure,"[26] with the emphasis on "order" (*taxis*) rather than "under" (*hypo*).[27]

Because forms of *hypotassein* introducing the relationship with basic social institutions is commonplace in ancient ethics, some interpreters have regarded 2:13—3:7 as an ethic of accommodation to societal norms.[28] However, the verb takes on a new dimension and motivation in Christian literature, especially 1 Peter. The author concludes this section with a summary, indicating the qualities of life that are appropriate for insiders and outsiders. He encourages the readers to have "unity of the Spirit" (*homophrones*), sympathy, and love for one another, a tender heart, and humility (3:8–9). Believers do not return evil for evil or abuse for abuse (3:9). In 5:5–6, submission is a dimension of humility. Indeed, Jesus was the submissive one who did not retaliate, leaving an example for his disciples to follow (2:23).

In response to the rumors that believers undermine the established order (2:12), Peter instructs believers not to rebel, but to demonstrate the good behavior that is expected of everyone (2:12). Peter encourages believers to be submissive to "every human institution" (2:13–17), including the emperor and governors, agreeing with Paul (Rom 13:1–2) that governmental institutions are sent by God to maintain order. Inasmuch as submission is not inconsistent with freedom (2:16), the task of believers is to use the freedom for good rather than evil (2:16–17), not provoking the state to violence against them. The stance of believers is summarized in the exhortation, "Honor everyone. Love the family of believers" (2:17), which distinguishes between the response to government (to honor) and the response to the community of believers (to love).

Like Ephesians and Colossians, 1 Peter includes a household code (cf. Eph 5:21—6:9; Col 3:18—4:1). Unlike these letters, however, Peter assumes that slaves and wives live in the households of unbelievers. He encourages slaves to be submissive even to harsh masters (2:18–19),[29] indicating that it is grace (*charis*) to suffer unjustly (2:19). The primary motivation is that submission to unjust suffering is the path of Jesus. To submit to unjust suffering is to follow "in his steps." The extended instructions to slaves, including

---

26. BDAG, 1042.

27. Goppelt, *Theology of the New Testament*, 2:168: the passage "wanted to say primarily: enlist yourselves in the institutions of society."

28. Cf. Balch, *Let Wives Be Submissive*; Balch, "Hellenism/Acculturation in 1 Peter."

29. See Schröger, *Gemeinde im 1. Petrusbrief*, 149: "Neither in the Jewish laws nor in Hellenistic wisdom nor in the Stoic lists of duties was it customary to address slaves." The early Christians were the first to address slaves. "Here they were not only subjects whose fate one decided, but people to whom one spoke."

the hymn-like summary of the suffering of Jesus (2:21–25), describes the path of discipleship for minority communities.[30]

Although wives who have become Christians without their husbands' consent have already exercised their freedom, Peter instructs them to be submissive, addressing them also with the verb *hypotassein*. Their attire (not by "braiding your hair, and by wearing gold ornaments or fine clothing") is a sign of chaste behavior (3:3) and of gentle and quiet spirit. That is, their attire indicates their submission to the norms of their society and their submission to their husbands.[31]

Peter instructs believers to respond to this hostile environment with behavior that is appropriate to the whole society. He instructs them to "do good" (*agathopoiein*) in order to silence the rumors about believers. By doing good the believers demonstrate that they live within the civic institutions. Slaves submit to their masters, "doing good" (2:20). Wives submit to their husbands in order to "do good" (3:6). Thus believers demonstrate by their good works that they live and work within the society and its institutions. They live an alternative way of life in the present social setting, demonstrating that they were not undermining society and its institutions. In any case, the community did not seek to exert social or political pressure but to give public witness to a new way of life.[32]

The ethical instructions in 1 Peter demonstrate that, while the community has separated its practices from those of society, becoming aliens in their own land because of their Christian confession, their values overlap with those of their society in important ways.[33] The community's task is to distinguish between the moral practices that constitute the holy life and the good works recognized by society. Even where the Christians' values overlap with those of their society, their motivation is different. Submission to society's institutions is for them the path of Jesus, their example of submission to injustice.

Exiles and the Missionary Task

Not only do the believers attempt to live peacefully within the pagan culture, but they also engage in missions. An alien community cannot change social structure, but it has a mission to the world. Like Israel, their vocation

30. See the discussion of 1 Pet 2:18–25 in ch. 9.

31. On the cultural expectations for feminine attire, see 1 Tim 2:9–10 and the discussion in ch. 9.

32. Volf, "Soft Difference," 20.

33. Williams, *Good Works in 1 Peter*, 257.

is not to retreat from the world but to "proclaim the mighty acts of him who called [them] out of darkness into his marvelous light" (2:9). By taking on the identity of Israel, the church also takes on its vocation, as the allusion to Isa 43:21 indicates that Israel has been called to be a "light to the nations" (Isa 49:6).

The proclamation of God's mighty acts is necessarily accompanied by appropriate Christian behavior. Continuing to live among the gentiles, they exhibit good behavior, which not only refutes the slanders against them but results in the positive response of their neighbors, who will see (*epopteu-ontes*) their "good works and glorify God when he comes to judge" (2:12, literally "on the day of visitation"). Their good deeds as citizens will silence those who slander them (2:15). Undoubtedly, the refusal of slaves to rebel will silence those who accuse Christians of undermining society. Wives submit to their husbands in the hope of winning them (3:1). Thus they witness to their neighbors both by words and deeds.[34] Believers respond to hostile questions about their hope by giving a defense (*apologia*) of their hope. According to Miroslav Volf:

> The distance from society that comes from the new birth into a living hope does not isolate from society. For hope in God, the Creator and Savior of the whole world, knows no boundaries. Instead of leading to isolation, this distance is a presupposition of mission. Without distance, churches can only give speeches that others have written for them and only go places where others lead them. To make a difference, one must be different.[35]

Although interpreters debate whether 1 Peter is a call for believers to distance themselves from their culture or to accommodate to it, one does not need to choose between these two approaches. This epistle expresses a tension between difference and enculturation. The dominant metaphor of alien stresses the separation from culture while "doing good among the gentiles" indicates that believers live within the structures of society and seek its common good. Even when Christians live within the institutions of society, they view them within the Christian focus on following in the footsteps of the one who suffered unjustly.

---

34. See Stenschke, "Mission and Conversion in the First Epistle of Peter," 236.
35. Volf, "Soft Difference," 24.

JAMES AND FRIENDSHIP WITH THE WORLD

In writing to "the twelve tribes of the dispersion" (1:1), James joins other NT writers in connecting his community with Israel's identity. The advice that he offers is consistent with the values expressed in Israel's wisdom literature. The author attempts to create communal solidarity in the way of life indicated in the series of imperatives. In addressing the readers as siblings (1:2, 9, 16, 19; 2:1, 14–15; 3:1; 4:11), he follows other New Testament writers in describing the church as a family that carries out familial obligations. If a brother or sister is in need, the believer's task is to take care of the needs of the body (2:14–15). The frequent use of "one another" (allēlōn) also points to the solidarity of the family. Members of the community do not speak evil of one another (4:11) or complain against one another (5:9). They confess their sins to one another and pray for one another (5:16).[36]

Communal solidarity is necessary for establishing boundaries. These sharp boundaries are indicated in James's distinction between God and the world. James uses "world" five times (1:27; 2:5; 3:6; 4:4 [bis]) to designate the culture system that is alien to the values of James's community. According to 1:27, "true and undefiled religion before God" is to "care for orphans and widows in their affliction, to keep oneself without defect from the world" (1:27). Thus he recognizes two poles: "before God" and "from the world."[37] For the community to remain "unstained from the world," it must maintain a line of separation between God's valuation and "the world." Readers are challenged to observe the boundary between the world's values and the will of God.

According to 4:4, believers face the choice between the two sets of values: those of the world and those of believers. On the one hand, James indicates that community members do not receive the answer to their prayers because they ask only for the benefit of their pleasures (4:3). They should know that "friendship with the world is enmity against God, and those who become friends of the world are enemies of God (4:4). The alternative to the world is for readers to submit to God (4:7) and draw near to God (4:8).

James offers a sharp distinction between the rich and the poor. Although he speaks of both in the third person (2:1–7), he identifies the believers with neither. He insists on impartiality toward both rich and poor when they enter their assembly, but gives special condemnation to the rich, declaring that the rich "oppress you and haul you into court" (2:6) and "blaspheme the good name by which you are called" (2:7). Thus James assumes that the community faces hostility from the society. Similarly, James

---

36. On allēlōn in family relationships, see Schäfer, "Gemeinde als "Bruderschaft," 25. See also Thompson, Moral Formation according to Paul, 57.

37. Lockett, "Strong and Weak Lines," 394.

addresses the rich in 5:1–6 in prophetic terms, declaring that they "murdered the just one."

Partiality is a violation of the "royal law" that "you shall love your neighbor as yourself" (2:8–9; cf. Lev 19:18). While Paul uses this passage to encourage love within the community, here it is not certain whether the love command extends outside the community, for James does not specify the identity of the poor.

In 3:13–18 he describes two types of wisdom: one is from below and the other is from above, and he encourages his readers to demonstrate the wisdom from above by their works. The wisdom from below is characterized by "envy and selfish ambition, . . . disorder and wickedness of every kind (3:16); it is "earthly, unspiritual, and devilish" (3:15). The wisdom from above is characterized by the opposite features; it is a life that is "pure, then peaceable, gentle, willing to yield, full of mercy and good fruits" (3:17). Those who exhibit the wisdom from above, therefore, have separated themselves from the values of the culture.

Although James draws sharp boundaries between the community and the world, the epistle reflects the author's good Greek education. Luke Timothy Johnson notes that the language of the epistle "is a form of clear and correct *koine* with some ambitions toward rhetorical flourish."[38] In addition to the author's mastery of grammar, the composition is rich in literary rhetorical features such as alliteration (1:2–3; 3:17), *parachesis* (the use of assonance, 1:24), and *paronomasia* (play on similar sounding words, 2:4, 20; 4:14).[39]

James also employs the diatribe, a familiar teaching method in the Greco-Roman world. This distinct teaching style appears in Jas 2:18–26 and includes an imaginary interlocutor's objection ("but some will say," 2:18), the direct address "you empty person" (2:19), and the use of rhetorical questions (2:20–21).[40]

Further evidence of Hellenistic influence may be observed in James's use of topics common in Greco-Roman moral teaching. Some of the moral topics used in James include the unity of virtue, the mirror as a source of self-reflection, the tongue as full of poison, the common images of the charioteer and pilot for self-control and the fundamental convictions that speech must be controlled, that friends correct each other, and that wars arise from one's passions.[41] When James says that "friendship with the world is enmity

38. Johnson, *Letter of James*.
39. Lockett, "Strong and Weak Lines," 400.
40. Lockett, "Strong and Weak Lines," 400.
41. Johnson, *Brother of Jesus, Friend of God*, 18.

against God," he urges the readers to separate from the values of the society: the pursuit of pleasure (4:1), jealousy, quarreling (3:16), the abuse of the poor (cf. 2:1–11), and the engagement in commerce without discerning the will of God (4:1–4). James urges the readers to be a counterculture that rejects the world's values and demonstrates a love for neighbors (2:8–11).

REVELATION AND THE ENDANGERED PEOPLE

The Apocalypse, whose author identifies himself as John (1:4, 9), was written at a time of great distress (*thlipsis*), which he shares with the seven churches to which he writes (1:9; 2:9, 10, 22; 7:14). Apparently, at least one has died (2:13), and others will be put into prison (2:10) for the sake of the gospel. The author is now in exile on the island of Patmos (1:9). The letters to the seven churches (chs. 2–3) indicate the church's tenuous status within the society and the prospect of overt persecution. Although tradition identifies the persecution with Domitian's reign (AD 81–96), the evidence for an organized persecution under Domitian remains uncertain.[42] However, the worship of the emperor was pervasive in the population, and believers evoked the hostility of the populace because of their rejection of the emperor cult. The New Testament witnesses consistently describe the hostility of the society toward Christ-believers, but only Revelation speaks consistently of the prospect of martyrdom at the hands of Rome.

The author offers a bleak portrayal of Roman power in chapters 12–18, describing the representatives of the Roman state in mythological language. The fiery dragon with seven heads makes war against the woman and her children (12:17). A beast rises out of the sea, having ten horns and seven heads, having blasphemous names on his heads (13:1). The world worships the beast (13:3–4). The great whore of Babylon—a code name for Rome— sits on the beast with blasphemous names; she is "drunk with the blood of the saints" (17:6). The "seven heads" of the beast are seven mountains on which the woman is seated. The reference is obviously to Rome, which sits on seven hills. The angel urges the church: "Come out of her, my people, so that you do not take part in her sins" (18:4). This plea is a call for clear distance between the church and the society.[43]

The consistent challenge to the church is to endure despite the persecutions that they will continue to face. John himself participates in the persecutions "with patient endurance" (*hypomonē*, 1:9). He praises the churches at Ephesus and Thyatira for their patient endurance (2:2–3, 19).

42. Klauck, "Gemeinde und Gesellschaft," 245.
43. See Klauck, "Gemeinde und Gesellschaft," 244.

When the beast threatens the community, he says, "This is a call for endurance of the saints" (13:10). When assimilation is the easy path (cf. 14:1–11), John again calls for the endurance of the saints (14:12). As the end of the drama indicates, the community endures because it looks beyond the persecutions of the moment to the new heavens and new earth.

CONCLUSION

Like the church throughout the ages, the churches addressed in the letters written in the latter part of the first century faced varying degrees of hostility from their culture. In some instances the readers were subject to discrimination, verbal abuse, and disdain. In other instances the churches faced overt persecution from their neighbors that resulted in death. With their confession that Jesus is Lord and call for conversion from all other deities, Christians disturbed the pluralism of ancient societies, separating believers from their family and friends. The authors addressed the pressure to assimilate to the culture by establishing a strong ecclesial identity for believers, maintaining that they were the privileged heirs of faithful people of the past and even the Lord himself, who faced the abuse of his contemporaries. They now cared for one another, replacing the families that had abandoned them.

In many respects, the contemporary church faces challenges that are similar to those faced in the first century. The overt persecution of Christians remains a reality in many parts of the world while in the Western world believers face the dilemma of living as exiles in their own land. The church has survived discrimination and oppression because of its refusal to accommodate to the values of the larger culture. Believers have not retreated from culture but have sought the public good, living as good citizens and loving their neighbors. Because they are separate from the culture, they conduct a mission to the culture.

9

Middle-Class Morality?

In George Bernard Shaw's *Pygmalion* (later adapted into the musical *My Fair Lady*), Alfred P. Doolittle laments that his new wealth has forced him to adopt "middle-class morality," a new set of rules that were never expected of him in his previous social class among the poorest citizens. "Middle-class morality" is an approximate rendering of "christliche Bürgerlichkeit," a term that Martin Dibelius used for the ethics of the Pastoral Epistles,[1] rendered in the English translation as "good citizenship." Dibelius introduced this phrase in an excursus on the instruction for believers to conduct a quiet and peaceful life (1 Tim 2:2). After Dibelius, other scholars applied the term *bürgerlich* (bourgeois, middle class) to the ethics of these letters. Siegfried Schulz has a chapter on "bürgerliches Christentum" in his *Neutestamentlichen Ethik*.[2] The slogan "bürgerliches Christentum" became commonplace among interpreters for describing the conventional morality in the culture adopted by Christians.

Two texts in the Pastoral Epistles that exemplify the conventional morality, according to Dibelius, are 1 Tim 2:1–2 and Titus 2:12. In 1 Tim 2:2,

1. Dibelius, *Die Pastoralbriefe*. The English translation of Dibelius renders the term "good citizenship."

2. *Semnos/semnotēs* is used to describe divinities and things pertaining to them. Applied to people, it refers to qualities that demand respect, fear, or reverence. It is especially used for conduct that is honorable and dignified. See Spicq, *semnos*, TLNT 3:244–45.

Paul appeals to the readers to pray for the rulers in order that the believers may "live a quiet and peaceful life in all godliness (*eusebeia*) and dignity (*semnotēs*)."[3] These categories are common in Hellenistic ethics but not in the undisputed letters of Paul.[4] In Titus 2:12 Paul encourages readers to put away the previous way of life and "to live lives that are self-controlled (*sōphronōs*), upright (*dikaiōs*), and godly (*eusebōs*)." According to Dibelius, 1 Tim 2:2 describes the characteristic "ethics of good citizenship": the peaceful relationship with authority, the wish for a "quiet and peaceful life," and the virtues of piety (*eusebeia*) and dignity (*semnotēs*). In Titus Greek cardinal virtues (*sōphonē*, *dikaiosynē*, and *eusebeia*) appear, all of which are part of the conventional morality of the period.

The ethics of "good citizenship" emerges with the loss of eschatological urgency, the end of a conflict with the authorities, the institutionalization of the church into established offices, and the assimilation to the values of the larger culture. The church no longer lives in the mode of "as if not" (cf. 1 Cor 7:29–31) but adapts to the conventional ethics of the larger society. The ethic of the family takes on a special significance in "christliche bürgerlichkeit," as the contrast between Paul's statements about the family in 1 Cor 7 and in the disputed letters indicates.

The ethics of "good citizenship," with its emphasis on the family, is particularly evident in the Pastoral Epistles and in the household codes of Ephesians, Colossians, and 1 Peter. According to S. Schulz, the household code is the symptom of a dangerous adaptation of early Christianity into the existing social relationships. "Instead of letting the eschatological message of the kingdom of God shape the dominant forms of authority, early Catholicism [i.e., Ephesians, Colossians, 1 Peter, and the Pastoral Epistles], drew the opposite conclusion by regarding the dominant order as divinely ordained."[5]

THE HOUSEHOLD CODES IN EPHESIANS AND COLOSSIANS

The household codes do not appear in the undisputed letters of Paul but appear in Colossians, Ephesians, and 1 Peter in various forms. First Timothy and Titus expand the household code to include members of the house church (cf. 1 Tim 2:1—3:16; 5:1—6:2; Titus 2:1—3:3). Numerous studies

3. In this chapter, I will identify the author of the Pastoral Epistles as Paul. While the actual authorship is disputed, the implied author is the apostle Paul.

4. In the undisputed letters of Paul, *semnos* appears only in Phil 4:8.

5. Schulz, *Neutestamentliche Ethik*, 567.

have compared these household codes, described by Luther as *Haustafeln*, to antecedents in ancient literature, maintaining that the household codes in the New Testament reflect the conventional morality of the period and the accommodation to the values of the society.

According to the dominant narrative of Christian origins, the inclusion of the *Haustafel* marks a radical break and conservative reaction to Paul's ethical instruction.[6] Paul is an egalitarian who joined the first generation of believers in proclaiming that "there is no longer slave or free, male and female" (Gal 3:28).[7] According to Elisabeth Schüssler-Fiorenza, "While a few scholars think that the demands for the obedience and submission of wives, children, and slaves are genuinely Christian, the majority sees the domestic code as a later Christian adaptation of a Graeco-Roman or Jewish-Hellenistic philosophical-theological code and the common morality of the day."[8] Thus the household code is commonly regarded as the reversal of Pauline countercultural egalitarianism of the first generation to adoption of conventional morality in the next generation. James Crouch suggested that it is a Christian creation in response to the cries for freedom among women and slaves.[9] Others argue that Christians appropriated it from the philosophical tradition via Hellenistic Judaism to mitigate the hostility of those who were offended by Christian egalitarianism.[10] According to this view, the household code is evidence of the surrender of the countercultural ethic and the accommodation to the culture.

Since the management of the household was a common theme in antiquity, the early Christian household codes had numerous antecedents but no precise parallels to all its features.[11] Whereas ancient household codes primarily addressed those in authority over the proper treatment of their subordinates, the household code in these letters addresses each member of the household, including those who have an inferior status. The use of the plural address reinforces the corporate nature of the community's hearing of these instructions.[12] Klaus Berger has observed the parallels to specific instructions in pagan and Jewish gnomic literature but does not find the combination of features that are present in the household codes in the New

6. See Stambaugh and Balch, *Social World of the First Christians*, 55.

7. See Crouch, *Origin of the Colossian Haustafel*, 124. Schüssler Fiorenza, *In Memory of Her*, 253–54; O'Brien Wicker, "First Century Marriage Ethics," 149.

8. Schüssler Fiorenza, *In Memory of Her*, 254.

9. Crouch, *Origin*, 124.

10. Balch, *Let Wives Be Submissive*, 80.

11. Hartman ("Code and Context," 188) speaks of a "rather developed root system."

12. Thompson, *Moral Formation according to Paul*, 191.

Testament. He is probably correct that "nests" of specific features existed in antiquity, which early Christians adapted for their own. Thus the *Haustafel* was probably not a static form, but existed in considerable variety from the beginning.

All the *Haustafeln* contain instructions for wives to be submissive to their husbands. That wives should submit to their husbands was commonplace in philosophical literature, in common folk wisdom,[13] in popular moral advice,[14] and in Jewish summaries of the law (Philo, *Hyp*.7.2–4; Josephus, *C. Ap.* 2.201). Similarly, the common expectation in ancient Hellenistic texts was for husbands to love their wives.[15] The obedience of slaves and children was also an unquestioned expectation.[16] Jewish and Hellenistic sources also attest to the responsibilities of masters and parents not to abuse those under their control. The *Haustafeln* are not unique among New Testament writings, however, in proposing commonplace morality. John Barclay's comment that "the Christian movement could hardly be expected, perhaps, to *invent* new vices"[17] is appropriate in describing virtues. While Christians apparently considered some vices and virtues from antiquity antithetical to their moral values, an acceptance of other moral values was inevitable.

While the household codes were largely consistent with conventional morality, Christ-believers did not uncritically adopt them from the culture. Indeed, the household codes in Colossians and Ephesians appear at the end of a lengthy paraenetic section in which Paul has described vices to "put to death" (Col 3:5) and "put away" (Eph 4:22, 25; Col 3:8) and moral practices to "put on" (Eph 4:24; Col 3:10). The vices listed belong to the old existence of believers (Eph 4:22; Col 3:7) when they shared the common practices of

13 The Delphic Precepts, composed of 145 commandments representing popular morality, included instructions for the honor that children owe to parents ("respect your parents," 4), the proper treatment of children ("Do not curse your sons," 94), and the husband's rule over the wife ("Rule your wife," 94), all in the apodictic form. Thus the commonplace values of antiquity called for the submission of wives, the obedience of children, and the obedience of slaves. See additional gnomic sentences in Berger, *Formen*, 197.

14 Cf. Plutarch, *Conj. praec.* 142E: "So is it with women also; if they subordinate (*hypotattousai*) themselves to their husbands, they are commended; but if they want to have control, they cut a sorrier figure than the subjects of their control" (LCL).

15. Charondas, *Frag.* 62; Theano, *Frag.* 199; Cf. 4 Macc 2:11; *Ps. Phoc.* 195. On Neopythagorean texts, see Balch, "Neopythagorean Moralists and the New Testament," 397.

16. Diogenes Laertius, *Lives* 7.120: "The Stoics approve also of honouring parents and brothers in the second place next after the gods." Cf. Josephus, *C. Ap.* 2.206: "Honor to parents is second only to honor to God." *Pseudo-Phocylides* warns fathers against abusing their children, instructing them, "Do not be harsh with your children, but be gentle" (207).

17. Barclay, "Ordinary but Different," 38.

their environment. Indeed, they belong to a community that is unlike any other in their society in which "there is no longer Greek and Jew, circumcised and uncircumcised, barbarian, Scythian, slave and free" (Col 3:11; cf. Eph 2:11–22). According to Ephesians, the believers are "the children of light," having once lived in darkness (5:8). Now their task is to recognize that the people in this new community are "members of one another" (Eph 4:25) who no longer live in darkness or associate with the "children of disobedience" (5:7, 11). The reciprocal response of members, reflected in the emphasis on "one another" (Eph 4:25, 32; 5:19; Col 3:9, 13, 16), indicates the family solidarity of the group, which unites the community and separates it from the surrounding culture.

The instruction to the household code in Ephesians, "Be submissive (*hypotassomenoi*) to one another in the fear of Christ" (Eph 5:21) is a bridge extending the emphasis on reciprocity within the community to existence within the household (Eph 5:21—6:9). Indeed, *hypotassein* is used elsewhere for the relationship of believers to each other (1 Cor 16:16). In Eph 5:22 it refers to the submission of wives.

While *hypotassein* is commonplace in ancient instructions for wives, its use in Ephesians, Colossians (3:18), and 1 Peter takes on a significance that it does not have in ancient societies, for it reflects the values of communities in which all members "submit to one another" (Eph 5:21), count others better then themselves (Phil 2:3), look to the interests of others, do not seek their own (Phil 2:4; cf. Rom 12:10). It is the expression of humility (*tapeinophrosynē*, Phil 2:3; Col 3:12) and the opposite of the grasping for power (cf. Rom 13:1–6). Indeed, both Jesus and Paul "humbled themselves" (*etapeinōsen*) by reversing the values of their own society. Jesus "humbled himself" at the cross (Phil 2:8), and Paul humbled himself by working with his hands (2 Cor 11:7). Paul's opponents criticized him for being "humble" (*tapeinos*, 2 Cor 10:1). Thus while the advice to wives to submit to their husbands corresponds to conventional morality, it takes on a new dimension within the community that is shaped by the reevaluation of humility and concern for others.[18]

While Paul does not reject the institutions of society mentioned in the household code, he places everyday activities under the sovereignty of the exalted Christ. Indeed, in a preface to the household code in Colossians, Paul encourages the community, "Whatever you do in word or deed, do all in the name of the Lord" (Col 3:17). This submission is "as is fitting in the Lord" (Col 3:18), and "as to the Lord" (Eph 5:22).

18. Thompson, *Moral Formation according to Paul*, 196.

Forms of *hypotassō* appear three times in the instructions for believers in 1 Peter (2:13, 18; 3:1). The first reference echoes the Pauline instruction to be submissive to government authorities (2:13; cf. Rom 13:1–7). The latter two references appear in the address to slaves (1 Pet 2:18) and wives (1 Pet 3:1) in the Petrine version of the household code in 2:18—3:7. The extended argument for the submission of slaves in 2:18–25 suggests that their situation is a central focus of the household code. Their submission is followed by the hymnic recitation of the Christian story. Indeed, the situation of slaves is paradigmatic for all believers. To suffer the indignities of slavery was nothing less than following in the footsteps of Jesus, who "suffered for you" (2:18), refusing to return abuse for abuse (2:23). To be submissive is not only the calling of slaves but to all who follow Jesus.

Addressing wives who have unbelieving husbands, Peter follows earlier tradition (Col 3:18; Eph 5:22), urging wives to be submissive to their own husbands. Although they have probably already displeased their husbands by becoming Christians,[19] they nevertheless practice submission, following the common expectation of both Jewish and Greco-Roman societies. Condemnation of luxury and extravagance was commonplace among Jewish, Greek, and Roman writers. Peter even insists that they dress in a way that demonstrates submission, conforming to ancient expectations for the chaste wife.[20] For example, Diodorus (*History* 12.28) mentions the wearing of gold jewelry or a garment with a purple border as signifying a "courtesan," and Epictetus (*Ench.* 40) laments that from an early age girls tend to beautify themselves with outward adornments. As a maxim in the *Sentences of Sextus* declares, "A wife who likes adornment is not faithful."[21]

---

19. Cf. Plutarch, *Conj. praec* 19. "Wherefore it is becoming for a wife to worship and to know only the gods that her husband believes in, and to shut the door tight upon all queer rituals and outlandish superstitions (LCL). Cf. Xenophon, *Oec.* 7.8; Dionysius of Hallicarnassus, *Ant. Rom* 2.25.1; Cicero, *Leg.* 2.8.19–22).

20. Cf. Plutarch, *Conj. praec.* 25: "The Sicilian despot sent clothing and jewellery of the costly kind to the daughters of Lysander; but Lysander would not accept them, saying, 'These adornments will disgrace my daughters far more than they will adorn them.'" Cf. *Conj. praec.* 142: "It is not gold or precious stones or scarlet that makes her such, but whatever invests her with that something which betokens dignity, good behavior, and modesty."

21. See Winter, *Roman Wives, Roman Widows*, 103–8. Winter refers to the Neo-Pythagorean letter Melissa to Kleareta (ca. first century AD), which states: "It is necessary then for the free and modest (*eleutherin kai sophrona*) wife to live with her lawful husband adorned with quietness, white and clean in her dress, plain but not costly, simple but not elaborate or excessive. For she must reject garments shot with purple or gold. For these are used by *hetairai* in soliciting men generally, but if she is to be attractive to one man, her own husband, the ornament of a wife is her manner and not her dress (*stole*), and a free and modest wife (*eleutherin kai sōphrona*) must appear

While the author shares the views of his contemporaries on the submission of wives, the motivations are "decidedly Christian in content and without parallel in the New Testament."[22] Subordination and holy conduct can win unbelieving husbands to the faith (3:1; cf. 1 Cor 7:12–16). It is also the will of God and consistent with the conduct of Sarah, the Jewish model and ancestor of women of faith.

Only in the instructions to men does the author not encourage submission (3:7). The instructions to live with consideration, like the instruction to wives, echoes ancient instructions to husbands to treat their wives appropriately. Like other ancient writers, Peter assumed that the wife is the "weaker vessel" who required special consideration.[23] First Peter, however, addresses Christian husbands who are "joint heirs of the grace of life," uniting with their wives in prayer. Thus while these instructions reflect common Greco-Roman values, they bring a new dimension in the motivation to husbands, who now share a common faith with their wives and join them in prayer.

After giving the instructions for the relations between believers and unbelievers in the institutions in which they are subordinate (2:13—3:7), Peter concludes with instructions to the whole community in their relationships with each other (3:8–12). As an exile community (2:11), they are encouraged to embody the moral qualities of unity of spirit (*homophrones*), sympathy (*sympathies*) love for one another (*philadelphoi*), tenderheartedness (*eusplagchnoi*), and humility (*tapeinophrosynes*). The instruction not to render evil for evil or abuse for abuse is intended not only for slaves but for the whole community as it follows the footsteps of Jesus.

In the other instructions, the writers adopt conventional practices, but they have a new motivation. That husbands should love their wives (Eph 5:25; Col 3:19; cf. 1 Pet 3:7) was commonplace in the moral teaching of antiquity. However, Ephesians offers a new dimension, defining love: "as Christ loved the church and gave himself for it" (Eph 5:25). Similarly, that children

---

attractive to her own husband, not to the man next door, having on her cheeks the blush of modesty (*opseos*) rather than of rouge and powder, and a good and noble bearing and decency and modesty (rather than gold and emerald)." P.Haun.II 13, ll. 1–42. Cited in Winter, *Roman Wives, Roman Widows*, 72–73.

22. See Elliott, *1 Peter*, 556.

23. On the weakness of females, see Plato, *Leg.* 6.781B, "The female nature in humankind is inferior in virtue to that of males." Plato also says, "The female is in all respects weaker (*astheneteron*) than the male" (*Resp.* 5; 5.455D). The weakness of the woman is a reason she should be restricted to the home and indoor matters: "For Providence made man stronger and woman weaker (*asthenesteron*), that he, in virtue of his manly prowess, may be more ready to defend the home") Ps. Aristotle *Oec.* 1.4, 1344a). According to the Jewish author in the *Epistle of Aristeas* (251), "the female requires a husband as 'pilot.'" For additional texts, see Elliott, *1 Peter*, 576.

should obey their parents was a common expectation in antiquity. That masters should treat slaves appropriately was also not uncommon in antiquity.

The new dimension in the household codes is the direct address to those in a subordinate position. Unlike ancient parallels, which were written for males in charge of the household, the instructions in Colossians, Ephesians, and 1 Peter address each of the groups in the household, including wives, slaves, and children. Although the proper treatment of slaves was a common topic in antiquity, the address to slaves in Col 3:22 and elsewhere (cf. Eph 6:5; 1 Tim 6:1–2; 1 Pet 2:18–25) is unparalleled in ancient sources. The direct address to slaves is an indication of their new status as members of the family and of the Christian community.[24] The direct address to children also reflects a community life unlike those of ancient associations. Thus while the instructions to those in a subordinate position correspond to Hellenistic moral values, the household codes in the New Testament are not merely the "middle-class morality" of the society. The household codes have both a distinctive Christian motivation and an ecclesiological dimension that recognizes the full membership of women, children, and slaves in the community.

THE EXPANDED HOUSEHOLD CODE (GEMEINDETAFEL): THE PASTORAL EPISTLES

Christ and Culture in 1 Timothy

First Timothy 2:1–2, identified by Dibelius as the expression of *bürgerlich* (bourgeois, middle-class) Christianity, introduces the expansion of the household code, which includes the entire house church. It is composed of men and women (2:8–15; 3:1–13), children (3:4), widows (5:1–16), old men (5:17–22), and slaves (6:1–2). Similarly, Titus 1 gives instructions for elders, and Titus 2 addresses old women, old men, young men, and slaves (2:1–10). The bishop is the paterfamilias of the household (1 Tim 3:1–5; cf. Titus 1:6), who manages both it and the church.[25] Similarly, the letter to Titus speaks of elders who have demonstrated their domestic responsibilities by having faithful children in a church that includes old women, old men, young men, and slaves (Titus 2:1–10). The task of the paterfamilias is to model

24. Thompson, *Moral Formation according to Paul*, 197.

25. The term *episkopos* occurs twice in the Pastorals (1 Tim 3:1; Titus 1:7; cf. Acts 20:28; Phil 1:1). Scholars debate the relationship between the overseer (*episkopos*) and the elder (*presbyteros*). A related question is whether the *episkopos* in 1 Timothy is generic or refers to a single individual. Comparison to all the other references suggests that *episkopos* and *presbyteros* are the same and thus refer to a plurality. See Towner, *Goal of Our Instruction*, 223–25.

appropriate behavior and to teach others how to behave in the household of God (1 Tim 3:15). Consequently, while the Pastoral Epistles frequently speak of "sound teaching" and recite the basic Christian confession, their focus is on the moral conduct of believers, that is, a life that is appropriate to sound teaching (Titus 2:1). The orderly household is necessary to combat the disorder caused by false teachers who threaten the church. The task of the paterfamilias is thus to model and teach proper conduct. While 2 Timothy is Paul's last will and testament, both 1 Timothy and Titus offer instructions on "how to behave in the household of God" (cf. 1 Tim 3:15), giving special focus on ethical conduct that is "appropriate to sound teaching" (Titus 2:1).

In all three Pastoral Epistles, the instructions are a response to the danger of false teachers who threaten the church. Although the false teaching is mentioned repeatedly (1 Tim 1:3–11; 4:1–6; 6:3–5; 6:20; 2 Tim 2:16–17; 3:1–9; Titus 1:10–14; 3:8–11), their actual teaching is never indicated in detail. Instead, Paul focuses on their immoral conduct, which is the result of their teaching, which is "like gangrene" (2 Tim 2:17). Paul insists repeatedly on "sound teaching" and the moral life that accompanies it, drawing a sharp contrast between the behavior of the believers and that of the false teachers.

Another concern of the Pastoral Epistles is the relationship of the house church to the larger society. These letters demonstrate an awareness of the boundary separating the church from the world and the importance of the church's reputation to outsiders. The prayers for the rulers (1 Tim 2:2), like the prayers for rulers among diaspora Jews, indicates the distinction between rulers and those who are under their power. The instructions for young widows to demonstrate proper behavior reflects a concern for the church's reputation among the adversaries (1 Tim 5:14). Only those who are "well thought of by outsiders" should be bishops (1 Tim 3:7). Slaves should honor their masters "so that the name of God and the teaching may not be blasphemed" (1 Tim 6:1). The same concern for the church's reputation among outsiders is present in Titus (2:5, 8, 10).

The relationship of believers to the culture is indicated in 1 Tim 2:1–2, as Dibelius observed. In the request for the prayers for "all people," Paul introduces the first of several noteworthy universalizing statements in 2:1–7, which suggest the community's relationship to the world. God wills the salvation of "all people" (2:4). Hence Jesus is the mediator between God and the people (2:5), having given his life a ransom "for all" (2:4). As 2:2 indicates, God "desires that all people be saved and come to the knowledge of the truth." The community not only creates no offense to the larger society but acknowledges the missionary implications of good behavior.

Prayer for the emperor

The transition from the concern for false teaching (1:18–20) to prayers for "all people," including kings and all those in authority (2:1), indicates the importance of social stability for Timothy's purpose in Ephesus.[26] This instruction recalls Paul's instruction for believers to be submissive to the authorities (Rom 13:7) and the similar instructions in Titus 3:1–2 (cf. 1 Pet 2:13–17). Thus contrary to Dibelius, the prayer for the governmental authorities is not evidence of accommodation to the culture, but the voice of a minority group, as the references in Rom 13:1–7 and 1 Pet 2:13–17 indicate.[27] Indeed, prayers for the ruling authorities were commonplace among diaspora Jews,[28] who prayed for rulers to maintain peace and security for themselves.

The encouragement of prayers for the imperial powers is a rhetorical strategy used by both Philo and Josephus, who indicate that Jews living during the imperial period demonstrate their loyalty to the emperor by praying and offering sacrifices to God on behalf of the emperor.[29] The early church continued this practice, as Tertullian indicates when he argues for the legitimate piety of Christians in their solemn prayers on behalf of the emperor's welfare (*Apol.* 30–34). In response to Roman suspicions about subversive intent of the Christians and the gatherings of all foreign cults, the prayers demonstrate that they do not foster sedition against imperial authority.[30]

The tenuous relationship of the house church to governmental authorities is suggested by the purpose statement in 2:2: "that we might live a quiet (*ēremos*) and peaceful (*hēsychion*) life in all godliness (*eusebeia*) and dignity (*semnotēti*)." The purpose clause indicates the community's separation from the authorities and its desire to live without repression. To live in quietness (*hēsychia*) is to live without disturbing Roman order.[31] This goal is consistent with Paul's instructions to the Thessalonians to "aspire to live quietly (*hēsychazein*), to mind [their] own affairs, and to work with their own hands" so that they may behave properly toward outsiders (1 Thess

26. Collins, *I and II Timothy and Titus*, 52.

27. Four kinds of prayers are mentioned: petitions (*deēseis*), prayers (*proseuchas*), invocations (*enteuxeis*), and thanksgivings (*eucharistias*).

28. Jer 29:7; Josephus, *Ant.* 19.349. Cf. Matt 5:44, "Love your enemies and pray for those who persecute you." According to 1 Macc 7:33, sacrifices were offered for the king. Prayers for Nebuchadnezzar were offered by the Jews (Bar 1:11).

29. See Hoklotubbe, *Civilized Piety*, 69. Cf. Philo, *Against Flaccus* 49: "For Jews all over the world, the starting point for reverence toward the household of Augustus is clearly [their] houses of prayer."

30. Hoklotubbe, *Civilized Piety*, 43.

31. Hoklotubbe, *Civilized Piety*, 76.

Piety

4:11). The concern for the reputation of the community among outsiders becomes a major focus throughout 1 Timothy.

To live "in all godliness (*eusebeia*)" is a central feature of the Pastoral Epistles (cf. 1 Tim 3:16; 4:7–8; 6:3, 5–6; 2 Tim 3:5; Titus 1:1), although it never appears in the undisputed letters of Paul and only rarely elsewhere in the New Testament (cf. Acts 3:17; 17:23; 2 Pet 1:3, 6; 3:11). The term is, however, a basic principle of Hellenistic religion. The stem *seb-* means "to shrink from" or have "reverent awe."[32] It was commonly used for one's religious duties towards the gods and the orders protected by them: family, neighbors, and government officers. It appeared in the earliest grouping of the four cardinal virtues.[33] Aeschylus (early fifth century BC) speaks of a pious (*eusebēs*), wise (*sōphrōn*), just (*dikaios*), good (*agathos*) man (*anēr*).[34] The Roman equivalent *pietas* played a special role in imperial ideology, signifying a devotion toward the gods, the nation, and family, which was epitomized in Augustus's vision of restoring Rome's ancestral traditions and values. Along with other virtues, it included valor, clemency, and justice, which were embodied in the emperor.[35]

The Pastoral Epistles, however, do not use *eusebeia* in the normal Greek sense. It refers both to the content of the Christian faith and the conduct that grows out of it.[36] The "mystery of godliness (*eusebeia*)" is the christological hymn in 1 Tim 3:16. The "teaching that is in accord with godliness" is the equivalent of the "sound words of our Lord Jesus Christ" (1 Tim 6:6 NRSV). Similarly, the "truth that is in accord with *eusebeia* (Titus 1:1) is the Christian message. The ethical dimension is evident in the author's desire that believers live a godly life (1 Tim 2:2; 2 Tim 3:12) and pursue godliness (1 Tim 4:7–8; 6:1). Thus *eusebeia* does not reflect the "middle-class" Christianity of accommodation to cultural values[37] but has been redefined in keeping with the Christian tradition. Similarly, to live "with dignity" (*semnotēs*) recalls Paul's instructions to live properly (*euschēmōs*) toward outsiders (1 Thess 4:11).[38] To live with dignity (*semnotēs*) was to live according to

32. Förster, *sebomai ktl.*, *TDNT* 7:170.

33. The four Platonic-Stoic principal virtues were *hē dikaiosynē kai hē phronēsis kai hē andreia kai hē sōphrosynē* (Diogenes Laertius, *Lives* 3.80). In the earliest period some variation existed in listing the four cardinal virtues. See Reiser, "Bürgerliches Christentum," 38.

34. Aeschylus, *Sept.* 610. Cited in Mott, "Greek Ethics and Christian Conversion," 23.

35. See the extended discussion of *pietas* in Hoklotubbe, *Civilized Piety*, 15.

36. See Thompson, *Moral Formation according to Paul*, 204.

37. Reiser, "Burgerliches Christentum," 35.

38. Reiser, "Bürgerliches Christentum," 37. *Semnos* (noble, serious, dignified) appears only once (Phil 4:8) in the undisputed Pauline letters but appears in the Pastoral

the Hellenistic values of good character. This language builds "linguistic bridges" between the church and the broader society.[39] Thus to "live a quiet and peaceful life" is not to accommodate to the culture but to ensure that outsiders find no occasion for hostility against the church (cf. 6:1; Titus 2:5).

Paul illustrates the good behavior that is necessary for living quiet and peaceful lives in 1 Tim 2:8–15, encouraging believers to embody practices that are consistent with Greco-Roman values. These instructions demonstrate to a suspicious public that Christians do not undermine public order. He extends the responsibilities of husbands and wives to the public assembly, describing the appropriate demeanor for both. The orderly lives of believers occur when men pray "without quarreling or wrangling" (2:8). The extended instructions for women probably reflect a special concern for the reputation of the church inasmuch as women were commonly confined to the household. They demonstrate the orderly life when they dress with modesty (*aidous*) and decency (*sōphrosynē*),[40] "not with braided hair, gold, pearls, or expensive clothes" but as befits a woman who professes godliness (*theosebeia*).[41] The conduct of the women is consistent with the injunction that "we may live a quiet and peaceful life in all godliness" (1 Tim 2:2), for the dress code conforms to the expectations of popular morality. Conduct that "befits a woman professing godliness" suggests the existence of common expectations for women in the society.

The instructions that the women "learn in silence in all subjection" (2:11) reflect the values of the day. According to Plutarch, the woman should conceal her presence and voice in public places (*Conj. praec.* 139C), "Whenever the moon is at a distance from the sun we see her conspicuous and brilliant, but she disappears and hides herself when she comes near him. Contrariwise a virtuous woman ought to be most visible in her husband's company, and to stay in the house and hide herself when he is away." The instructions that a woman not "teach or have authority over men" in the assembly also conforms to popular expectations, extending her submissiveness in the household to the assembly. That she should learn "in quietness"

Epistles at 1 Tim 3:8; Titus 2:2). *Semnotēs* (dignity, seriousness) appears only in the Pastoral Epistles (1 Tim 2:2; 3:4; Titus 2:7. It is widely used in Greek ethics for excellence of character. See texts in Spicq, *semnos*, TLNT 3:246.

39. Hoklotubbe, *Civilized Society*, 74.

40. *Sōphrosynē* is one of the Greek cardinal virtues. It connotes the "exercise of care and intelligence appropriate to circumstances" (BDAG, 986). On modesty (*aidos*), see Plutarch, *Conj. praec.* 10: "Herodotus was not right in saying that a woman lays aside her modesty (*aido*) along with her undergarment. On the contrary, a virtuous woman puts on modesty (*aido*) in its stead, and the husband and wife bring into their mutual relations the greatest modesty as a token of greatest love."

41. On the reputation of women who wear luxurious clothes, see above.

(*hesychia*) is an example of the quiet life Paul encourages for the whole church (cf. 2:1) in demonstrating that the community does not subvert the order of society. To have authority over men would also undermine the reputation of the community.[42]

The reason that women are not permitted to teach is that it was not Adam who was deceived in the beginning but Eve (Gen 3), who represents all women. While Paul uses this story in 2 Cor 11:3 to indicate the vulnerability of the whole church, only Eve is the one who is deceived in 1 Tim 2:13. This argument indicates that the author holds the culture's common stereotype of women. She is thus the archetype of the gullibility of women.[43] As Paul indicates in 2 Timothy, women were vulnerable to false teachings because they were led away by the passions (2 Tim 3:6). Instead, her role is to bear children (2:14–15), the expected role of the woman in that society (cf. 1 Tim 5:14; Titus 2:3–5).

Having limited the authority of women and declared that their proper role is childbearing (1 Tim 2:15), Paul describes the role of the bishop as the legitimate authority. Bishops manage the house church, having demonstrated that they can manage their own households (1 Tim 3:4). In the context of the threatening false teachers, they are the authorized teachers of the church. As the list of virtues indicates (3:2–7), overseers are distinguished by their character. These qualities of bishops are not mentioned in the undisputed Pauline letters but are common in Greco-Roman discourse.[44] Dibelius has demonstrated that the qualifications for the office closely resemble the qualifications for a good general.[45] The ideal of being "blameless" (*anegklētos*) covers the entire catalogue of virtues and forms an *inclusio* with the last in the series, "having a good witness to those who are outside" (3:7). These virtues are not limited to overseers, however, but are also expected of deacons and women (1 Tim 3:8).[46] That is, the focal point is that their moral

42. On the relationship between the activities of women and the community's reputation, see 1 Tim 5:14.

43. Cf. Philo, *QG* 46: "Woman is more accustomed to be deceived than man. For his judgment, like his body, is masculine, and is capable of dissolving or destroying the designs of deception; but the judgment of the woman is more feminine, and because of softness she easily gives way and is taken in by plausible falsehoods which resemble truth."

44. Johnson, *First and Second Letters to Timothy*, 213.

45. Dibelius, *Die Pastoralbriefe*, 25. According to Onasander, one must choose a general who is "temperate, self-restrained, vigilant, frugal, hardened to labor, alert, free from avarice, neither too young nor too old, indeed a father of children if possible, a ready speaker, and a man with a good reputation" (*The General* 1.1).

46. Inasmuch as the topic in 3:8–13 is the qualification for servers (*diakonoi*), the women in 3:11 are evidently female servers.

behavior represents the highest expectations in the culture. These instructions describe how one behaves in the household of God (1 Tim 3:15).

While the community exemplifies some of the moral ideals of the culture, its message places it in tension with its surroundings. First Timothy repeatedly recalls the Christian message that separates it from the larger culture. As a preface to the instructions for men and women in the assembly, Paul says:

> There is one God;
> There is also one mediator between God and humankind,
> Christ Jesus, himself human,
> Who gave himself a ransom for all. (1 Tim 2:5)

After describing the qualities of those who live appropriately in the household of God, Paul concludes:

> He was revealed in flesh,
> Vindicated in spirit,
> Seen by angels,
> Proclaimed among Gentiles,
> Believed in throughout the world,
> Taken up in glory. (1 Tim 3:15–16)

The Pastoral Epistles consistently recall the Christian message (cf. 1 Tim 4:10; 2 Tim 1:9–10; 2:8–13; Titus 1:1–4; 2:11–14; 3:3–7), the confession that distinguishes believers from the larger society. This claim gives a missionary motivation, for God wants all people to be saved and come to the knowledge of the truth (1 Tim 2:4).

Paul also insists on moral values that were not commonplace in the culture. The focus on faith and love (1 Tim 1:5; 2:15; 4:11; 6:11) distinguishes the moral vision from that of the surrounding culture. He also condemns the same vices that are condemned in the undisputed letters of Paul, including fornication (1 Tim 1:10), homosexual practices (1 Tim 1:10; cf. 1 Cor 6:9), and subservience to the lusts (1 Tim 6:9; cf. 2 Tim 2:22; 3:6; Titus 2:12). The requirement that both bishops and deacons be "husband of one wife" (1 Tim 3:2, 11) also distinguishes the community from the larger culture.

Christ and Culture in Titus

In Titus, Paul instructs his emissary to ordain elders in every city in order to combat the false teachers. The qualifications for elders are closely parallel to those listed in 1 Timothy. They exhibit moral behavior that is in sharp contrast to the behavior of the false teachers (1:5–16). According to Titus 2, the entire house church is expected to maintain the same moral conduct as the elders, demonstrating a life that "is appropriate to sound teaching" (2:2). The instructions for the whole community indicate the qualities that are the expectations for the whole church.

The instructions for old men repeat the earlier virtues of the bishops and deacons. They are to be temperate (*nēphalios*, cf. 1 Tim 3:2, 11), honorable (*semnos*, cf. the characteristics of deacons, 1 Tim 3:8), and sober (*sōphrōn*, cf. 2:12; 1 Tim 3:21), qualities that are common in Greek ethics. Similarly, the older women conform to a Greek ethical ideal; they are to be reverent (*hieroprepei*, literally "fitting for a priest").[47] The old women and young women also exemplify the common values of the day. Old women are not to be slanderers or enslaved to wine, but should teach the young women to practice the common morality of the day: to love their husbands and their children, to be self-controlled (*sōphronōs*), chaste (*hagnas*), keepers of the household (*oikourgos*), and submissive to their own husbands (cf. Col 3:18; Eph 5:21; 1 Pet 3:1). Similarly, young men are encouraged to be self-controlled (*sōphronein*, 2:6), and Titus himself (presumably one of the young men) is encouraged to be a model of good works and demonstrate integrity (*aphthoria*), gravity (*semnotēta*), and sound speech in his teaching. Likewise, slaves are expected to submit to their masters (cf. Col 3:22–25; Eph 6:5–9; 1 Tim 6:1–2; 1 Pet 2:18–25). While distinctly Christian values are present, including faith, love, and endurance (2:2), the ethical values for the church, like the ethical values for the leaders (1 Tim 3:1–15), reflect the values of the larger society. One may observe especially the repetition of forms of *sōphron* (2:4, 6) and *semnos* (2:2, 7), which play a dominant role elsewhere in the Pastoral Epistles (1 Tim 2:2; 3:4, 8; 2 Tim 1:7), as well as the traditional expectation of submission of the wives and slaves.

Having addressed the conduct of specific groups within the house church (2:2–10), describing the life that is appropriate to sound teaching (2:1), Paul summarizes the moral life of the entire community in 2:11–15. Their challenge is to live "soberly (*sōphonōs*), righteously (*dikaiōs*) and godly (*eusebōs*) in this present world" (2:12). These qualities have been a consistent feature of the ethics of the Pastoral Epistles (cf. *sōphron-* in 1 Tim 3:2; Titus 2:2, 5–6; 2 Tim 1:7; *dikaios-* in 1 Tim 6:11; *euseb-* in 1 Tim 2:2; 3:16;

---

47. This word is used nowhere else in Scripture. *Hieroprepēs* is used in antiquity for religious processions that are conducted in an appropriate and dignified way. It came to refer to the reverent life that is appropriate for a priest. In 4 Macc 9:25, the oldest of the brothers is described as "a saintly" (*hieroprepeis*) young man who had defended the law before he was killed. The word is used frequently in Philo for a holy person. One may also compare *hieroprepēs* in Titus 2:3 with *theosebein* in 1 Tim 2:10. See the discussion in Spicq, *hieroprepēs*, TLNT 2:215–16.

4:7–8; 6:3, 5–6; 2 Tim 3:5; Titus 1:1); thus they offer a general summary of the ethics of these letters. These qualities conform to three of the cardinal virtues in antiquity; thus they would have resonated with a Greek audience.

Interpreters have maintained that the frequent use of Hellenistic ethical values is an indication of the accommodation of the Pastoral Epistles to the larger society. Jürgen Roloff, for example, has argued that the Hellenistic values in the Pastoral Epistles indicate that the author presents the community as living according to the highest ideals of Hellenistic society.[48] While the ethical categories would have resonated with a Hellenistic audience, they take on a new meaning in the Pastoral Epistles. As Reiser argues, "Here Christianity does not conform to Hellenistic ethics, but Hellenistic ethics conforms to Christianity."[49] As the larger context of Titus 2:12 indicates, the moral life conforms to "sound teaching" (2:1). The call to live "soberly, righteously, and godly in this present world" is (in Greek) a part of a single sentence that begins in 2:11 and ends in 2:14. The rejection of earthly lusts (2:12) is the presupposition for the adoption of the cardinal virtues; it does not fit with the common understanding of the cardinal virtues. Furthermore, the motivation for the moral life is the incarnation and redemptive death of Jesus (2:14), who cleansed a people to engage in good works (2:14). Titus 3:3–7 follows the familiar Pauline once-now, describing the sharp distinction between the community's former behavior (cf. Titus 3:3) and the new existence (Titus 3:4–6), which is antithetical to the conduct of those in their surroundings (cf. 1:12).

The life that is appropriate to sound teaching (2:1) is intended to have an evangelistic impact. The advice to specific groups is repeatedly followed by a purpose clause, indicating the motivation for appropriate behavior. Young wives conform to the common expectations of their culture "in order that the word of God not be discredited" (2:5). Young men should behave appropriately so that "any opponent will be put to shame, having nothing evil to say of us" (2:8). Slaves should be submissive in accordance with common expectations "so that in everything they may be an ornament to the doctrine of God our Savior" (2:10). Similarly, the slaves of 1 Timothy are instructed to honor their masters "in order that the name of God and the teaching may not be blasphemed" (1 Tim 6:1). He expects young widows to marry and have children in order "to give the adversary no reason to revile us" (1 Tim 5:14).

48. Roloff, *Der erste Brief an Timotheus*, 384.
49. Reiser, "Bürgerliches Christentum," 38.

CONCLUSION

The Pastoral Epistles reflect an acute awareness of the separation of the community from its culture. While the primary issue in the Pastoral Epistles is the internal confrontation with false teachers, the relationship of the church to society is also a major concern. Undoubtedly, the Christian message, which is reaffirmed periodically in these letters (cf. 1:15; 2:5–6; 3:16; 6:15–16; 2 Tim 2:9–10; Titus 2:11–14; 3:3–7), has separated the community from its surroundings, creating adversaries (1 Tim 5:14) who slander the community (5:14; 6:2), claiming that it undermines the order of society.

The Pastoral Epistles present a moral vision that is consistent with Paul's desire that the community live "quiet and peaceful lives" as a minority group conscious of its reputation. On the surface, the ethical instructions appeal to the highest ideals of Hellenistic culture, employing many terms that are unprecedented in the undisputed Pauline letters. These letters also assume the societal expectations for the submission of wives and slaves and the authority of the paterfamilias, depicting the community as an extended household. By praying for rulers, the community demonstrates its desire to live peacefully with its culture.

However, the community has accepted only those Hellenistic values that are consistent with their own identity, and it has redefined the Greek virtues that play an important role in the epistles. Contrary to Dibelius and others, the Pastoral Epistles do not reflect an accommodation to the culture. Indeed, 2 Timothy is the testimony of the apostle as he faces death at the hands of the governmental authorities (2 Tim 1:8, 12, 17; 2:9). He declares that all who live godly lives (*eusebōs*) will be persecuted (4:12), and he challenges Timothy to join him in suffering for the gospel (1:8; 2:3). If 2 Timothy is included with 1 Timothy and Titus as a single collection, as most scholars believe, it is evidence of the tensions between Christ and culture and the reasons for the church's concern for its reputation.

Because God "wants all people to be saved" (1 Tim 2:4), the church does not retreat from the world but declares the Christian message—"the mystery of godliness" (3:16)—and lives in a way that is appropriate to it (cf. Titus 2:1). Good behavior will thus make the faith attractive to outsiders (Titus 2:10) and ensure that others do not slander believers (cf. 1 Tim 5:14; 6:1; Titus 2:5, 8).

Conclusion

Christ and Culture: Lessons from the Past

In the era when mainline Protestant Christianity was dominant in the United States, H. Richard Niebuhr wrote *Christ and Culture*, arguing that Christianity can have a transforming effect on the culture. While Niebuhr was responding to those who questioned the benefit of Christianity for society, today we ask the question of Christ and culture at a time when Christianity is no longer dominant but is declining throughout the West. Because believers have become a "cognitive minority" that deviates from the views of the majority culture, one may ask how it can survive in this changing situation. Sociologists describe the challenges of maintaining a set of convictions when one is immersed in a culture that does not share them or even regards them with disdain.[1] For us the question is existential: How do we respond to a post-Constantinian situation? In the words of the psalmist, "How could we sing the Lord's song in a foreign land" (Ps 137:4)? Can the church survive when it is a minority in a land that is increasingly less hospitable? What form of Christianity will survive?

We are not lacking for answers. For decades, believers have aligned themselves with political parties in hopes of restoring the Constantinian era, making their own understanding of Christian values a matter of public policy. Others maintain that the church should take measures to become more attractive to the values of the twenty-first century. It would be more attractive, for instance, if it abandoned the exclusive claims of the Christian confession and accepted its place in a pluralistic society, no longer engaging in the mission of converting others. Or perhaps the church could be more attractive if it removed boundaries and became more inclusive to all

---

1. See Zimmermann, "Diasporafähiger Glaube," 50.

alternative lifestyles. Undoubtedly, multiple ways exist to make Christianity more attractive.

Two questions emerge from the alternative approaches. First, one may ask the pragmatic question: would accommodation to contemporary values actually be effective for the survival of Christianity? That is, when the church accommodates to the culture, does a compelling reason exist for becoming or remaining a Christian? One must also ask the theological question: what is in the DNA of the Christian faith that defines its relation to culture? Niebuhr looked to the New Testament to articulate options and to commend a course of action. As I indicated in the introductory chapter, Niebuhr's categories rarely fit the message of the respective writers in the New Testament. In this study, I have examined the response of the first-century Christ-believers to the problem of Christ and culture to discover models for the church today.

We cannot simply reproduce the early Christian experience in the present, as Hans-Josef Klauck has argued, for the temporal distance is too great. To do so would be to become a museum piece for those with historical interests. The vast distance from the pre-Constantinian to the post-Constantinian period requires caution as we look to antiquity for models for facing the marginalization that believers now experience, for we are tempted to begin with our own conclusions and superimpose them on the historical evidence.[2] Nevertheless, we will benefit from determining which factors in the Christian existence in antiquity are relevant for the contemporary church.[3] As Talcott Parsons demonstrated, movements that survive and flourish share common strategies.[4] We turn to the New Testament for models, for it records the roots of the movement that unleashed the new

2. See Gäckle, "Die (Un)Attraktivität der frühen Christentum," 239 (239–62); Frey, "Die Ausbreitung des frühen Christentums," 87.

3. Frey, "Die Ausbreitung des frühen Christentums," 111.

4. Movements that survive in the midst of the majority culture, according to Talcott Parsons, must meet several conditions. 1) They must first establish boundaries, designating the differences and agreements between it and the world around it. 2) The group has a founder who defines its identity and 3) rituals that bind the people together, (4) an understanding of its place in history, and (5) a public claim that makes it intelligible to others. The new movement develops its own language, establishing its own identity (6), and (7) succeeds only when it has a comprehensive ethical and ideological worldview and set of values that can be understood within the surrounding societal and cultural systems. (8) This worldview and value system must include signals of both differentiation and integration and distinguish itself by subordinating the opposing values. Parsons's assessment is not limited to a specific era but applies to movements in different eras. The early church, which began as an insignificant splinter movement of Judaism, grew because it established a strong identity and differentiated itself from the larger culture.

dynamic that remains today. "Those who wish to shape the future must first understand the past and know their roots."[5] We learn from history, but the application of what we have learned requires a process of discernment because the restoration of all early Christian and ancient conditions is neither possible nor desirable. Our discernment requires a hermeneutical reflection on which features of Christian existence in the early church are meaningful for the task of the church today.[6] The New Testament demonstrates that, in a pluralistic and syncretistic world of religions, Christian identity exists neither through absorption into the culture nor through total withdrawal but through dialogue and critique.[7]

THE ANCIENT AND CONTEMPORARY CONTEXTS

We now face a situation that resembles that of the earliest Christians in many respects inasmuch as the pre-Constantinian world has similarities to the post-Constantinian environment.[8] Like the churches in the first generation, contemporary believers will be increasingly marginalized in a secular culture, existing as a "cognitive minority."[9] Similarly, the contemporary church, like the ancient communities, exists in a pluralistic society. Romans and Greeks did not doubt the existence of strange gods; thus they were open to the claims of various religions. The growth of the mystery religions is evidence of openness to new religious expressions, and the mobility of the people also created a climate for growth.

The pluralism of a multicultural society once provided the environment for the growth of Christianity.[10] Similarly, in the post-Constantinian situation, Christians live in a pluralistic society that is a marketplace of ideas and values. While its message may be rejected by most of society, some will find the foundation for their lives and the place to belong in the communities of faith, as in the first generation.

5. Klauck, "Gemeinde und Gesellschaft," 246.
6. Gäckle, "Die (Un)Attraktivität der frühen Christentum," 239.
7. Klauck, "Gemeinde und Gesellschaft," 246.
8. See Frey, "Ausbreitung," 86–87.
9. The term was used by Peter Berger in *A Rumor of Angels* (1969).
10. Schnelle, *First Hundred Years of Christianity*, 142.

GROWTH AND RESISTANCE IN EARLY CHRISTIANITY

Christianity grew in this pluralistic society prior to Constantine. While precise data on the growth of Christianity in the first three centuries are not available, we can draw conclusions from the comments of ancient writers and the informed estimates of historians. In AD 25, this movement did not exist, and contemporary writers took little notice of it.[11] One hundred years later, Pliny writes to the emperor Trajan to inquire about the prosecution of Christians, complaining about their growth. "It is not only the towns, but villages and rural districts too which are infected through contact with this wretched cult" (Pliny, *Ep.* 10.96.9–10 LCL). Rodney Stark estimates that in AD 200 there were around 200,000 Christians.[12] He estimates that in AD 300 there were around six million Christians.[13] It nevertheless remained a minority group before Constantine as it flourished in the midst of the hostility of the populace. Thus numerical growth was consistently accompanied by the hostility of the majority.

While the New Testament says little about the numerical growth of the movement in the first generation,[14] the existence of churches throughout the empire indicates the spread of Christianity. The hostility to the movement, which is evident in almost every book of the New Testament, is an indication of the growth of a movement as it divided families and separated believers from civic and commercial life. The success of Christianity was undoubtedly the source of the hostility that believers faced, for believers were perceived as a threat to existing institutions. Not only was Paul consistently persecuted, but the communities that he left behind also faced hostility from their relationships, leaving them with an uneasy relationship with their culture. Before persecutions were officially mandated, believers suffered discrimination and abuse from their neighbors in the local communities (cf. Phil 1:28; 1 Thess 3:1–5) because of their refusal to accommodate fully to the culture.

11. See Klauck, "Gemeinde und Gesellschaft," 225–26. "Christianity was practically nonexistent for outsiders in the first century. It was not noticed. One does not even need the fingers of one's hand to count the incidental remarks by Roman historians." Only in the references by Tacitus (*An.* 15:44.2) and Suetonius (*Nero* 16.2) is Christianity mentioned.

12. On the numerous references *to* Christians by pagan authors in the second century, see Klauck, "Gemeinde und Gesellschaft," 227.

13. Stark, *Rise of Christianity*, 6–7.

14. Only Acts offers statistics stating numerical growth (2:41; 4:4). While rapid growth in the earliest church is a certainty, most scholars are skeptical of the precise numbers. Frey, "Ausbreitung," 90.

THE UNATTRACTIVENESS
AND ATTRACTIVENESS OF
CHRISTIANITY: THEN AND NOW

Early Christians lived between the two poles of withdrawing from their culture and taking their place within it. That is, it was unattractive to the majority and attractive to the minority who accepted the Christian message. As Paul indicates in 1 Corinthians, the Christian message was attractive to a minority of the population, but most people were offended by the message of a crucified Savior (cf. 1 Cor 1:18–28) and the call to turn away from local religions.[15]

The Exclusive Claim and the Rejection of Pluralism

The claim that "for us there is one Lord, Jesus Christ" (1 Cor 8:6) was attractive to those who rejected polytheism, but the exclusive claim was offensive to the majority. The movement spread because the early Christians believed that what they had found to be true was true for the whole world. As the author of Hebrews indicates, God has spoken his final word "in these last days" (1:2). Paul insists that believers "turn from idols"—all ancient religion—to "serve the living God" (1:10). While the message resulted in the conversion of some, it also created hostility among others. The Christian message thus disturbed the pluralism of the ancient culture.

Both the growth and the hostility experienced by the church were the result of the absolute claims that "there is no other name" by which people are saved (cf. Acts 4:12). This claim remains an offense to our own culture. The celebration of diversity in the current climate precludes any claim to possess the ultimate truth for all. In a postmodern society, all claims are to be entertained except those that claim to be true. Consequently, the claim that God has been revealed singularly in Jesus Christ is offensive to the pluralism of our time just as it was in antiquity.

The earliest Christians flourished not because they accepted their place within the pluralism of their time or minimized the offense of the gospel but because they claimed that their message was true for the whole world and declared a message that people would accept or reject. As Paul said when he faced the apparent failure of his message, "And even if our gospel is veiled,

---

15. See Gäckle, "(Un) Attraktivität," 241. "A distinctive characteristic of historical research into early Christianity is that one finds it easier to describe the unattractiveness of this movement to Hellenistic-Roman eyes than to describe the attractiveness that brought about its astonishing growth." Cf. Feldmeier, *Die Christen als Fremde*, 119: "From the worship of a crucified one to the justification of the sinner, the Christians trampled all that was holy and divine in ancient culture."

it is veiled to those who are perishing. In their case the god of this world has blinded the minds of unbelievers, to keep them from seeing the light of the gospel of the glory of Christ, who is the image of God. For we preach not ourselves but Jesus Christ as Lord" (2 Cor 4:3–5).

The clarity of this confession provided Karl Barth and his colleagues the strength to resist those who adapted the gospel to the social and intellectual currents of the time. According to the first article of the Barmen Declaration, written by Barth in response to the German Christians, who had accommodated the church to the Third Reich, the words of the Gospel of John remain true.

> I am the way, and the truth, and the life: no one comes to the Father, but by me." (John 14:6). "Truly, truly, I say to you, he who does not enter the sheepfold by the door but climbs in by another way, that man is a thief and a robber. . . . I am the door; if anyone enters by me, he will be saved. (John 10:1, 9)

Barth knew that an acculturated gospel could no longer offer a critique of idolatries of his own time.[16] In the same way, the church lives to declare "that the gospel is the unique and radical thing that it is: as the Truth which has no other foundation than the God revealed in Israel and Jesus Christ."[17] Believers follow the model of Paul, who neither "peddles" God's word like merchandise (2 Cor 2:17) nor "tampers" with it (2 Cor 4:2) in order to win others.

This claim inevitably creates boundaries between believers and unbelievers—between church and society—in their convictions and way of life. The basic Christian confession requires consistent elaboration and defense. Consequently, Paul's model is still appropriate as catechesis involves the repetition of the church's confession and its application in all situations. In preaching and worship, the church is reminded of the confession that defines its identity. The elaboration on the confession is the church's resource for resisting the false gods of the current era. The reminder of the one who emptied himself offers an alternative vision of morality to the current emphasis on the rights of the individual. The consistent reaffirmation and catechesis create an alternative plausibility structure to the dominant one in the culture.[18]

---

16. See Wood, *Contending for the Faith*, 9.

17. Wood, *Contending for the Faith*, 19.

18. Zimmermann, "Diasporafähiger Glaube," 56.

Christians as Strangers in Their Own Land

The Christian confession unites believers who accept it and creates boundaries separating it from the existing society. The Johannine literature demarcates believers from the world that hates them (John 15:18), and Paul distinguishes between believers and unbelievers, insiders and outsiders. A common image identifying believers was that of citizens of another country, a colony of outsiders in their own lands. Paul indicates that their citizenship is in heaven (Phil 3:20), and both the authors of Hebrews and 1 Peter describe believers as "aliens and exiles" (cf. Heb 11:13–16; 13:13–14; 1 Pet 2:11). Thus they knew sharp boundaries between themselves and the world.

The metaphor of the exile and alien is still useful for believers. As Martin Niemöller said when the German church was oppressed, "We do not want to forget that even the German fatherland means a foreign exile to us, as for the man who had nothing as he lay in the manger because he laid down his head out of love for the people."[19] While believers continue to be good citizens, they recognize that political parties, national interests, business, and commerce are only penultimate values for those who are exiles in their own land.

Love for One Another

All the witnesses of the New Testament describe an alternative society with its own identity and ethos. The Sermon on the Mount portrays the identity and the ethos that is applicable only within the circle of disciples, exceeding the "righteousness of the Pharisees" (Matt 5:20). Paul's letters consistently describe a pattern of life that is "worthy of the gospel" and encourage the moral formation of a community that is "blameless at the day of Christ" (cf. Phil 1:10). At the heart of the community's existence is love for one another as the community replaced the functions that had belonged to the families from whom they were separated. The command to "love one another" is shared by the Johannine literature (John 13:34–35; 1 John 1:7), Paul (Rom 12:9; Gal 5:14; 1 Thess 3:12), Hebrews (Heb 10:24), and 1 Peter (4:8). Indeed, the prominence of "one another" in the exhortations in the New Testament reflects the distinctive community ethic of believers who are separated from their society. The *Epistle of Diognetus* summarizes the ways in which believers demarcated themselves from values of the societies in which they lived. They did not expose infants; they maintained marital

---

19. Niemöller, *Exile in the Fatherland*, 124.

fidelity, and loved everyone. Nevertheless, they were regarded with suspicion and were outsiders in their own lands.[20]

Openness to All

While the early church established boundaries from its culture, it was open to all. Among the associations of the ancient world, a community that included multiple ethnic groups and social classes, women, and children was unprecedented. While their love for one another reflects special concern for members within the community, their practice was attractive to the larger culture and a means of evangelism. Indeed, the rigorous ethic required throughout the New Testament was attractive to Greeks and Romans who were searching for a means of self-control. Only by separating from their culture could the early Christians "shine as lights in the world" (cf. Phil 2:15). Similarly, in the current climate, a vibrant community of mutual care and support can be the place where people can find a place to belong, and the demanding ethic can provide structure for those who have lost a moral compass.

A Missionary Movement

The claim to exclusive truth was the foundation of the missionary efforts of the earliest Christians. Unlike both Judaism and Hellenistic religions, Christians engaged in mission to convert their contemporaries to their own confession. If one understands by mission an activity of intentional recruitment and action based on a global, established eschatological claim to exclusive truth in order to win others to a clearly definable group, then early Christianity brought a new dimension into the history of ancient religions. The aim of the early Christian mission was not to offer people an additional religion; rather, it combined with the exclusive claim a requirement for the abandonment of all previous religious commitments.[21]

Like the ancient society, today's pluralistic society is skeptical of all attempts to evangelize or engage in foreign missions to convert others. Believers nevertheless engage in missions, anticipating the time when "every knee will bow and every tongue confess that Jesus is Lord," sharing the ancient conviction that Jesus Christ is Lord of the world. As in ancient times, believers bear witness to their faith within the family (cf. 1 Cor 7:16; 1 Pet 3:1) and other close relationships.

20. Klauck, "Gemeinde und Gesellschaft," 232.
21. Schnelle, *First Hundred Years*, 145.

Engagement with the World

Despite the boundaries, early Christians did not retreat from their culture. Believers lived between the two poles of withdrawal from the local populace and engagement with it. As the *Epistle of Diognetus* explained (see ch. 8), Christians were participants in society. They spoke the language of their fellow citizens, lived in the cities without withdrawing into ghettos, married, had families, and lived as good citizens, looking out for the public good. While their citizenship was in heaven, they acted as good citizens, recognizing the legitimate authority of government officials. None of these earthly institutions, however, were of ultimate importance (1 Cor 7:29–32), for they belonged to the world that is passing away.

While Paul encouraged his converts not to behave "like the gentiles" (1 Thess 4:5), the Christians accepted many of the ethical norms of antiquity. They were conscious of conducting themselves in a way that outsiders would approve (1 Thess 4:12; cf. 1 Pet 3:3). Thus the existence of boundaries does not involve a retreat from the world but the engagement with it. Only by having boundaries can the church be a light to the world (cf. Phil 2:15). Paul's statement comes shortly after he has told the story of the one who emptied himself.

Although believers withdrew from many functions of the society, they lived in the cities where education and literature played an important role in their community formation. Udo Schnelle indicates that "no religious figure (earlier or later) gave rise to a literature as quickly and totally as Jesus Christ!"[22] The literacy rate of Christians was impressive. The Christians demonstrated a knowledge of the basic Greek literature and created their own new forms of literature. Paul adapted the epistle from Greek predecessors to engage in community formation. He employed Stoic arguments on natural law for his own purposes (Rom 1; 1 Cor 11). He demonstrates an awareness of the conflict between the philosophers and rhetoricians and engages in anti-Sophistic rhetoric. The author of Hebrews demonstrates a knowledge of Middle Platonism. However, these writers do not uncritically accept the Stoic or Platonic systems. As Paul says to the Corinthians, his task is to take every thought captive to Jesus Christ (2 Cor 10:8).

According to Schnelle, the growth of the early Christian mission can be explained only with the assumption of a high capacity to speak intelligibly to an audience immersed in Jewish and Greco-Roman streams of tradition. The transformation of Greco-Roman concepts within the Christian tradition did not begin with the second-century apologists but with Paul. Like

---

22. Schnelle, *First Hundred Years*, 492.

no one else, he was capable of combining Jewish and Greco-Roman thought and creating an open and intellectual system in which both Jews and Greeks could participate. Similarly, other Christian authors appropriated Greco-Roman literary models to make their arguments. This twofold capacity for connection could be attained not by rejection but only through a conscious participation in the debates that were taking place in the environment of the churches. The early Christian missionaries participated aggressively in the religious, ethical, and philosophical discussions of their time. "A new cultural system like early Christianity could emerge only because it was in a position to connect with existing cultural movements and produce new organizations of concepts and traditions. Intentional communication and desired conviction are here at the beginning!"[23]

Believers do not retreat from the intellectual challenges of the world. As Paul and the author of Hebrews indicate, believers engage in the intellectual conversation, at times acknowledging their benefits but also offering a critique. As 1 Peter indicates, as believers interact with outsiders, they are prepared to give a defense (*apologia*) of their hope (3:15). The apologists of the second century continued the task of meeting the intellectual challenges of their environment.

SUMMARY

If the church in Western society is now marginalized, it joins the earliest believers as well as Christians throughout the ages who have experienced situations more perilous than our own. While some have suffered from overt persecution, others have experienced marginalization and discrimination. This experience is not a misfortune but belongs to the DNA of the Christian faith, for the gospel was offensive to the majority from the beginning. The task of believers is to be faithful even when Christian belief is not plausible to major parts of the population. As the first Christians learned, the offensive gospel evokes both growth and hostility.

While the New Testament does not provide a complete pattern that the church can duplicate, it offers insights demonstrating that the Christian community can flourish in difficult circumstances when it maintains a clear identity and a confidence in its message. It flourishes neither by accommodating to the world's values nor by total withdrawal from the world. With its eschatological vision of the new age, the church is an alternative community that offers a critique of the values of individualism, nationalism, politics, and commercialization that dominate the culture.

23. Schnelle, *First Hundred Years*, 561.

Bibliography

Agamben, Giorgio. *The Time That Remains: A Commentary on the Letter to the Romans.* Translated by Patricia Dailey. Stanford, CA: Stanford University Press, 2005.

Alexander, Loveday. "Paul and the Hellenistic Schools: The Evidence of Galen." In *Paul in His Hellenistic Context,* edited by Troels Engberg-Pedersen, 60–83. Minneapolis: Fortress, 1995.

Backhaus, Knut. *Der Hebräerbrief: Übersetzt und erklärt von Knut Backhaus.* Regensburger Neues Testament. Regensburg: Pustet, 2009.

Badiou, Alan. *Saint Paul: The Foundation of Universalism.* Stanford: Stanford University Press, 2003.

Balch, David L. "Hellenism/Acculturation in 1 Peter." In *Perspectives on First Peter,* edited by C. H. Talbert, 79–102. National Association of Baptist Professors of Religion Special Studies 9. Macon, GA: Mercer University Press, 1986.

———. *Let Wives Be Submissive: The Domestic Code of 1 Peter.* Society of Biblical Literature Monograph Series 26. Chico, CA: Scholars, 1981.

———. "Neopythagorean Moralists and the New Testament." In *Aufstieg und Niedergang der Römischen Welt,* edited by H. Temporini and W. Haase, 2:380–411. Berlin: de Gruyter, 1992–.

Balz, H. βάρβαρος, EDNT 1.197–98.

———. κῆνσος, EDNT 2.287.

Barclay, John M. G. *Jews in the Mediterranean Diaspora: From Alexander to Trajan (323 BCE–117 CE).* Edinburgh: T & T Clark, 1996.

———. "'Neither Jew nor Greek': Multiculturalism and the New Perspective on Paul." In *Ethnicity and the Bible,* edited by Mark. G. Brett, 197–214. Leiden: Brill, 1996.

———. "Ordinary but Different: Colossians and Hidden Moral Identity." *Australian Biblical Review* 49 (2001) 34–52.

———. "Paul and the Philosophers: Alain Badiou and the Event." *New Blackfriars* 91 (2010) 171–84.

———. *Pauline Churches and Diaspora Jews.* Grand Rapids: Eerdmans, 2011.

———. "Why the Roman Empire Was Insignificant to Paul." In *Pauline Churches and Diaspora Jews,* 363–87. Grand Rapids: Eerdmans, 2011.

Bargár, Pavol. "Niebuhr's Typology Reconsidered: Reading Christ and Culture through the Lenses of the Praxis Matrix." *Communio Viatorum* 56 (2014) 294–316.

Barton, Stephen C. "Sanctification and Oneness in 1 Corinthians with Implications for the Case of 'Mixed Marriages' (1 Corinthians 7:12–16)." *New Testament Studies* 63 (2017) 38–55.

Batey, Richard A. "Sepphoris and the Jesus Movement." *New Testament Studies* 46 (2001) 408–9.

Becker, Eve-Marie. *Paul on Humility*. Translated by Wayne Coppins. Waco, TX: Baylor University Press, 2020.

Becker, Jürgen. *Paul: Apostle to the Gentiles*. Translated by O. C. Dean. Louisville: Westminster John Knox, 1993.

Bennema, Comelis. "The Identity and Composition of *oi Ioudaioi* in the Gospel of John." *Tyndale Bulletin* 60 (2009) 239–63.

Berger, Klaus. *Formen und Gattungen im Neuen Testament*. Uni-Taschenbücher 2532. Tübingen: Francke, 2005.

Berger, Peter. *A Rumor of Angels: Modern Society and the Rediscovery of the Supernatural*. New York: Doubleday, 1969.

Bermejo-Rubio, Fernando. "Jesus and the Anti-Roman Resistance: A Reassessment of the Arguments." *Journal for the Study of the Historical Jesus* 12 (2014) 1–105.

Betz, Hans Dieter. "2 Cor 6:14–7:1: An Anti-Pauline Fragment?" *Journal of Biblical Literature* 92 (1973) 88–108⁻

———. *Galatians: A Commentary on Paul's Letter to the Churches of Galatia*. Hermeneia—A Critical and Historical Commentary on the Bible. Philadelphia: Fortress, 1979.

Bird, Michael F. *An Anomalous Jew: Paul among Jews, Greeks, and Romans*. Grand Rapids: Eerdmans, 2016.

Boyarin, Daniel. *A Radical Jew: Paul and the Politics of Identity*. Berkeley: University of California Press, 1994.

Briones, David E. "Paul and Aristotle on Friendship." In *Paul and the Greco-Roman Philosophical Tradition*, edited by Joseph R. Dodson and Andrew W. Pitts, 55–74. Library of New Testament Studies 527. London: T & T Clark, 2017.

Brookins, Timothy A. "Natural Hair: A 'New Rhetorical' Assessment of 1 Cor. 11.14–15." In *Paul and the Greco-Roman Philosophical Tradition*, edited by Joseph R. Dodson and Andrew W. Pitts, 173–98. Library of New Testament Studies. London: T & T Clark, 2017.

Brox, N. *Der erste Petrusbrief*. Evangelisch-Katholischer Kommentar zum Neuen Testament. Neukirchen-Vluyn: Benziger, 1979.

Brunk, George R. *Galatians*. Believers Church Bible Commentary. Harrisonburg, VA: Herald, 2015.

Bryan, Christopher. *Render to Caesar: Jesus, the Early Church, and the Roman Superpower*. New York: Oxford University Press, 2005.

Buell, Denise, and Caroline E. Johnson Hodge. "The Politics of Interpretation: The Rhetoric of Race and Ethnicity in Paul." *Journal of Biblical Literature* 123 (2004) 235–51.

Bultmann, Rudolf. *Theology of the New Testament*. Translated by Kendrick Grobel. London: SCM, 1955.

Burke, Simeon R. "'Render to Caesar the Things of Caesar and to God the Things of God': Recent Perspectives on a Puzzling Command (1945–Present)." *Currents in Biblical Research* 16 (2018) 157–90.

Campbell, David F., Geoffrey C Layman and John Clifford Green. *Secular Surge: A New Fault Line in American Politics*. Cambridge: Cambridge University Press, 2021.

Cancik, Hildegard. *Untersuchungen zu Senecas Epistulae morales*. Spudasmata: Studien zu klassischen Philologie und ihre Grenzgebieten 18. Hildesheim: Olms, 1967.

Carson, D. A. *Christ and Culture Revisited*. Grand Rapids: Eerdmans, 2008.

Carter, T. L. "The Irony of Romans 13." *Novum Testamentum* 46 (2004) 209–28.

Collins, John J. *Between Athens and Jerusalem: Jewish Identity in the Hellenistic Diaspora*. New York: Crossroad, 1986.

Collins, Raymond F. *I and II Timothy and Titus: A Commentary*. New Testament Library. Louisville: Westminster John Knox, 2002.

Constantineanu, Cornelius. "The Bible and the Public Arena: A Pauline Model for Christian Engagement with Society with Reference to Romans 13." *Kairos* 4 (2010) 135–58.

Cosgrove, Charles H. "Did Paul Value Ethnicity." *Catholic Biblical Quarterly* 68 (2006) 268–90.

———. "Paul and Ethnicity: A Selective History of Interpretation." In *Paul Unbound: Other Perspectives on the Apostle*, edited by Mark D. Given, 71–98. Peabody, MA: Hendrickson, 2010.

Crouch, James E. *The Origin of the Colossian Haustafel*. Forschungen zur Religion und Literatur des Alten und Neuen Testaments. Göttingen: Vandenhoeck & Ruprecht, 1972.

Croy, N. Clayton "'Show Me the Money': Jesus, Visual Aids and the Tribute Question." *Tyndale Bulletin* 71 (2020) 191–206.

de Gruchy, John W. *Daring, Trusting Spirit: Bonhoeffer's Friend Eberhard Bethge*. Minneapolis: Fortress, 2005.

de Vos, Craig S. "Once a Slave, Always a Slave? Slavery, Manumission and Relational Patterns in Paul's Letter to Philemon." *Journal for the Study of the New Testament* 82 (2001) 89–105.

Deissmann, Adolf. *Light from the Ancient East*. Translated by L. R. M. Strachan. Repr. London: Hodder and Stoughton, 1965.

Deming, Will. "A Diatribal Pattern in 1 Cor 7:21–22: A New Perspective on Paul's Directions to Slaves." *Novum Testamentum* 17 (1995) 130–37.

deSilva, David. *Fourth Maccabees and the Promotion of Jewish Philosophy: Rhetoric, Intertexture, and Reception*. Eugene, OR: Cascade, 2020.

———. *Introducing the Apocrypha*. Grand Rapids: Baker Academic 2002.

Dibelius, Martin. *Die Pastoralbriefe*. Handbuch zum Neuen Testament 13. Tübingen: J. C. B. Mohr [Paul Siebeck] 1931.

Dillon, John. *The Middle Platonists*. London: Duckworth, 1977.

Divjanović, Kristin. *Paulus als Philosoph: Das Ethos des Apostels vor dem Hintergrund antiker Populärphilosophie*. Neutestamentliche Abhandlungen n.f. 58. Münster: Aschendorff, 2015.

Dodson, Joseph R., and Andrew W. Pitts. *Paul and the Greco-Roman Philosophical Tradition*. Library of New Testament Studies. London: T & T Clark, 2017.

du Toit, Andrie. "Revisiting the Sermon on the Mount: Some Major Issues." *Neotestamentica* 50 (2016) 59–91.

Dunn, James D. G. *Jesus Remembered*. Vol. 1 of *Christianity in the Making*. Grand Rapids: Eerdmans, 2003.

———. *Romans*. 2 vols. World Biblical Commentary 38A and 38B. Grand Rapids: Zondervan Academic, 2017.

———. "Romans 13: A Charter for Political Quietism?" *Ex Auditu* 2 (1986) 55–68.

———. "The Thought World of Jesus." *Early Christianity* 1 (2010) 321–43.

Elliott, John H. *1 Peter: A New Translation with Introduction and Commentary*. Anchor Bible 37B. New York: Doubleday, 2000.

———. *A Home for the Homeless: A Sociological Exegesis of 1 Peter, Its Situation and Strategy, with a New Introduction*. Minneapolis: Fortress, 1990.

Engberg-Pedersen, Troels. *Paul and the Stoics*. Louisville: Westminster John Knox, 2000.

———. "Stoicism in Philippians." In *Paul in His Hellenistic Context*, edited by Engberg-Pedersen, 256–90. Minneapolis: Fortress, 1995.

———. *Paul on Identity: Theology as Politics*. Minneapolis: Fortress, 2021.

———. "Paul, Virtues, and Vices." In *Paul in the Greco-Roman World: A Handbook*, edited by J. Paul Sampley, 608–33. Harrisburg, PA: Trinity Press International, 2003.

———. "Paul's Stoicizing Politics in Rom 12–13: The Role of 13:1–10 in the Argument. *Journal for the Study of the New Testament* 29 (2006) 163–72.

Erbse, Hartmut. "Die Bedeutung der Synkrisis in den Parallelbiographen Plutarchs." *Hermes* 84 (1956) 398–424.

Esler, Philip Francis. *The First Christians in Their Social Worlds: Social-Scientific Approaches to New Testament Interpretation*. London: Routledge, 1994.

Eusebius. *Preparation for the Gospel*. Grand Rapids: Baker, 1981.

Feldmeier, Reinhard. *Die Christen als Fremde: Die Metapher der Fremde in der antiken Welt, im Urchristentum, und im 1. Petrusbrief*. Wissenschaftliche Untersuchungen zum Neuen Testament 64. Tübingen: Mohr Siebeck, 1992.

Fiore, Benjamin. *The Function of Personal Example in the Socratic and Pastoral Epistles*. Analecta Biblica 105. Rome: Biblical Institute Press, 1986.

Fitzgerald, John T. *Cracks in an Earthen Vessel: An Examination of the Catalogues of Hardships in the Corinthian Correspondence*. Society of Biblical Literature Dissertation Series 99. Atlanta: Society of Biblical Literature, 1988.

———. "Paul and Friendship." In *Paul in the Greco-Roman World*, edited by J. Paul Sampley, 319–43. Harrisburg, PA: Trinity Press International, 2003.

———. "Philippians in the Light of Ancient Discussions of Friendship." In *Friendship, Flattery, and Frankness of Speech*, 141–62. Supplements to Novum Testamentum 82. Edited by John T. Fitzgerald. Leiden: Brill, 1996.

———. "Vice/Virtue Lists." In *Anchor Bible Dictionary*, 6:857–59. New York: Doubleday, 1992.

Fitzmyer, Joseph A. *The Letter to Philemon: A New Translation and Commentary*. Anchor Bible 34c. New York: Doubleday, 2000.

Flusser, David. "The Jewish Origins of the Early Church's Attitude toward the State." In *Judaism of the Second Temple Period* vol. 1, *Qumran and Apocalypticism*, 299–304. Grand Rapids: Eerdmans, 2007.

———. *Judaism of the Second Temple Period*. Vol. 1, *Qumran and Apocalypticism*. Grand Rapids: Eerdmans, 2007.

Forbes, Christopher. "Comparison, Self-Praise and Irony: Paul's Boasting and the Conventions of Hellenistic Rhetoric." *New Testament Studies* 32 (1986) 1–30.

Förster, Niclas. *Jesus und die Steuerfrage: Die Zinsgroschenkperikope auf dem religiösen und politischen Hintergrund ihrer Zeit.* Wissenschaftliche Untersuchungen zum Neuen Testament 294. Tübingen: Mohr Siebeck, 2012.

Förster, W. *Sebomai ktl., TDNT* 7.170.

Frey, Jörg. "Die Ausbreitung des frühen Christentums: Perspektiven für die gegenwärtige Praxis der Kirche." In *Kirche zwischen postmoderner Kultur und Evangelium,* edited by M. Reppenhagen, 86–112. Neukirchen-Vluyn: Neukirchener Verlag, 2010.

Gäckle, Volker. "Die (Un)Attraktivität der frühen Christenheit." *Kerygma und Dogma* (2017) 239–62.

Geertz, Clifford. *The Interpretation of Cultures.* New York: Basic Books, 1973.

Gillihan, Y. M. "Jewish Laws on Illicit Marriage, the Defilement of Offspring, and the Holiness of the Temple: A New Halakhic Interpretation of 1 Corinthians 7:14," *Journal of Biblical Literature* 121 (2002) 711–44.

Gnilka, Joachim. *Das Evangelium nach Markus (Mk 8,26–16,20).* Evangelisch-Katholischer Kommentar zum Neuen Testament. Neukirchen-Vluyn: Benziger, 1999.

Goppelt, Leonhard. *Theology of the New Testament: The Variety and Unity of the Apostolic Witness.* Translated by John Alsup. Grand Rapids: Eerdmans, 1982.

Gorman, Michael J. *Abide and Go: Missional Theosis in the Gospel of John.* Eugene, OR: Cascade, 2018.

———. "John: The Nonsectarian, Missional Gospel." *The Canadian-American Theological Review* 7 (2018) 138–62.

Grässer, Erich. *An die Hebräer.* Evangelisch-Katholischer Kommentar. 3 vols. Zurich: Benziger, 1990.

Gruen, Erich S. *The Construct of Identity in Hellenistic Judaism.* Berlin: de Gruyter, 2016.

Gürtner, Daniel M. *Introducing the Pseudepigrapha of Second Temple Judaism.* Grand Rapids: Baker Academic, 2020.

Gustafson, James M. Preface to *Christ and Culture* by H. Richard. Niebuhr, xxi–xxxv. New York: HarperCollins, 1951.

Hahn, Ferdinand. *Theologie des Neuen Testaments.* 2 vols. Tübingen: Mohr Siebeck, 2002.

Harrill, J. Albert. "Paul and Slavery." In *Paul in the Greco-Roman World: A Handbook,* edited by J. Paul Sampley, 575–607. Harrisburg, PA: Trinity Press International, 2003.

Harrison, James R. "Paul and the Imperial Gospel at Thessaloniki." *Journal for the Study of the New Testament* 25 (2002) 71–96.

Hartman, Lars. "Code and Context: A Few Reflections on the Paranesis of Col 3:6–4:1." In *Understanding Paul's Ethics,* edited by Brian. S. Rosner, 177–91. Grand Rapids: Eerdmans, 1995.

Hauerwas, Stanley, and William Willimon. *Resident Aliens: A Provocative Christian Assessment of the Culture and Ministry for People Who Know That Something Is Wrong.* Nashville: Abingdon, 1989.

Heil, Christoph. "Die Sprache der Absonderung in 2 Kor 6,17 und bei Paulus." In *The Corinthian Correspondence,* edited by Reimund Bieringer, 717–29. Leuven: Leuven University Press, 1996.

Heilig, Christopher. *Hidden Criticism? The Methodology and Plausibility of the Search for a Counter-Imperial Subtext in Paul.* Wissenschaftliche Untersuchungen zum Neuen Testament 2.392. Tübingen: Mohr Siebeck, 2015.

Hengel, Martin. *The Charismatic Leader and His Followers*. Studies of the New Testament and Its World. Translated by James Greg. New York: Crossroads, 1981.

———. *Judaism and Hellenism: Studies in Their Encounter in Palestine during the Early Hellenistic Period*. Philadelphia: Fortress, 1981.

Himes, Paul. "First Peter's Identity Theology and the Community of Faith: A Test-Case in How Social Scientific Criticism Can Assist with Theological Ethics via Biblical Theology." *Evangelical Quarterly* 89 (2018) 115–32.

Hinkle Shore, Mary. "The Freedom of Three Christians: Paul's Letter to Philemon and the Beginning of a New Age." *Word and World* 38 (2018) 390–97.

Hogg, M. A. "Social Categorization, Depersonalization, and Group Behavior." In *Blackwell Handbook of Social Psychology; Group Processes*, edited by M. A. Hogg and R. W. Tindol, 56–85. Oxford: Blackwell, 2001.

Hoklotubbe, T. Christopher. *Civilized Piety: The Rhetoric of Pietas in the Pastoral Epistles and the Roman Empire*. Waco, TX: Baylor University Press, 2017.

Holladay, Carl R. "Jewish Responses to Hellenistic Culture in Early Ptolemaic Egypt." In *Ethnicity in Hellenistic Egypt*, edited by Per Bilde et al., 139–63. Studies in Hellenistic Civilization 3. Aarhus: Aarhus University Press, 1992.

———. "Paul and His Predecessors in the Diaspora: Some Reflections on Ethnic Identity in the Fragmentary Hellenistic Jewish Authors." In *Early Christianity and Classical Culture: Comparative Studies in Honor of Abraham J. Malherbe*, edited by John T. Fitzgerald et al., 429–59. Novum Testamentum Supplements 110. Leiden: Brill, 2003.

Horn, F. W. "Christen in der Diaspora: Zum Kirchenverständnis des 1. Petrusbriefs." *Kerygma und Dogma* 63 (2017) 21–16.

Horrell, David. "The Peaceful, Tolerant Community and the Legitimate Role of the State: Ethics and Ethical Dilemmas in Romans 12:1–15:13." *Review and Expositor* 100 (2003) 81–99.

Horsley, Richard A. *Jesus and the Powers: Conflict, Covenant, and the Hope of the Poor*. Minneapolis: Fortress, 2011.

———. "Rhetoric and Empire—and 1 Corinthians." In *Paul and Politics: Ekklesia, Israel, Imperium, Interpretation; Essays in Honor of Krister Stendahl*, edited by Richard A. Horsley, 72–102. Harrisburg, PA: Trinity Press International, 2000.

Horton, Michael. *Christless Christianity: The Alternative Gospel of the American Church*. Grand Rapids: Baker, 2008.

Hurtado, Larry. *Destroyer of the Gods: Early Christian Distinctiveness in the Roman World*. Waco, TX: Baylor University Press, 2016.

Huttunen, Niko. "Stoic Law in Paul?" In *Stoicism in Early Christianity*, edited by Tuomas Rasimus et al., 39–58. Grand Rapids: Baker Academic, 2010.

Jervis, L. Ann. "1 Corinthians 14:34–35: A Reconsideration of Paul's Limitation of the Free Speech of Some Corinthian Women." *Journal for the Study of the New Testament* 17 (1995) 51–74.

Johnson, Luke Timothy. *Brother of Jesus, Friend of God: Studies in the Letter of James*. Grand Rapids: Eerdmans, 2004.

———. *Constructing Paul: The Canonical Paul*. Grand Rapids: Eerdmans, 2020.

———. *The First and Second Letters to Timothy: A New Translation with Commentary*. New Haven: Yale University Press, 2008.

———. *The Letter of James: A New Translation with Commentary* Anchor Bible 7. New York: Doubleday, 1995.

———. *The Writings of the New Testament*. 3rd ed. Minneapolis: Fortress, 2010.

Johnson Hodge, Caroline. *If Sons, Then Heirs: A Study of Kinship and Ethnicity in the Letters of Paul*. Oxford: Oxford University Press, 2007.

———. "Married to an Unbeliever: Households, Hierarchies, and Holiness in 1 Corinthians 7:12–16." *Harvard Theological Review* 103 (2010) 1–25.

Judge, E. A. "The Early Christians as a Scholastic Community." *Journal of Religious History* 1 (1960–61) 4–15.

———. *The First Christians in the Roman World*. Wissenschaftliche Untersuchungen zum Neuen Testament 229. Tübingen: Mohr Siebeck, 2008.

———. "Paul's Boasting and Contemporary Professional Practice. *Australian Biblical Review* 16 (1968) 37–50.

———. "St. Paul and Socrates." *Interchange* 14 (1973) 106–16.

Kallas, James. "Romans XIII.1–7: An Interpolation." *New Testament Studies* 11 (1964–65) 365–74.

Kamesar, Adam. "Biblical Interpretation in Philo." In *The Cambridge Companion to Philo*, edited by Adam Kamesar, 65–91. Cambridge: Cambridge University Press, 2009.

Käsemann, Ernst. *Commentary on Romans*. Translated by G. W. Bromiley. Grand Rapids: Eerdmans, 1980.

Kennedy, George A. *A New History of Classical Rhetoric*. Princeton: Princeton University Press, 1994.

———. *Progymnasmata: Greek Textbooks of Prose Composition and Rhetoric*. Atlanta: Society of Biblical Literature, 2003.

Kierspel, Lars. *The Jews and the World in the Fourth Gospel: Parallelism, Function, and Context*. Wissenschaftliche Untersuchungen zum Neuen Testament 2.220. Tübingen: Mohr Siebeck, 2006.

King, Andrew M. "Idolatry and Jewish Identity in Wisdom 13–15." *Conversations with the Biblical World* 36 (2016) 76–96.

Klassen-Wiebe, Sheila. "In the World but Not of the World: A Johannine Perspective on the Church-World Relationship." In *The Church Made Strange for the Nations: Essays on Ecclesiology and Political Theology*, edited by Paul J. Doerksen and Karl Koop, 9–20. Eugene, OR: Pickwick, 2011.

Klauck, Hans-Josef. "Die Bruderliebe bei Plutarch und im vierten Makkabäerbuch." In *Alte Welt und neuer Glaube: Beiträge zur Religionsgeschichte und Theologie des Neuen Testaments*, 83–98. Göttingen: Vandenhoeck & Ruprecht, 1994.

———. "Gemeinde und Gesellschaft im frühen Christentum: Ein Leitbild für die Zukunft?" *Antonianum* 76 (2001) 225–46.

———. *4 Makkabäerbuch*. Gütersloh: Gütersloher Verlag, 1989.

Klausner, Joseph. *Jesus of Nazareth: His Life, Times, and Teaching*. New York: MacMillan, 1925.

Kneepkens, C. H. "Comparatio." In *Historisches Wörterbuch der Rhetorik*, edited by Gert Ueding, 293–99. Tübingen: Niemeyer, 1994.

Kok, Kobus. "As the Father Has Sent Me, I Send You: Towards a Missional-Incarnational Ethos in John 4." In *The Moral Language in the New Testament*, edited by Ruben Zimmermann et al., 168–93. Wissenschaftliche Untersuchungen zum Neuen Testament 2.296. Tübingen: Mohr Siebeck, 2010.

Krentz, Edgar. "Logos or Sophia: The Pauline Use of the Ancient Dispute between Rhetoric and Philosophy." In *Early Christianity and Classical Culture: Comparative*

Studies in Honor of Abraham J. Malherbe, edited by John T. Fitzgerald et al., 277–90. Supplements to Novum Testamentum 110. Leiden: Brill, 2003.

Lampe, Peter. "Das korinthische Herrenmahl im Schnittpunkt hellenistich-römischer Mahlpraxis und paulinischer Theologia Crucis (IKor 11,17–34)." *Zeitschrift für die neutestamentliche Wissenschaft* (1991) 183–213.

Lategan, Bernard. "Reconsidering the Origin and Function of Galatians 3:28." *Neotestamentica* 20 (2012) 274–86.

Lee, Michelle. *Paul, the Stoics, and the Body of Christ.* Society for the Study of the New Testament Monograph Series. Cambridge: Cambridge University Press, 2008.

Lim, Sung U. "A Double-voiced Reading of Romans 13:1–7 in the Light of the Imperial Cult." *Hervormde Teologiese Studies* 71 (2015) 1–10.

Lockett, Darian. "Strong and Weak Lines: Permeable Boundaries between Church and Culture in the Letter of James." *Revue and Expositor* 108 (2011) 391–405.

Lohfink, Gerhard. *Jesus and Community: The Social Dimension of Christian Faith.* Translated by John P. Galvin. Philadelphia: Fortress, 1982.

MacIntyre, Alasdair. *After Virtue: A Study in Moral Theory.* Notre Dame: University of Notre Dame Press, 1981.

Malherbe, Abraham. "'Gentle as a Nurse': The Cynic Background to 1 Thessalonians 2." *Novum Testamentum* 12 (1970) 35–48.

———. *The Letters to the Thessalonians: A New Translation with Introduction and Commentary.* Anchor Bible 32b. New York: Doubleday, 2000.

———. "Paul's Self-Sufficiency (Philippians 4:11)." In *Texts and Contexts: Biblical Tests in Their Textual and Educational Contexts: Essays in Honor of Lars Hartman*, edited by Tord Fornberg and David Hellholm, 813–26. Oslo: Scandinavian University Press, 1995.

Marrow, Stanley. "Kosmos in John." *Catholic Biblical Quarterly* 64 (2002) 90–102.

Marsden, George. "Christianity and Cultures: Transforming Niebuhr's Categories." *Insights* 115 (1999) 4–15.

Marshall, Peter. *Enmity at Corinth: Social Conventions in Paul's Relation to the Corinthians.* Wissenschaftliche Untersuchungen zum Neuen Testament 2.23. Tübingen: Mohr Siebeck, 1987.

Martin, Michael. "Philo's Use of Syncrisis: An Examination of Philonic Composition in the Light of the Progymnasmata." *Perspectives in Religious Studies* 30 (2003) 271–97.

Martyn, J. Louis. *Galatians: A New Translation with Introduction and Commentary.* Anchor Bible 33A. New York: Doubleday, 1998.

———. "Galatians 3:28, Faculty Appointments, and Overcoming Christological Amnesia." *Katallagete* 81 (1982) 39–44.

Matera, Frank J. *New Testament Theology: Exploring Diversity and Unity.* Louisville: Westminster John Knox Press, 2007.

———. *Romans.* Paideia. Grand Rapids: Baker Academic, 2010.

Meeks, Wayne A. "The Ethics of the Fourth Evangelist." In *Exploring the Gospel of John: In Honor of Moody Smith*, edited by R. Alan Culpepper and C. Clifton Black, 317–26. Louisville: Westminster John Knox, 1996.

———. *The First Urban Christians.* New Haven: Yale University Press, 1983.

———. "The Man from Heaven in Johannine Sectarianism." *Journal of Biblical Literature* 91 (1972) 44–72.

Merk, O. *archōn*, EDNT 1:167–68.

Metzger, Paul Louis. "Christ, Culture, and the Sermon on the Mount Community." *Ex Auditu* 23 (2007) 22–46.

Miller, Paul D. *The Religion of American Greatness: What's Wrong with Christian Nationalism.* Downers Grove, IL: IVP Academic, 2022.

Mitchell, Margaret M. *Paul and the Rhetoric of Reconciliation.* Louisville: Westminster John Knox, 1991.

Mott, Stephen Charles. "Greek Ethics and Christian Conversion: The Philonic Background of Titus II 10–14 and III 3–7." *Novum Testamentum* 20 (January 1978) 22–48.

Murphy-O'Connor, Jerome. "1 Corinthians 11:2–16 Once Again." *The Catholic Biblical Quarterly* 50.2 (April 1988) 256–74.

Myers, Alicia D. "Just Opponents? Ambiguity, Empathy, and the Jews in the Gospel of John." In *Johannine Ethics: The Moral World of the Gospel and Epistles of John,* edited by Sherri Brown and Christopher W. Skinner, 159–96. Minneapolis: Fortress, 2017.

Najman, Hindy. "The Law of Nature and the Authority of the Mosaic Law." *Studia Philonica Annual* 11 (1999) 55–73.

Niebuhr, Karl-Wilhelm. *Gesetz und Paränese: Katechismusartige Weisungsreihen in der frühjüdischen Literatur.* Wissenschaftliche Untersuchungen zum Neuen Testaments 2.28. Tübingen: J. C. B. Mohr (Paul Siebeck), 1987.

Niebuhr, H. Richard. *Christ and Culture.* New York: HarperCollins, 1951.

Niemöller, Martin. *Exile in the Fatherland.* Grand Rapids: Eerdmans, 1986.

Norden, Eduard. *Die antike Kunstprosa vom VI. Jahrhundert v. Chr. bis in die Zeit der Renaissance.* Leipzig: Teubner, 1898.

Oakes, Peter. *Galatians.* Paideia. Grand Rapids: Baker Academic, 2015.

Oberlinner, L. *diapherō,* EDNT 1:315.

O'Brien Wicker, Kathleen. "First Century Marriage Ethics: A Comparative Study of the Household Codes and Plutarch's Conjugal Precepts." In *No Famine in the Land: Studies in Honor of John L. McKenzi,* edited by James W. Flanagan, 141–53. Missoula, MT: Scholars, 1975.

Okure, Teresa. *The Johannine Approach to Mission.* Wissenschaftliche Untersuchungen zum Neuen Testament 2.31. Tübingen: J. C. B. Mohr (Paul Siebeck), 1998.

Pennington, Jonathan T. *The Sermon on the Mount and Human Flourishing: A Theological Commentary.* Grand Rapids: Baker Academic, 2018.

Pesch, Rudolf. *Das Markusevangelium.* Herders theologischer Kommentar zum Neuen Testament. Freiburg: Herder, 1991.

Pilhofer, Peter. "Philippi zur Zeit des Paulus: Eine Ortsbegehung." *Bibel und Kirche* 64 (2009) 11–17.

Plümacher, Eckhard. "Die Rätsel der Ἡρῳδιάνοι im Markusevangelium." *Zeitschrift für die neutestamentliche Wissenschaft* 106 (2015) 115–25.

Pogoloff, Stephen M. *Logos and Sophia: The Rhetorical Situation of 1 Corinthians.* Atlanta: Scholars, 1990.

Pohlenz, M. *Die Stoa: Geschichte einer geistigen Bewegung.* Göttingen: Vandenhoeck & Ruprecht, 1964.

Popkes, W. "Zum Thema 'Anti-imperiale Deutung neutestamentlicher Schriften." *Theologische Literaturzeitung* 127 (2002) 850–62.

Raabe, Paul. "A Dynamic Tension: God and World in John." *Concordia Journal* 21 (1995) 132–47.

Rabens, Volker. "Paul's Rhetoric of Demarcation: Separation from 'Unbelievers' (2 Cor 6:14–7:1)." In *Theologizing in the Corinthian Conflict: Studies in the Exegesis and Theology of 2 Corinthians*, edited by Reimund Bieringer et al., 229–53. Leuven: Peeters, 2013.

Reese, James M. *Hellenistic Influence on the Book of Wisdom and Its Consequences.* Analecta Biblica 41. Rome: Biblical Institute, 1970.

Reinbold, Wolfgang. *Propaganda und Mission im ältesten Christentum: Eine Untersuchung zu den Modalitäten der Ausbreitung der frühen Kirche.* Forschungen zur Religion und Literatur des Alten und Neuen Testaments 188. Göttingen: Vandenhoeck & Ruprecht, 1998.

Ranieri, Philippo. "Virtue." In *Brill's New Pauly*, edited by Hubert Cancik and Helmut Schneider, 15:458–59. Leiden: Brill, 2010.

Reiser, Marius. "Bürgerliches Christentum in den Pastoralbriefen?" *Biblica* 74 (1993) 27–44.

Rieff, Philip. *My Life among the Deathworks: Illustrations of the Aesthetics of Authority.* Charlottesville: University of Virginia Press, 2006.

Robinson, Laura. "Hidden Transcripts? The Supposedly Self-censoring Paul and Rome as a Surveillance State in Modern Scholarship." *New Testament Studies* 67 (2021) 55–72.

Roloff, Jürgen. *Der erste Brief an Timotheus.* Evangelisch-Katholischer Kommentar zum Neuen Testament. Neukirchen: Zurich, 1988.

Ruiz, Miguel Rodríguez. *Der Missionsgedanke des Johannesevangelium: Ein Beitrag zur johanneischen Soteriologie und Ekklesiologie.* Forschung zur Bibel 55. Würzburg: Echter Verlag, 1987.

Sandnes, Karl Olav. *A New Family: Conversion and Ecclesiology in the Early Church with Cross-Cultural Comparisons.* New York: Peter Lang, 1994.

Schäfer, Peter. *Gemeinde als "Bruderschaft": Ein Beitrag zum Kirchenverständnis des Paulus.* Europäische Hochschschriften. New York: Peter Lang, 1989.

Schenck, Kenneth. *A Brief Guide to Philo.* Louisville: Westminster John Knox, 2005.

Schmeller, Thomas. *Der zweite Brief an die Korinther (2Kor 7,5–13,13).* Evangelisch-Katholischer Kommentar. Neukirchen-Vluyn: Neukirchener Verlag, 2015.

Schnelle, Udo. *Apostle Paul: His Life and Theology.* Translated by M. Eugene Boring. Grand Rapids: Baker Academic, 2005.

———. *Die getrennten Wege von Römern, Juden und Christen.* Tübingen: Mohr Siebeck, 2019.

———. *The First Hundred Years of Christianity: An Introduction to Its History, Literature, and Development.* Translated by James W. Thompson. Grand Rapids: Baker Academic, 2020.

———. *Theology of the New Testament.* Translated by M. Eugene Boring. Grand Rapids: Baker Academic, 2009.

Schrage, Wolfgang. *Der erste Brief an die Korinther.* Evangelisch-katholischer Kommentar. Vol. 7. Zurich: Benziger, 1991.

———. "Die Stellung zur Welt bei Paulus, Epiktet und in der Apokalyptik." In *Kreuzestheologie und Ethik im Neuen Testament: Gesammelte Studien*, 59–86. Göttingen: Vandenhoeck & Ruprecht, 2004.

Schröger, Friedrich. *Gemeinde im 1. Petrusbrief: Untersuchungen zum Selbstverständnis einer christlichen Gemeinde an der Wende vom 1. zum 2. Jahrhundert.* Katholische Theologie. Passau: Passavia Universitatsverlag, 1981.

Schulz, Siegfried. *Neutestamentliche Ethik*. Zürcher Grundrisse zur Bibel. Zurich: Theologischer Verlag, 1987.

Schüssler Fiorenza, Elizabeth. *In Memory of Her: A Feminist Theological Reconstruction of Christian Origins*. New York: Crossroad, 1983.

Schwartz, Daniel R. "Philo, His Family, and His Times." In *The Cambridge Companion to Philo*, edited by Adam Kamesar, 9–31. Cambridge: Cambridge University Press, 2009.

Scroggs, Robin. "Paul and the Eschatological Woman." *Journal of the American Academy of Religion* 40 (1972) 283–303.

Seland, Torrey. *Strangers in the Light: Philonic Perspectives on Christian Identity in 1 Peter*. Biblical Interpretation Series. Boston: Brill Leiden, 2005.

Selwyn, E. G. *The First Epistle of St. Peter*. London: Macmillan, 1964.

Skinner, Christopher W. "Love One Another: The Johannine Love Command in the Farewell Discourse." In *Johannine Ethics: The Moral World of the Gospel and Epistles*, edited by Sherri Brown, 25–42. Minneapolis: Fortress, 2017.

Spicq, Ceslas. "*Alētheia*." In *Theological Lexicon of the New Testament*, 1:66–86. Peabody, MA: Hendrickson, 1994.

———. "*Epiphaneia*." In *Theological Lexicon of the New Testament*, 1:65–68. Peabody, MA: Hendrickson, 1994.

———. "*Hieroprepēs*." In *Theological Lexicon of the New Testament*, 2:215–16. Peabody, MA: Hendrickson, 1994.

———. "*Kapēlos*." In *Theological Lexicon of the New Testament*, 2:254–57. Peabody, MA: Hendrickson, 1994.

———. "*Parepidēmos*." In *Theological Lexicon of the New Testament*, 3:41–43. Peabody, MA: Hendrickson, 1994.

———. "*Parousia*." In *Theological Lexicon of the New Testament*, 3:53–55. Peabody, MA: Hendrickson, 1994.

———. "*Parrhēsia*." In *Theological Lexicon of the New Testament*, 3:56–62. Peabody, MA: Hendrickson, 1994.

———. "*Phōs*." In *Theological Lexicon of the New Testament*, 3:470–91. Peabody, MA: Hendrickson, 1994.

———. "*Semnos*." In *Theological Lexicon of the New Testament*, 3:244–45. Peabody, MA: Hendrickson, 1994.

———. "*Splachna*." In *Theological Lexicon of the New Testament*, 3:273–75. Peabody, MA: Hendrickson, 1994.

———. *Theological Lexicon of the New Testament*. Translated and edited by James D. Ernest. 3 vols. Peabody, MA: Hendrickson, 1994.

Stark, Rodney. *The Rise of Christianity*. San Francisco: HarperCollins, 1996.

Stambaugh, J., and David L. Balch. *The Social World of the First Christians*. London: SPCK, 1986.

Starling, David. "The ἄπιστοι of 2 Cor 6:14: Beyond the Impasse." *Novum Testamentum* 55 (2013) 45–60.

Stenschke, Christoph. "Mission and Conversion in the First Epistle of Peter." *Acta Patristica et Byzantina* 19 (2008) 221–63.

Still, Todd D. "More Than Friends? The Literary Classification of Philippians Revisited." *Perspectives in Religious Studies* 39 (2012) 53–66.

———. "Pauline Theology and Ancient Slavery: Does the Former Support or Subvert the Latter?" *Horizons in Biblical Theology* 27 (2005) 21–34.

Stowers, Stanley K. "Paul and Self-Mastery." In *Paul in the Greco-Roman World*, edited by J. Paul Sampley, 524–50. Harrisburg, PA: Trinity Press International, 2003.
———. *A Rereading of Romans: Justice, Jews and Gentiles.* New Haven: Yale University Press, 1994.
———. "Social Status, Public Speaking and Private Teaching: The Circumstances of Paul's Preaching Activity." *Novum Testamentum* 26 (1984) 59–82.
Strecker, Christian. "Taktiken der Aneignung: Politische Implikationen der paulinischen Botschaft im Kontext der römischen imperialen Wirklichkeit." In *Neues Testament und politische Theorie: Interdisziplinäre Beiträge zur Zukunft des Politischen*, edited by Eckart Reinmuth, 114–61. Stuttgart: Kohlhammer, 2011.
Taubes, Jacob. *The Political Theology of Paul.* Translated by Dana Hollander. Stanford: Stanford University Press, 2004.
Taylor, Charles. *A Secular Age.* Cambridge: Harvard University Press, 2007.
Taylor, N. H. "Herodians and Pharisees: The Historical and Political Context of Mark 3:6; 8:15; 12:13–17." *Neotestamentica* 34 (2000) 299–310.
Tellbe, Michael. *Paul between Synagogue and State: Christians, Jews, and Civic Authorities in 1 Thessalonians, Romans, and Philippians.* Coniectanea Biblica: New Testament Series 34. Stockholm, Almqvist & Wiksell, 2001.
Termini, Christina. "Philo's Thought within the Context of Middle Judaism." In *The Cambridge Companion to Philo*, edited by Adam Kamesar, 95–123. Cambridge: Cambridge University Press, 2009.
Theissen, Gerd. *Social Reality of the Early Christians: Theology, Ethics, and the World of the New Testament.* Minneapolis: Fortress, 1992.
Thiselton, Anthony. *The First Epistle to the Corinthians: A Commentary on the Greek Text.* New International Greek Testament Commentary. Grand Rapids: Eerdmans, 2000.
Thompson, James W. *Apostle of Persuasion: Theology and Rhetoric in the Pauline Letters.* Grand Rapids: Baker Academic, 2020.
———. *The Beginnings of Christian Philosophy.* Washington, DC: Catholic Biblical Association, 1982.
———. *The Church according to Paul: Rediscovering the Community Conformed to Christ.* Grand Rapids: Baker Academic, 2014.
———. "Creation, Shame, and Nature." In *Early Christianity and Classical Culture: Comparative Studies in Honor of Abraham J. Malherbe*, edited by John T. Fitzgerald et al., 237–58. Supplements to Novum Testamentum 110. Leiden: Brill, 2003.
———. *Moral Formation according to Paul: The Context and Coherence of Pauline Ethics.* Grand Rapids: Baker Academic, 2011.
———. "What Has Hebrews to Do with Middle Platonism?" In *Reading the Epistle to the Hebrews: A Resource for Students*, edited by Eric F. Mason and Kevin B. McCruden, 31–52. Atlanta: Society of Biblical Literature, 2011.
Thompson, James W., and Bruce Longenecker. *Philippians and Philemon.* Paideia. Grand Rapids: Baker Academic, 2016.
Thorsteinsson, Runar M. "Paul and Roman Stoicism: Romans 12 and Contemporary Stoic Ethics." *Journal for the Study of the New Testament* 29 (2006) 139–61.
Tolmie, D. Francois. "Research on the Letter to the Galatians: 2000–2010." *Acta Theologica* 32 (2012) 118–57.

Towner, Philip H. *The Goal of Our Instruction: The Structure of Theology and Ethics in the Pastoral Epistles*. Journal for the Study of the New Testament Supplement Series 34. Sheffield: JSOT Press, 1989.

Trebilco, Paul. *Outsider Designations and Boundary Construction in the New Testament: Early Christian Communities and the Formation of Group Identity*. Cambridge: Cambridge University Press, 2017.

Trueman, Carl R. *The Rise and Triumph of the Therapeutic Self*. Wheaton, IL: Crossway, 2020.

Tucker, J. Brian. *"Remain in Your Calling": Paul and the Continuation of Social Identities in 1 Corinthians*. Eugene, OR: Pickwick, 2011.

Ukpong, Justin S. "Tribute to Caesar, Mark 12:13–17 (Mt 22:15–22, Luke 20:20–26)." *Neotestamentica* 33 (1999) 433–44.

Uzukwu, Gesila Nneka. *The Unity of Male and Female in Christ: An Exegetical Study of Galatians 3.28c in Light of Paul's Theology of Promise*. Library of New Testament Studies 531. London: Bloomsbury T & T Clark, 2015.

van der Watt, Jan G. "Ethics and Ethos in the Gospel according to John." *Zeitschrift für die neutestamentliche Wissenschaft und die Kunde der älteren Kirche* 97 (2006) 147–76.

———. "Radical Social Redefinition and Radical Love: Ethics and Ethos in the Gospel of John." In *Identity, Ethics, and Ethos in the New Testament*, edited by Jan G. van der Watt, 107–34. Berlin: de Gruyter, 2006.

Vögtle, Anton. *Die Tugend- und Lasterkataloge im Neuen Testament*. Neutestamentliche Abhandlung. Münster: Aschendorf, 1936.

Volf, Miroslav. "Soft Difference: Theological Reflections on the Relation between Church and Culture in 1 Peter." *Ex Auditu* 10 (1994) 15–30.

Vollenweider, Samuel. "Der 'Raub' der Gottgleichheit: Ein religionsgeschichtlicher Vorschlag zu Phil. 2,6(-11)." In *Horizonte neutestamentlicher Christologie: Studien zu Paulus und zur frühchristlichen Theologie*, 263–84. Tübingen: Mohr Siebeck, 2002.

———. "Politische Theologie im Philipperbrief?" In *Paulus und Johannes*, edited by Dieter Sänger and Ulrich Mell, 458–68. Tübingen: Mohr Siebeck, 2011.

von Soden, Hans. *Hand-Commentar zum Neuen Testament*. Zweite Abtheilung: *Hebräerbrief, Briefe des Petrus, Jakobus, Judas*. 3rd ed. Freiburg: Mohr, 1899.

Weber, Reinhard. *Das Gesetz im hellenistischen Judentum: Studien zum Verständnis und zur Funktion der Thora von Demetrios bis Pseudo-Phokylides*. Arbeiten zur Religion und Geschichte des Urchristentums 10. Frankfurt am Main: Peter Lang, 2000.

Welborn, Lawrence. *Politics and Rhetoric in the Corinthian Epistles*. Macon, GA: Mercer University Press, 1997.

Wengst, Klaus. *Pax Romana and the Peace of Jesus Christ*. Philadelphia: Fortress, 1987.

Wibbing, Siegfried. *Die Tugend- und Lasterkataloge im Neuen Testament und ihre Traditionsgeschichte unter Berücksichtigung der Qumran-Texte*. Berlin: Töpelmann, 1959.

Willimon, William H. "Been There, Preached That: Today's Conservatives Sound Like Yesterday's Liberals." *Leadership: A Practical Journal for Church Leaders* (1995) 74–76.

Williams, Travis B. *Good Works in 1 Peter: Negotiating Social Conflict and Christian Identity in the Greco-Roman World.* Wissenschaftliche Untersuchungen zum Neuen Testament 337. Tübingen: Mohr Siebeck, 2011.

Winston, David. *The Wisdom of Solomon: A New Translation and Commentary.* New York: Doubleday, 1979.

Winter, Bruce W. *After Paul Left Corinth: The Influence of Secular Ethics and Social Change.* Grand Rapids: Eerdmans, 2001.

———. "The Entries and Ethics of Orators and Paul (1 Thessalonians 2:1–12)." *Tyndale Bulletin* 44 (1993) 55–74.

———. "Is Paul among the Sophists?" *Reformed Theological Review* 53 (1994) 28–38.

———. *Roman Wives, Roman Widows: The Appearance of New Women and the Pauline Communities.* Grand Rapids: Eerdmans, 2003.

———. "The Seasons of This Life and Eschatology." In *Eschatology in Bible and Theology: Evangelical Essays at the Dawn of a New Millennium*, edited by K. E. Brower and M. W. Elliott, 323–34. Downers Grove, IL: InterVarsity Press, 1997.

Witherington, Ben. *Grace in Galatia: A Commentary on St Paul's Letter to the Galatians.* Grand Rapids: Eerdmans, 1998.

Wood, Ralph C. *Contending for the Faith.* Waco, TX: Baylor University Press, 2003.

Wright, N. T. *Jesus and the Victory of God.* Vol. 2 of *Christian Origins and the Question of God.* Minneapolis: Fortress, 1996.

———. "The Letter to the Romans." In *The New Interpreter's Bible, Volume IX: Acts, Introduction to Epistolary Literature, Romans 1 & 2, Corinthians, Galatians*, 395–770. Nashville: Abingdon, 1994.

———. "Paul and Caesar: A New Reading of Romans." In *A Royal Priesthood: The Use of the Bible Ethically and Politically; a Dialogue with Oliver O'Donovan*, edited by Craig G. Bartholomew, 173–93. Carlisle, Cumbria: Paternoster, 2002.

———. "Paul and Empire." In *The Blackwell Companion to Paul*, edited by Stephen Westerholm, 285–87. Oxford: Blackwell, 2011.

———. *Paul and the Faithfulness of God: Christian Origins and the Question of God.* Vol. 2. Minneapolis: Fortress, 2013.

———. "Paul's Gospel and Caesar's Empire." In *Paul and Politics: Ekklesia, Israel, Imperium, Interpretation; Essays in Honor of Krister Stendahl*, edited by Richard A. Horsley, 160–83. Harrisburg, PA: Trinity Press International, 2000.

Yoder, John Howard. "How H. Richard Niebuhr Reasoned: A Critique of *Christ and Culture*." In *Authentic Transformation: A New Vision of Christ and Culture*, edited by Glen H. Stassen et al., 15–30. Nashville: Abingdon, 1996.

Zimmermann, Johannes. "Diasporafähiger Glaube: Eine Herausforderung für christliche Gemeinden in einer pluralen Gesellschaft." In *Kirche zwischen postmoderner Kultur und Evangelium*, edited by Martin Reppenhagen, 39–62. Neukirchen-Vluyn: Neukirchener Verlag, 2010.

Index of Names

Index of Subjects

accommodation, 4, 7, 9, 11, 12, 13, 14, 15, 17, 19, 32, 99, 153, 155, 159, 162, 169, 170, 171, 175, 176, 178, 180, 182, 186
acculturated resistance literature, 26
Age of Enchantment, 12
allegory, 19, 20, 20n, 21, 28, 71
alternative Community, 34, 36, 37, 46, 147, 186
assimilationist, 5, 14, 15, 19, 26, 30, 159, 161,

cardinal virtues,, 25, 27, 118, 120, 121, 122, 161, 170, 171, 175
Christ above culture, 5
Christ against culture, 4, 11, 125
Christ and culture in paradox, 5, 9, 66
Christ and culture, 1, 1n, 2, 2n, 4, 4n, 6, 6n, 9, 10, 10n, 11, 12, 48, 54, 55, 66, 125, 125n, 127n, 128n, 148, 167, 173, 176, 177, 178
Christ the transformer of culture, 5, 11, 125
Constantinian Era, 2, 4, 6, 7, 9, 177, 178, 179
culture of authenticity, 4

diatribe, 157

egkyklios paideia, 19
Enlightenment, 2, 3, 9

epideictic oratory, 26
eschatological banquet, 36
evangelicals, 7, 8, 9,

family values, 2, 7
fundamentalism, 7

haustafel, 162
Hellenism, 10, 13, 13n, 14, 16n, 32n, 153n
Hellenization, 15, 24
Herodians, 42, 42n
holiness, 13, 16, 51,53, 60
household codes, 11, 77, 161, 162, 163, 167
humility, 89, 90, 122, 153, 164, 166

John the Baptist, 32, 33, 35, 40, 41, 43, 139

kingdom of God, 31, 33, 36, 37, 45, 50, 56, 161

Levitical code, 52, 147
liberals, 5, 7, 9, 199

Maccabean literature, 10, 15
mainline Protestants, 5, 9, 177
Middle Platonism and Stoicism, 20

Neo-Pythagoreans, 120

Index of Ancient Sources